WOMEN
TALK ABOUT
GYNECOLOGICAL
SURGERY

WOMEN TALK ABOUT GYNECOLOGICAL SURGERY

From Diagnosis to Recovery

AMY GROSS *and* DEE ITO

CLARKSON POTTER / PUBLISHERS
New York

DISCARD

Copyright © 1991 by Amy Gross and Dee Ito

Published by Clarkson N. Potter, Inc., 201 East 50th Street, New York, New York 10022.
Member of the Crown Publishing Group.

CLARKSON N. POTTER, POTTER and colophon are trademarks of
Clarkson N. Potter, Inc.

Manufactured in the United States of America

LIBRARY OF CONGRESS CATALOGING-IN-PUBLICATION DATA
Gross, Amy.
Women talk about gynecological surgery : from diagnosis to recovery : how to go
through it in the smartest, calmest way / by Amy Gross and Dee Ito.—1st ed.
p. cm.
Includes bibliographical references (p. 344) and index.
1. Generative organs, Female—Surgery—Popular works.
2. Generative organs, Female—Patients—Interviews. I. Ito, Dee.
II. Title.
RG104.G763 1991
362.1′981′00922—dc20   90-7669
ISBN 0-517-58055-1

Text design by Beth Tondreau Design / Mary A. Wirth
10 9 8 7 6 5 4 3 2 1

First Edition

*Once again—for the women, our heroines,
who gave us their stories and taught us
how to get through surgery*

ACKNOWLEDGMENTS

We are tremendously grateful to the doctors, nurses, and health professionals who generously and patiently explained what they do and how they think: Karen Blanchard, M.D.; Anthony Calanog, M.D.; Joel Ito, R.Ph.; Robert Korn, M.D.; Marilyn Kritchman, M.D.; Jerold Kurzban, M.D.; Louis Lapid, M.D.; Pat McGuier; Marilyn Miklau; Lila Nachtigall, M.D.; Fredrica Preston, R.N., M.A., O.C.N.; Ruth Ravich; and J. Victor Reyniak, M.D.

Our thanks, also, to our editor, Carol Southern, for her continued support and enthusiasm.

CONTENTS

THREE · *Consultations with Specialists*

O N E

Introduction

THE PATIENT AS EXPERT

This book, and its predecessor, *Women Talk About Breast Surgery*, began when we realized that we could offer women facing surgery a form of reassurance they weren't getting anywhere else: the expertise and wisdom of patients who've been through the surgery.

It was 1985, and four of our friends were scheduled for, or recovering from, a hysterectomy. Even though the women are well-informed and sophisticated, the surgical process took them by surprise. The women who were on their way into the hospital were nervous, alarmed about procedures ("What's this I hear about a catheter?"), and searching for information and advice. We'd relay their questions to our friends who were now veterans of the surgery, and circle back with the answers. The six of us established a kind of network and we saw how useful and comforting that network was—how it answered questions that weren't being addressed by all the shelves of books and magazine articles on women's health.

We decided to re-create the network on a bigger scale. As we noted in the first *Women Talk . . .* , surgery is still a mysterious process and it shouldn't be. Ignorance is not bliss, and it's not protection. What you don't know in this area can hurt you; it can throw you just because it's unexpected. Doctors used to say, "A little knowledge is a dangerous thing." We ask: Dangerous for whom? The answer may be: For the doctor, because answering a patient's long list of questions is more complicated—and more time-consuming—than simply issuing doctor's orders. During our research, we met women whose doctors never explained that a complete hysterectomy was going to jolt them into sudden, premature menopause. We met women who weren't prepared for the gas pains that almost always follow abdominal surgery, and women who were afraid something was wrong with them because they still tired easily a few months after a major operation.

Knowing what to expect would have protected them from some

3

of the shock of surgery. Thanks to drug management, pain is no longer the major hurdle of surgery; fear is, whether the procedure is considered minor or major. Some fear is a reasonable reaction to a disease or to the risks of surgery and general anesthesia. But for the informed patient, the anxiety of the unknown is lessened. Instead of panicking when a doctor says you need surgery, you can choose how you want to proceed. Instead of feeling victimized and disembodied by hospital routines, you can understand the purpose of a procedure; you can even refuse it. Instead of feeling blown in like Dorothy waking in Oz, you can rest in the knowledge that you mapped your own route.

Some women faced with surgery get themselves through it by putting their trust in one doctor and following instructions. Other women crave facts. They are reassured by knowing what to expect and having a say in the process. This book is for them. It is a compilation of conversations with women who have been through surgery. Their collective experience adds up to the inside story of surgery. The talk ranges from the patients' emotional and physical reactions to the details a doctor is too busy to list, doesn't know, or is reluctant to share for various reasons. (Doctors, for instance, are afraid of planting a suggestion of a side effect—they think that if they don't tell you a drug could nauseate you, maybe it won't. They don't want to scare you with possible complications. And they don't want to say anything that might make them vulnerable to a lawsuit.)

The underlying power of the women's stories is that they are proof that one survives these experiences. The voices have all been to the front and returned to tell what happened. In a sense, these are adventure stories. They are about heroics, about fighting back, being brave, keeping your wits about you. They're also lessons in how to be the smartest possible patient—how to get the best possible care for yourself.

We were awed by the thoroughness with which some women attacked the project of surgery. They might have been planning a war. They applied the same energy, competence, sense of responsibility, and urge to *manage* that make many of them tremendous successes in their work. They researched their medical condition, comparison-shopped for doctors, investigated experimental high-tech surgical approaches. As one woman said of her calm the night before surgery, "I felt that I'd done my homework, and I was confident in my choices. Now I could relax."

When we began, we planned only to interview patients, relying on them as the experts. We quickly ran into a problem precisely because of their expertise. Their stories were heavily embellished with medical information, and we needed to talk with doctors, specialists in anesthesia, endocrinology, and radiology, as well as other medical personnel to clarify procedures and to explain the new techniques some of the patients had tried successfully.

We track the women from the first time they noticed a symptom to their recovery. Our aim is to clarify: What is it like to go through this operation? What can you expect in the way of procedures, physical discomfort, emotional reactions, recovery time? Our focus is always on the operation and how it affects a woman physically and emotionally. A woman who is going to have a hysterectomy for fibroids will find useful information in the experience of a woman who had a hysterectomy for endometriosis. The nature of the specific disorder will color the experience, but the operations, the hospital routines, and the healing will be similar.

The women range in age from their twenties to sixties. They are all middle class, with enough money to afford whatever medical care was required, so we suspect that—for better or worse—they've drawn a portrait of American medical care at its finest. All had had their surgery within the past five or six years. The cut-off was necessary because the procedures and the doctor-patient dynamic have changed so rapidly. That doesn't mean the medical establishment is now all that it should be. But it does suggest that women are beginning to see themselves as consumers of medical care and that doctors are under pressure to adapt to what the customers want. As one woman gynecologist told us, "Doctors know where their bread is buttered."

The patients are not scientists (except for the gynecologist), and they are not saints. Their personalities, as you'll see, shape their experience, as do their personal health theories, their fears, their values. We checked their medical information and, when possible, their theories. A few women, for instance, went into training before surgery on the hunch that if they were thin and "in good shape" before surgery, the surgeon would find it easier to operate, and they would recuperate more quickly. We wondered if this theory was simply fitness mania pushed to new heights, but according to two of the surgeons we interviewed, the women were right. Fitness counts.

We learned, too, that reactions to different aspects of surgery are idiosyncratic. One woman found the sonogram an "excruciating experience"; another described it as absolutely pain free. Being shaved on the pubic area before surgery can be experienced as horribly embarrassing or dismissed with an airy, "Absolutely nothing to it."

One of the themes running through the interviews is the patient's need for a sense of control. Surgery is more than a physical assault; it can be emotionally battering. You're in a weakened condition, in an unfamiliar, impersonal environment. You're dependent on strangers, at the mercy of the nurse who's slow to bring the painkiller, a sitting duck for medical students eager to practice on you and for yet another person in a white coat who wants to draw blood. Many of the women's organizational strategies—from bringing a certain kind of mattress to the hospital to planning their aftercare—were geared toward creating a sense of control. One woman eased herself through chemotherapy by arranging for sessions with a hypnotist and a nutritionist and petitioning for THC pills (the active ingredient in marijuana, said to reduce nausea caused by chemotherapy). All that effort, she says, made her feel that "I was a little bit in control, that I hadn't given up all my rights, that I wasn't kneeling at the altar of the medical profession to cure me."

The sense of being in control, keeping a grip on what's happening to her, is not simply "nice" for the patient. We suspect that unnecessary surgeries take place when a doctor is intimidating, moves to schedule an operation too quickly, and frightens the patient into submissiveness. The most important information this book offers may be the reassurance—the insistence—that a patient can always take the time to research, get other opinions, and make the important decisions thoughtfully—beginning with the decision to have the surgery or not.

The women we talked to were, for the most part, lucky. Their doctors didn't make big mistakes, and the complications of surgery were, by and large, minor. The women's angriest complaint was about the brusqueness of surgeons, their withholding of information as well as gestures of simple humanity. One doctor "never had the grace to sit down in my room," a patient raged. Another doctor frustrated a patient by his stinginess with facts: "I wish he had answered my questions, I wish he had told me exactly what he was going to do, what feelings I would be having.

He just said, 'Oh, it's nothing.' It was much more than I had anticipated. I was perfectly willing to accept what this thing is, as long as he would give me some information about it."

Women like the ones interviewed here are pushing doctors to open up the medical sanctorum, to involve patients in making decisions. Yet at some point, we noticed, even the most compulsively responsible patient chooses to relinquish control to the surgeon. First, because she must. "I realized I couldn't operate on myself," one woman said. Second, because one yearns, in this vulnerable position, to believe in the surgeon's authority, benevolence, and superhuman competence. "When I started out, I wanted to know everything," one woman said. "By the time I'd seen three doctors, all I wanted was somebody I liked to take care of it."

"There comes a moment," another woman said, "where I'm hesitant to learn more, where I think, Okay, I know enough—the doctor is the boss. I still want doctors to be authority figures. I want to rely on them. It's true they know more about it than I do or than I could learn through conversation."

Regression is probably inevitable. The question is, when do you give up, relax, and trust? The answer is, after gathering enough information to make decisions, after doing your homework.

Wanting it both ways makes for a delicate doctor-patient relationship. It asks the doctor to respect the patient as a partner in making decisions and then be compassionate—not condescending—when she switches to dependency. It also demands more time and both the verbal skills and patience necessary to explain rather than just prescribe.

On the other hand, the ideal new doctor-patient relationship also asks more of the patient. The old-style patient assumed she was incapable of understanding anything medical; she put herself in the hands of the doctor as though she were a child. Now, total passivity is no longer totally comfortable: the awareness that doctors are fallible impels us to educate ourselves. The modern patient can't just lie back and smile gratefully at her surgeon, the god. She's got to take responsibility for her own health; she's got to see herself as *hiring* a surgeon rather than crawling to Lourdes. She's got to stay alert.

This is no easy job—resisting the process of becoming hypnotized into dumb acquiescence, the "good patient" role. But it's worth the effort because women who know what to expect are more likely to get what they want. The information required must be made accessible and nonthreatening. One woman we interviewed had an idea: "I think there should be some sort of support system before you go in, where you could talk, as we're talking now, with somebody who has had the surgery, answering questions the doctor will never answer, and making it more acceptable."

It's mystifying to us that such a system isn't in place for patients facing all kinds of surgery. We hope this book will serve as that sort of support and encourage hospitals and doctors to invent such systems. We want this book to be both a source of information and a place of comfort—offering reassurance, courage, and perspective from the women who have been through the surgeries. These experiences, imagined as insurmountable, can be managed. The stories here are evidence of that. They are inspiring because the storytellers are just regular women. They are us, and if they can do it, we can do it, you can do it.

IS THIS SURGERY NECESSARY?

Gynecology is a specialty under siege. This is where the medical consumer movement began, in the late sixties. In the course of reexamining their lives, women became outraged by the way they were treated as gynecology patients. They resented everything from the cold shock of the metal speculum to the hours spent in the waiting room (the implication being that a woman's time wasn't valuable) to the way doctors talked to them —as though women were children, and doctors, like Daddy, knew best.

Now, you have only to notice your gynecologist's warming the speculum under hot water, or the nurse's presence in the room during the examination, to see doctors' responsiveness to their demanding new patients. But women have gone beyond correcting medical manners. As you'll read in the following interviews, they are stepping into areas formerly cordoned off from the layperson. They want to discuss the kind of incision and anesthesia they'll have, and they research alternatives to traditional procedures. They accuse gynecologists of performing unnecessary surgery and of making simple procedures and easily diagnosed—and easily treated—conditions seem unnecessarily complicated.

The question of unnecessary surgery is to gynecology what the Eiffel Tower is to Paris: it dominates the landscape. Thanks to the medical-consumer movement, the idea that gynecological procedures are performed promiscuously in the United States has become widely known. Our rate of hysterectomy is twice that of Great Britain's.* Our percentage of cesarean sections increases every year, rising from 14.1 percent in 1979 to 23 percent in 1985,

---

* Some health activists claim the U.S. rate is three times Great Britain's, but according to figures from the National Center for Health Statistics, they're exaggerating. In 1985 670,000 hysterectomies were performed in the United States, compared with 66,170 in England. Correcting for the difference in population size (ours is about five times greater than Great Britain's), we find the U.S. rate is twice Great Britain's.

the last year surveyed—while in Great Britain that year only 10 percent of births were by C-section.* The litigious American patient is in part responsible for the difference. The majority of all U.S. obstetrician-gynecologists have been sued, according to the National Women's Health Network. As technological advances like the fetal monitor alert the medical team to dangers they formerly would not have been able to detect during labor, the patient is more likely to hold the obstetrician responsible if anything goes wrong. The *Mayo Clinic Health Letter* (February 1988) noted, "When faced with a difficult pregnancy . . . a doctor may consider advising cesarean section to be sure all precautions are taken." More and more doctors are likely to play it safe and rush into surgery at any sign of trouble. The C-section offers a degree of control that is increasingly irresistible.

The assumption is that American doctors like to perform surgery and are strongly guided by the threat of malpractice suits. This is an assumption we share. If we harbor it to a lesser extent now than when we started writing this book, still we think that every recommendation to have an operation must be toughly questioned and tested. Hysterectomy is one of the most commonly performed operations in the country. The odds of an American woman getting through life with her uterus intact are less than 40 percent. National statistics for hysterectomy indicate that approximately one-fifth of all hysterectomies are performed for reasons other than those considered uncontroversial (cancer, hyperplasia, fibroids, endometriosis, prolapse.)†

What could these reasons be? Somewhere in this country, we worry, a woman is having a hysterectomy because she doesn't want to have any more children—though a tubal ligation is all that's required for sterilization. Or she's having a hysterectomy because she has small, innocuous fibroid tumors—though they

---

* s o u r c e : The American College of Obstetricians and Gynecologists, and the National Institutes of Health.
† s o u r c e : National Center for Health Statistics study of hysterectomies performed between 1985 and 1987 (the most recent survey made by diagnosis):

> 593,000 HYSTERECTOMIES FOR FIBROIDS
> 372,000 FOR ENDOMETRIOSIS
> 318,000 FOR UTERINE PROLAPSE
> 198,000 FOR CANCER
> 114,000 FOR ENDOMETRIAL HYPERPLASIA
> 372,000 FOR ALL OTHER REASONS

might never bother her. Or because she's bleeding heavily as she nears menopause—though "in a vast majority of cases," according to endocrinologist Lila Nachtigall, M.D., the bleeding "can be reversed within two or three months of treatment with progesterone." (Another approach is to burn out the lining of the uterus with laser, which permanently stops the bleeding yet leaves the uterus in place.)

These are clear-cut cases of unnecessary surgery. The women we interviewed presented no such obvious examples. We are assuming that we met a particularly knowledgeable group of women. One did have a laparoscopy for an ovarian cyst when hormonal treatment might have been tried first. Another had a hysterectomy plus oophorectomy (removal of the ovaries) when a cone biopsy, a much simpler operation, was an option. But she was the one who made the decision to have the more radical procedure—she, and not some knife-happy surgeon. The cone biopsy carries with it a 5 percent chance of recurrence of cervical cancer; hysterectomy is a complete cure. Regular and frequent Pap tests would spot a recurrence, one doctor reassured her, but she didn't want to live with fear.

For us, the question of unnecessary surgery turned out to be complex rather than simple. It may well be that American doctors are knife-happy. But it may also be that American women are less willing to tolerate discomfort and are more receptive to surgical solutions. The combination of the two adds up to a lot of surgery.

FIBROIDS

Consider hysterectomy for fibroids, benign tumors growing in the uterine wall. The surgery is described as elective: fibroids won't kill you, and if you can hold out until menopause, the tumors will vanish naturally—they're fed by the hormone estrogen, and with menopause the supply of estrogen essentially dries up. Yet over a fourth of all hysterectomies are performed because of these tumors. Two factors make surgery seem essential: size and the risk of malignancy.

Many doctors insist that surgery for fibroids becomes absolutely necessary when the tumor has reached a certain size— usually that of a twelve-week fetus.

Doctors describe fibroid size in one of two ways:

1. In terms of fruits—lemon or plum is relatively small; grape-fruit is large. (The normal uterus is the size of a pear, says Louis Lapid, M.D., a gynecologist at Mount Sinai Hospital in New York City, "an inverted pear, about eight to ten centimeters by six centimeters.")

2. In terms of gestation size—the fibroids have expanded the uterus to the size it would be if the woman were, say, eight weeks pregnant (three-month size is considered large).

Side effects of such large tumors may include very heavy bleeding with each monthly period, anemia, fatigue. Yet if the woman has no symptoms, her doctor may warn her that it's only a matter of time before she does, and that the fibroid soon will "press" on other organs.

Once the threat of surgery is raised, it nags like an unanswered question. The woman becomes obsessed with the fibroid. The persistent awareness of the tumor compromises her image of herself as healthy: she tires more easily, her stomach may bulge, she's bleeding heavily. Why wait, when surgery seems inevitable? Can she hold out until menopause? There's an impulse to solve the problem, to end the ambiguity.

She and her doctor discuss surgery: for the sake of "the quality of life," hysterectomy seems desirable. And usually, after it's all over, she wishes that she'd done it years before.

To resist surgery in a situation like this takes either great courage or great fear. One gynecologist repeatedly told a woman with fibroids that she must have a hysterectomy. He threatened that her periods were so heavy she was on the verge of anemia and added ominously that her fibroids were so large he could no longer feel her ovaries. Determined to avoid surgery, she went for one opinion after another until the fourth doctor told her she was in no real danger and the choice was hers: her decision should depend on how much discomfort she was willing to bear. She preferred discomfort to a hysterectomy. Fortunately she went into menopause relatively early, at forty-five, and that was the end of her fibroid problem.

The point here is that the surgery is elective. Fibroid size alone should not be an absolute indication for surgery, Louis Lapid,

M.D., told us. No matter how large the fibroids, he said, sonograms now enable a doctor to check regularly on the health of the ovaries, as well as the position of fibroids in relation to other organs.

FIBROIDS AND CANCER

If side effects, or the threat of side effects, don't push a woman with fibroids into surgery, the fear of cancer will. Roughly a fourth of the women we interviewed learned, during a routine gynecological visit, that their fibroids were "suddenly growing rapidly." The implication was that the tumor might be malignant rather than benign. An implication like that seems to take the elective out of elective surgery.

All of the women went on to have hysterectomies, and all were found to have ordinary fibroids. We, hearing their stories, were sorry that they went into surgery saddled with the threat of cancer. The fact is that the odds of their having cancer was statistically tiny. *Fibroids rarely become malignant: the incidence is at most .5 percent.* Why were so many doctors scaring so many women into surgery?

As you'll see, we asked this question of the gynecologists we interviewed. The doctors all explained that medical ethics (and we interpret that as malpractice guidelines) demand that they warn the patient of the possible dangers. "It is the doctor's responsibility to inform her that the tumor is growing very fast and to pressure her into decision making," one surgeon said. Though the chances of a fibroid "degenerating" into a leiomyosarcoma (cancer) are very small, a rapidly growing tumor *could* be a sarcoma. In fact, one doctor had just heard from the lab that a patient diagnosed as having fibroids actually had a sarcoma. He was clearly rattled. "This is the first time in twelve years for me," he said. "It's a very rare situation—it's one in a million."

So we learned that fibroids "rarely" turn out to be anything other than fibroids, yet rarely doesn't mean never, and every doctor can recall an incident where the worst-case scenario was played out. We concluded that preparing a patient for the possibility of cancer is in the doctor's best interests—if not always the patient's. And there's an irony here: judging from the women we interviewed, a doctor's presurgery assessment of whether a patient has a malignancy or a benign condition rarely correlates with the ultimate diagnosis. The patient should keep in mind that the odds are powerfully in favor of her having garden-variety fibroids.

FIBROIDS: CHOICES IN SURGERY

A woman who decides to have surgery for fibroids has several options.

1. *Myomectomy vs. hysterectomy:* Sometimes it's possible to remove the fibroids from the uterus rather than cut out the whole uterus. This operation, called a myomectomy, is more delicate than a hysterectomy. It will be the preference of any woman who hopes to become pregnant and any woman who feels very strongly about having the least possible surgery. The disadvantage of myomectomy is the 15 percent chance that fibroids will recur after the surgery, making another operation necessary— either another myomectomy or a hysterectomy.* Two new techniques have improved the myomectomy and made it a sensible choice for many. (See interviews pp. 110–123.)

2. *Bikini vs. vertical—the incision:* One way to spot the change in medical practice is to note the topics women want to discuss with their surgeon before surgery—for instance, the choice of surgical incision. Instead of ignoring the question as beyond their understanding, many of the women requested the so-called bikini cut. (One woman pasted a sign on herself as she went into surgery: "GIVE ME A LOW BIKINI CUT.") The bikini is the most common incision for both hysterectomy and myomectomy: a horizontal line following the top of the pubic hair. The alternative is the vertical incision, running from below the navel to the top of the pubic hair.

The bikini cut is not only more attractive and less noticeable than the vertical; it is stronger. Also, a bikini cut does not interfere with abdominal enlargement during pregnancy.

Even for cesarean section, the horizontal is recommended. According to the *Mayo Clinic Health Letter* (February 1988), women who have had the vertical cut are not able to have vaginal delivery in future pregnancies; women who have the "lower uterine transverse incision" have a chance. Also, the horizontal incision heals better, with less chance of rupture.

* S O U R C E : *Current Therapy in Surgical Gynecology.*

The vertical allows the surgeon greater visibility and is used when there's a strong possibility of finding a malignancy. Doctors warn patients that the vertical might be necessary if the fibroids are enormous; but in the operations described here, the surgeon always managed to get the fibroids out through the horizontal cut.

3. *Abdominal vs vaginal surgery:* The development of technology makes it possible, in some cases, to perform both hysterectomy and myomectomy through the vagina. By avoiding an abdominal incision, the vaginal approach dramatically reduces the patient's discomfort, lowers the risk of complications and infection, greatly shortens the recovery time, and leaves the patient without a scar.

Not everyone is a candidate for such surgery. If there's any fear of finding a malignancy, most surgeons will insist on the greater visibility allowed by an abdominal incision. If the fibroids are growing from the outer wall of the uterus into the abdominal cavity, obviously the vaginal approach is useless. And if the fibroids are of a size vaguely referred to as "large," doctors will insist on abdominal surgery (though one doctor mentioned a process called morcellation, in which even large fibroids are removed in pieces).

Robert S. Neuwirth, M.D., described the vaginal approach as an option with fibroids "if the uterine cavity is not larger than ten centimeters. With a young woman who hoped to have children, it would be better to do an abdominal myomectomy. But if a woman is forty-five and bleeding, and she's trying to make it to menopause [without major surgery], and we know by virtue of the laparoscope and/or ultrasound that the mass is in fact fibroids, then sure, we will go in vaginally and take out the submucous fibroid or burn out the rest of the endometrium."

For all the guidelines, the greatest obstacle to vaginal surgery is doctors' seeming preference for abdominal surgery. According to Karen Blanchard, M.D., "The vaginal approach requires a higher level of skill than the abdominal." For some reason this method is most commonly performed in the central United States, she says, "but I would think that in any large city, there'll be skilled vaginal surgeons." Judging from the experiences of the women we interviewed who had vaginal surgery, those surgeons are worth hunting out.

PREVENTIVE MEASURES TO AVOID SURGERY FOR FIBROIDS

We began our research with the hope that certain diets, in conjunction with exercise, could reduce the size of fibroids. We still are convinced that good nutrition and health practices are valuable, and we've learned that someone who is fit and lean is going to have an easier time recovering from surgery. But we have seen no evidence that fibroids can be controlled by any regimen. The effort itself, we found, induces a sense of frustration and failure.

We were distressed to learn of some holistic-medicine theories suggesting that fibroids have a psychological component. One woman was told that fibroids are caused by tension, intensity, and "pelvic anger." In effect, these theories, which are totally unfounded, hold the woman responsible for her fibroids. Whenever bad things happen to good or bad people, the question arises: "Why did this happen to me?" The psychological theories of fibroid growth are a false and punishing answer to that question.

SURGERY AS THE BIG SWEEP:
THE OVARIAN CONTROVERSY

In gynecological surgery, we noticed, an attitude of efficiency prevails. "While we're in there, we might as well clean out the ovaries," a forty-six-year-old woman facing a hysterectomy for fibroids was told. Nothing was wrong with her ovaries, and she might reasonably have expected them to supply her with a few years more of natural hormone therapy.

The urge to "clean out" a woman has its roots in the traditional surgical rule: If you don't need it, take it out. By removing the ovaries, the doctor is eliminating a woman's chances of developing ovarian disease. To many gynecologists, a woman who's had all the children she's planning to have—or who knows she'll never want children—no longer "needs" her ovaries. Neither does the "older" patient, though what constitutes hoary age, gynecologically, is chilling. For example, a thirty-five-year-old male gynecologist, identifying himself as one of those at the forefront of medical thinking, said he always tries to save the ovaries unless the patient is "old." "What's old?" we asked. "Forty," he replied.

If a surgeon thinks in terms of statistics rather than about the well-being of a particular woman, it makes sense to follow tradition. Why run the risk of ovarian cancer or a cyst? Ovarian cancer is hard to detect, and it's a virulent killer. On the other hand, it's relatively uncommon (it strikes one in a hundred women, compared with one in ten for breast cancer). Doctors may overstate the risks. One doctor advised a woman to have an oophorectomy along with her hysterectomy, saying "the odds" were she'd get a cyst "sometime." You would not want this man to bet on horses for you: his understanding of odds is eccentric. Only 6 or 7 percent of women will require surgery for ovarian cysts or tumors during their lifetime, according to Hugh Barber, M.D., in his book *Ovarian Cancer: Etiology, Diagnosis, and Treatment*.

Two other studies, cited in *Understanding Your Body*, persuade us that the "odds" are very much in a woman's favor. One study of women who had hysterectomies and kept their ovaries found that only 1 to 2 percent of them subsequently needed surgery for "an ovary or tube problem." And, curiously, the other study reported, only one in a thousand of these women developed ovarian cancer: that rate is *ten times lower* than the average.

Why hysterectomy correlates with a lower incidence of ovarian cancer is not understood. The authors speculate that perhaps the age of the women is a factor: the older the patient, the lower the rate. "It is also possible," they write, "that removing the uterus might in some way protect against later cancer in the ovary, or that women in these studies had lower than average risk factors."

If you want to play odds, there's a 100 percent chance that after oophorectomy, the premenopausal woman will suddenly find herself in surgical menopause, an emotionally and biochemically disruptive event. The ovaries manufacture hormones that regulate the menstrual cycle as well as pregnancy, protect a woman against heart attack, stroke, and bone loss, keep her skin looking young, prevent atrophy of her vaginal tissues, and make it easier for her to lose weight than it is for a postmenopausal woman. After oophorectomy, she may want to start hormone replacement therapy, unless she cannot take estrogen.*

The art of hormone therapy has never been more highly developed, but as one woman was told by a gynecologist-friend, "If

---

* The hormone estrogen is not advised for women with a family tendency toward breast, ovarian, or colon cancer, or a history of stroke, heart, liver, or gall bladder disease, diabetes, or "serious high blood pressure," according to *Understanding Your Body*.

you were my wife, I'd tell you to leave your ovaries in. They're a very good drugstore. It isn't like you walk in and take Premarin the first time and get the right dose. It's a lot more complicated than that, and you're really taking a chance by having them out."

Even for the postmenopausal woman, the loss of her ovaries is not insignificant. "There is increasing evidence that the ovaries do produce hormones well past menopause," according to Susanne Morgan, Ph.D., in *Coping with a Hysterectomy*. "In addition, the ovaries produce many hormones, not just estrogen. Thus estrogen replacement drugs do not fully replace the function of the ovaries."

In response to women's increasing sophistication, medical practice is changing. Many of the doctors we interviewed encouraged us to think that a shift in attitude is taking place. The new surgical guideline, one said, is "if there's nothing wrong with it, leave it alone." Another doctor acknowledged, "I'm becoming more and more conservative with removal of the ovaries. Nobody says to the forty-year-old male who has had a prostatectomy [removal of all or part of the prostate gland], 'Oh, while we're in there, why don't we take out your testicles?' Incidental ovariectomy is no longer incidental."

What we learned from the interviews is that the woman herself can often make the decision to keep her ovaries or have them removed. It's a difficult decision. Some of the women fought to keep surgery to the minimum; others were relieved that the more radical surgery freed them from the fear of further gynecological problems. To absolutely prohibit your doctor from doing what turns out to be necessary, we learned, can backfire. Most women, at the end of their research, made a deal with their doctors: the women entrusted them with the final decision-making power in return for their doctor's promise to remove the ovaries only if they appeared diseased.

The trick is to choose a doctor who respects your right to have a point of view. This may require your finding a new surgeon. A forty-one-year-old mother of two was going into surgery for a cyst on one ovary and a tumor on the other. She asked her doctor to leave as much of the ovaries as he could. "That's really going to be a surgical exercise," he answered, with what she heard as irritation. The surgeon managed to leave part of an ovary, enough to keep her menstruating; however, during the operation, he decided that her uterus was "enlarged" and removed it—despite the biopsy report that it was normal.

It may sound whimsical to suggest leaving a doctor because you don't like his tone of voice, but such intuitive judgments are not to be dismissed. The women who were most content with their surgical experience usually admitted that after all their research, they chose their doctor on the basis of intuition; they trusted their "gut" reactions.

The particular nature of the doctor-patient relationship in the field of gynecology certainly makes such quick moves difficult. The doctor who suggests surgery is usually the woman's long-term gynecologist or obstetrician, the person who has been treating her benignly for years, who delivered her children, or who "has always been very nice." When the doctor tells the woman she needs an operation, she may simply go along, as in the past she trustingly filled prescriptions for medication, birth control, whatever. To question the doctor's skill as a surgeon or attitude may seem disloyal. Worse, it means the patient must become detached and analytical just at the moment anxiety over her health would make her want to lean. She must become a researcher at the moment she is most unnerved by a diagnosis. Her gynecologist's opinion should be checked by another doctor who is not a colleague of the first and, ideally, is affiliated with another hospital. This puts her in a solitary posture and puts the responsibility for the decision on her, where, alas, it belongs. She must, finally, rely on her own research and intuition to decide whether or not she will have surgery and who will do it. The reward is the sense of her own competence and the comfort of knowing that she's done everything she can to get herself the best medical care.

T W O

Gynecological Surgery: The Stories

DILATION AND CURETTAGE (D&C)
DILATION AND EVACUATION (D&E)
LAPAROSCOPY
CONE BIOPSY
OVARIAN SURGERY
TUBAL LIGATION
TUBOPLASTY
CESAREAN SECTION
PELVIC REPAIR
MYOMECTOMY
HYSTERECTOMY

DILATION AND CURETTAGE (D&C)
DILATION AND EVACUATION (D&E)

Dilation and curettage is the most commonly performed surgical procedure for women, according to a 1984 Metropolitan Life Insurance Company study. Women who have abnormally heavy or frequent periods, or who have bleeding after menopause, may have a D&C to find out why. The D&C takes only about fifteen minutes, and you're able to leave three or four hours later. The cervix (the opening to the uterus) is gradually stretched with metal dilators of increasing size. Second, a curette—a long, curved, spoonlike instrument—reaches through the cervix into the uterus and scrapes off samples of the lining.

In many cases the D&C is therapeutic as well as diagnostic. If the cause of the bleeding turns out to be polyps (small, benign growths), those are easily clipped out during the procedure. If the lining of the uterus has thickened in response to hormonal imbalance, scraping alone may stabilize it. "The bleeding stops, and there's instant relief," says Victor Reyniak, M.D. "With other problems, the D&C will only provide diagnosis; it won't cure. If there's a big intracavity fibroid causing the bleeding, D&C will do nothing."

Some doctors will offer to perform the procedure in their office with a local anesthetic, but from our interviews we gather that it is best performed in the hospital under a light general anesthesia. "Discomfort is caused by dilating the cervix," Louis Lapid, M.D., explains. "You can do a local to block that, but when you go in with a curette, it hurts, and a patient could start moving. I wouldn't do it that way."

All of the women who were given the choice had their D&C in the hospital, even though several were anxious about going under anesthesia. After surgery a few had some mild cramping and bleeding, but all returned to normal activity within a day.

D&C may also be performed for the purpose of abortion during the first three months of pregnancy. (If it's early enough into the pregnancy, a D&C isn't necessary. Vacuum aspiration can be performed without dilation and with only a local anesthetic.) After a miscarriage a D&C will make sure all the residual embryonic tissue is flushed out.

If a miscarriage or an abortion takes place in the second trimester (up to twenty-four weeks), the procedure is similar to a D&C but is somewhat more complicated. Called a dilation and evacuation (D&E), it requires greater dilation of the cervix and uses vacuum aspiration as well as a curette.

"I KNOW IT'S A SIMPLE PROCEDURE, BUT I FELT ANGRY THAT IT HAD TO BE DONE, MOSTLY BECAUSE I WAS SCARED."

An actress and writer in her early fifties who had a D&C to remove a polyp. She is divorced, with no children.

What symptoms did you have before being diagnosed?
I was staining way past my period each month. I kept track of it for about a year, and finally the doctor said he thought it was abnormal, because the pattern had continued for so long.
What action did the doctor recommend?
At first he planned to do an endometrial biopsy in the office to check the lining of the uterus. But then he said, "Why don't we do a D&C, and that way I can find out everything I need to know." He thought the problem might be a polyp, but it could have been something more serious.

He had said he could do the endometrial biopsy with tranquilizers and Novocain in the office, so I asked about having the D&C done the same way. I really didn't want to be knocked out. He said he had done D&Cs with no anesthesia but wouldn't recommend it because it's very painful. He also said he had done D&Cs with Novocain, but that the procedure was harder to control with the patient awake than under general anesthesia. Based on that and the fact that I get a hyperreaction to Novocain, I decided to have it done in the hospital under general anesthesia; go to sleep and wake up knowing it was done.

How did you feel about having surgery?
I hated the idea. I know it's a simple procedure, but I felt angry that it had to be done, mostly because I was scared! I'd never been in a hospital.

On the day of the surgery, what happened?
I went by myself. The setup looked like a field hospital in World War I. The thing that was most striking to me was that the little hospital rags they give you to put on are so wrinkled; there are even wrinkled mittens for your feet. You feel thoroughly unattractive. Then my doctor came out, and he looked as though he were in his pajamas. You don't expect that. I thought it would be like the hairdresser—you know, neat, pressed little gowns.

He said, "Are you ready?" and told me I had to sign the usual release form saying that if it's necessary, they reserve the right to remove the uterus or whatever. So I said, "My feminist instinct and training tells me I can't sign." He said, "Don't worry, just cross out everything you don't like." So I did. Then we walked to the operating room together, down long corridors, the two of us padding along trying to make conversation. It felt like death row to me! I was so scared of the anesthesia, I was trembling!

Can you tell us about the anesthesia?
He had said, "We'll meet the anesthesiologist on the way to the operating room." Suddenly, a door opened. I had expected—for some reason—a petite, upwardly mobile feminist. Somehow that image made me feel very comfortable. Out came someone who looked like a linebacker for the Chicago Bears. He was the anesthesiologist. We went into the operating room. It looked dingy and unglamorous, not like in the movies at all. They took my blood pressure, and I said, "What's going to happen?" The anesthesiologist said, "We're going to put you to sleep." He was cheerful. He said, "I have never seen anyone so scared in my life," and burst out laughing. I lay down and he hooked this thing in my arm. I must have looked ashen because my doctor then did a very nice thing. He came over and just put his hand on my cheek, and that made me feel so comforted. They started putting the stuff in me,

and the anesthesiologist said, "You can wash up now." And that's the last thing I remember.

What happened when you awakened in the recovery room?
There was this roar in my head, and they had an oxygen mask on me. I remember shoving it off my face and immediately knowing where I was and what had happened. There was no pain. The thing I hated most was I don't know what happened to my life during that hour under anesthesia—I hated being so out of control.

There was a nurse standing next to me, and she said, "Oh, you can wake up now. You've been asleep a long time." That's why she gave me some oxygen, because I'd been in the recovery room for about twenty-five or thirty minutes, and I was still out. They took off the mask and I started passing out. I thought I was dying. I said that I felt horrible, and this orderly glanced at a monitor and said brusquely, "Your vital signs are fine." They weren't nice at all. I was freezing cold and I just wanted to get out. That was the only unpleasant thing about it.

In about a half hour, the nurse said, "I know you're anxious to leave." I stood up, and then blood went all over the place—all over my gown and all over everything. The orderlies were standing there, and the nurse said, "Oh . . ." and put a screen around me and gave me a sanitary napkin. She said, "Look, we don't have a belt. Could you just sort of hold it while you walk through to get your clothes?" She really expected me to walk through the waiting room all covered with blood. Finally she gave me something to wrap around me. It wasn't frightening. It was just something to deal with.

How did you feel after you left the recovery room?
My sister was waiting for me, and someone gave me a cup of tea, and I felt absolutely fine. It was quite an adventure.

I had what seemed like jet lag for about a day—I would suddenly feel sleepy. Then I was completely clear. I could have done anything.

The doctor told me to call him when I got home, so I did. He said I was fine, that I'd had a polyp, but he'd removed it. Within hours the staining stopped, but there was a mucus discharge for the next few days which the doctor said was perfectly normal. After that I could hardly remember I'd had surgery at all.

"EVEN THOUGH A D&C IS A FAIRLY BENIGN PROCEDURE, IT'S IMPORTANT TO UNDERSTAND WHY—AND IF—YOU REALLY NEED IT."

An artist with a very complicated gynecological history, including polyps and fibroids. She's forty-eight, married, has three children, and has had D&Cs for both diagnostic and therapeutic reasons.

Why did you have the most recent D&C?
I was having irregular bleeding over a long period of time. In the past, I had a D&C that showed a proliferative endometrium, meaning there's more endometrium being produced than you would expect. They tested it, and there were some precancerous changes: they won't say it's cancer, but they'll say they're beginning to see cellular changes. Once that happens, they become concerned when there's sudden irregular bleeding. So this particular physician wanted me to have a D&C for two reasons. One, to know what was going on inside my uterus. The only way to do that is to clear out the whole thing with a D&C. An endometrial biopsy, which is a simpler office procedure that doesn't require general anesthesia, has only 95 percent accuracy, and my doctor wanted to be absolutely sure. Two, cleaning out the uterus with a D&C, even if there's nothing wrong, sometimes just puts the whole system back into whack again.

Was your D&C an office or hospital procedure?
Hospital. It's usually a same-day procedure, but I checked into the hospital the day before the surgery because I was over forty, and once you hit that magic number, they feel you are more at risk for everything. You're taking general anesthesia, and they want to know that all of your vital signs are good.

The big risk in an office procedure, as I understand it, is that they don't have the backup equipment you might need if for any reason you have to change to total anesthesia. That's why, for a D&C, I prefer to be in the hospital.

I didn't have to have the regular blood test and X-rays because I had had a number of them recently. But I have a heart murmur and had to be premedicated with penicillin so I wouldn't get bacterial endocarditis. That's an infection of the heart. It's a potential risk if there's anything amiss with your heart when you're having any work done in the vagina, mouth, or respiratory system: there's heavy bacteria in these areas that can go into your bloodstream.

Couldn't a heart murmur become a serious complication during surgery?

The heart murmur turned out to be more of an issue than the D&C. I had had about three or four D&Cs from 1974 to 1983 for irregular bleeding problems, and I had done just fine. But after the one just before this, I was weak and sick for days. I could barely raise my head or get out of bed. When I was discharged from the hospital, my family took me for a walk and they practically had to carry me home.

So when this D&C had to be done, I was in a state of alarm. It was one of those horrible situations where you have to be your own advocate. I spoke to my doctor about my reaction, and she'd never heard of such a thing but said that I should certainly take it upon myself to talk to the anesthesiologist the day before the D&C. I had to implore him to please check out my past records. He said there was absolutely nothing he uses that has ever given anyone an allergic reaction. But he finally trusted me and got the records. He discovered that, prior to anesthesia the last time, I had been given Fentanyl, [a sedative] known to produce the reaction I had. So this time I was fine.

Is the D&C an anxiety-provoking procedure?

I've had so many other gynecological assaults in my life—stillbirths, miscarriages, and whatnot—that I don't consider the D&C scary. It's a brief, routine, and innocuous procedure. It's not invasive the way abdominal surgery is. The anxiety for me always had to do with the risk of general anesthesia, which is something to avoid if you can. But I've had a D&C with just local anesthetic, and I don't think I'd ever consider doing that again. The pain was unforgettable, and you can usually forget pain. I know many women who, when they have elective abortions, will go to their gynecologist's office and have an aspiration procedure done with just a local anesthetic—an injection to the cervix—and have no problems. Different people have different relationships to their bodies. Someone has a great recovery from something, and someone else has a lousy one. But the great advantage of general anesthesia is that you have *no* pain.

How is the recovery from a D&C?

It's really like recovering from a bad period. Maybe you'll have some cramping. You have to take some precautions afterward—no intercourse for two weeks and showering instead of bathing for a week or so. But, basically, you're absolutely fine, able to go out and do you name it. And within six weeks you have a period again.

What would you advise women considering a D&C?

Even though a D&C is a fairly benign procedure, it's important to understand why—and if—you really need it. And what the alternatives are to having it. What the risks are *to* having it and what the risks are to *not* having it.

"I HAD NO DISCOMFORT AFTERWARD AT ALL—EXCEPT MY THROAT HURT FROM THE TUBE THEY PUT IN TO HELP YOU BREATHE. NO ONE TOLD ME THAT WOULD HAPPEN."

A thirty-three-year-old graphic designer, married, with no children. She had a D&E after a miscarriage, a year before this interview.

Could you tell us what the circumstances were around your miscarriage?

I was about day sixty-one of a pregnancy. I started having a slight discharge about four in the afternoon. I called my doctor, but her office was closed, so I talked to her the next day, about five-thirty in the evening when I got home from work. She told me that it was really too early to do anything, that I should just stay in bed and call her if anything else happened. About four in the morning I woke up and was really discharging. I thought, Well, that's it. There's nothing we can do at this point other than cry. I called the doctor about nine in the morning. She wasn't in, but her nurses called me back—it's a very good practice. They said to stay in bed and not to move. I was bleeding very heavily, and I presumed I had miscarried. The doctor called and told me to come in. And when she examined me, she told me I was still pregnant and sent me for ultrasound.

Based on the ultrasound, my doctor's recommendation was to

go ahead and do a D&E. I was feeling ill by this point and upset. My doctor said, "We can wait and see what happens tomorrow, but I think everything that was there has gone." She said she could do it in the office, but when I said, "That's going to be painful, isn't it?" she arranged to do it in the hospital at five o'clock that day. So I went home, called my husband at work, and he came to get me.

How was your emotional state?

We were just really sad. We had been sad the first night, Thursday, when I realized something was wrong. Friday had just been a day of dealing with the doctors and nurses. It's an odd kind of situation, trying not to burst out crying.

What do you remember about the procedure?

They wheeled me into the operating room and were very, very nice. The anesthesiologist talked to me and was really gentle. He gave me the anesthetic in my hand. I got groggy at that point. They placed something over my legs that felt like rubber leggings, and the next thing I remember was thinking I was dying. I was choking, I couldn't talk, I couldn't open my eyes, and I couldn't breathe. I didn't seem to be able to get anybody's attention. Then everyone was around me and telling me to calm down.

They must have put a breathing tube down your throat—did they take it out?

Yes, but I didn't feel them take it out. Just, all of a sudden, they were saying it was okay. But I could feel that my throat was bruised. No one told me that would happen. I found out later that the same thing happened to a friend of mine who had a miscarriage about six months before.

How long was the surgery?

The doctor talked to us beforehand. She said, "It will be either ten minutes or much longer." If everything was straightforward, I would only be in for ten or fifteen minutes. If it was a tubal pregnancy or anything complicated, I gave her permission to go in and sort it out. When I first came to, I looked at the clock and I was so relieved—it was only fifteen minutes after I'd gone in, so I knew it had been a simple D&E.

How did you feel in the recovery room?

The anesthesiologist kept asking me a lot of questions—how old I was, where I was born, the date of my last period. I wondered if she was doing some kind of survey. I guess she was just trying to see how alert I was. I wanted water, and they could only give me a piece of lemon soaked in water. I probably felt better than I had during the last fifteen hours because I didn't hurt anymore. I had no discomfort afterward at all.

I was there about an hour. They said I had to wait until I could urinate, and then I could go home. I was still a little dizzy. My leg hurt because they had given me a sedative in my thigh, right in the muscle. My thigh hurt for about two weeks.

Did you have any other problems after the D&E?
No, the doctor told me she'd found some fibroids, which were no big deal, she said, because they were small, and she'd removed them. I went back for a checkup about four weeks later. I'd been told I might bleed for two weeks, but I only bled for about five days, and it wasn't heavy. I didn't have a period for about six or seven weeks afterward.

When did you resume sex?
Two weeks after the D&E. There was no problem.

How would you assess the D&E?
It wasn't difficult. I didn't ache afterward, and other than my throat and my leg, I had no discomfort.

"I HAD A DIAPHRAGM, BUT I WASN'T USING IT."
A student in her early twenties who chose to have a D&E when she discovered she was pregnant.

What were the circumstances leading to the abortion?
I was traveling in Italy and had missed a period, but I thought I was late because of the time difference. Also, I never have regular periods and during that time I kept getting slight cramps, so I was sure I would be getting a period at any time. But when I came back home, after almost two months without a period, I went to a student clinic at college and had a blood test. And the results were positive.

How did you feel about that?
Well, I didn't take it lightly. But I knew I couldn't keep the child. If I didn't have the choice of an abortion, I don't know what I would have done. I wasn't married, it was something I had to do. But I had no money. I couldn't borrow from my family, and I wasn't working. My roommate was so good about it—she lent me the money.

Did the college clinic recommend a doctor?
Yes. They referred me to a doctor who gave me a regular gynecological examination. He said I was farther along than the four
or five weeks I thought I was. It turned out I was eight or nine
weeks pregnant.

How soon did you have the abortion?
About a week later. The doctor made an appointment for me at
an abortion clinic, where I was registered as his private patient
rather than as a clinic patient.

What was the procedure at the clinic?
They gave me a sonogram and a blood test. I had more trouble
with the blood test than I did with anything else. I have very low
blood pressure, so it takes a long time to have my blood drawn.
The guy was a little impatient with me. I signed a form stating I
hadn't had anything to eat or drink within the last twelve hours,
and that if I died while under the anesthesia, it wasn't the doctor's fault. That really freaked me out. I never thought you could
die under anesthesia. They took a complete family medical history, where I listed every medical condition that existed in my
family from allergies to ragweed to who had diabetes and heart
disease. And then the doctor told me, "You will be completely
out. We're going to dilate your cervix and then we're going to
place the machine into your cervix and use the suction method."

How long did the whole thing take?
Fifteen minutes.

Were you in any pain afterward?
A little bit, not too much. They pick you up after you wake up and
put you in a wheelchair and wheel you to the recovery room. The
only problem I had was, the nurse told me to get up too soon.
You're supposed to rest there for half an hour, and I knew I hadn't
been there for half an hour. I was weak and had cramps, but I
managed to start dressing. They gave me a sanitary pad attached
to this little garter thing. I wasn't bleeding heavily at all. By the
time I got dressed, I felt fine.

How long was it before you could resume sex?
They said not to have sex for at least two weeks and, when I did,
to use birth control. They also gave me a little pamphlet that
stressed that abortion was not a form of birth control.

What kind of birth control did you use after the abortion?
Oh, the Pill, and immediately.

What were you using when you got pregnant?
I had a diaphragm, but I wasn't using it—it was too much trouble.

———————

"PHYSICALLY, IT WAS AS SIMPLE AND EFFICIENT AS I
CAN IMAGINE IT BEING. AND AS UNINTIMIDATING. THE
REAL STRESS OF IT FOR ME WASN'T PHYSICAL—IT WAS
EMOTIONAL."
A thirty-three-year-old choreographer with no children.

At what point in the pregnancy did you have the abortion?
I must have been eight weeks pregnant. We knew earlier, but apparently there's a better chance of getting everything if you wait until eight weeks.
Was it done in the hospital or your doctor's office?
In the hospital, on an outpatient basis. I was scheduled for surgery at 11 A.M. They tell you to get there an hour in advance. When I arrived they said to me, "We've got nobody in the operating room, so just come on in." Looking back, it was a good thing they did me forty-five minutes early, because I was very nervous. I had never been under general anesthesia before. I had never checked into a hospital before.
Did you have a workup before the procedure?
One week before surgery, I had to go to the hospital and have an EKG, chest X-ray, a lot of blood tests, and a urine test to make sure you're in good enough shape for general anesthesia.
Any rules about not eating before surgery?
Yes, I wasn't allowed to eat or drink anything after six o'clock the night before. I had a nightmare that I woke up and took a drink and screwed everything up. I didn't have to have an enema or anything like that.
Did you go to the hospital alone?
No, Dan [the man she'd been seeing for a year] went with me. He took the day off from work. Everyone was very nice. I expected to be processed through some mill. And I expected a lot more formality around the operating room. I pictured operating rooms the way you see them in movies, as these closed amphitheaters with people wheeling in and out. It was nothing like that!

They showed me where to change—it was like a locker room! Then they led me into this room that had maybe five beds in it, where the anesthesiologist was waiting. My doctor came in and talked to me for two minutes and said, "Well, why don't we start?" So they took me into this adjoining room, which was the operating room. There was no dramatic demarcation between one thing and another. It was just sort of, "Well, here's the table, hop on."

Where was Dan—in the waiting room?

He was very nervous, and he wasn't allowed to smoke in the waiting room, so he spent the whole day on the lawn in front of the hospital.

What happened once you hopped on the table?

The anesthesiologist started an IV on top of my hand. I was lying there and she said, "Now you should be getting a little drowsy." My limbs felt very relaxed, but my mind, I remember, was racing. I thought, They'll never put me out like this. The next thing I knew, they were slapping me in the face and calling my name. I had read somewhere that when you're put out under general anesthesia, your mind picks up exactly where it left off—there's no notion of time having elapsed. So I was thinking, Well, when are they going to do it? And I was in the recovery room. It was that simple.

The other funny thing was that when we started, I had my knees bent to make it easy for them to put my feet into the stirrups—but the nurse kept saying, "Relax, straighten your legs." I guess they just push you into position once you're out. And when I woke up, I was lying there with my legs straight and thought, They've never done the surgery.

How much time did the whole thing take?

I think it was twenty minutes. I had read the night before, in *Our Bodies, Ourselves*, that this procedure was now simpler than a tonsillectomy, which gave me great confidence.

How did you feel in the recovery room?

I felt perfectly fine. I could have just gotten up and walked out. A nurse kept coming by and taking my temperature. The sheets were soaked with blood—which I wasn't aware of until I got up. They brought me some very sugary tea and a couple of Saltines. Dan called from downstairs, and they told him that I was fine and that I was resting. I remember being amazed at how long they made me stay there. I think they didn't let me go until about two—and they'd started me at about ten-fifteen.

One of the first things I thought about when I woke up was how different my body felt. I don't know if this is psychosomatic or not. Even though I was only eight weeks into the pregnancy, I'd felt as though my body were changing. I'd been very aware that my breasts were bigger, that I was retaining water. And then, when I was lying in the recovery room, I had that feeling you have on the first day of your period—when you've been retaining all this water and suddenly it's gone. You feel kind of cleaned out and streamlined. I remember feeling a kind of euphoria then.

Anyway, Dan came up at two to get me. I changed and went home. I was very tired, but that was really the only effect. In fact, I went out for dinner with Dan that night.

Did you continue to bleed?

I did, but not for as long as you would bleed with a period—maybe that day and the next, and that was it.

No other aftereffects?

None. No achiness, no reaction to the anesthesia. It was very simple. Physically speaking, it was as simple and efficient as I can imagine it being. And as unintimidating. I think the real stress of it for me was not physical—it wasn't what was happening with my body—so much as it was emotional.

Were you ambivalent about having it done?

I didn't feel there was really a choice to be made—my life was not such that I could have done anything else—but it was a very hard decision for both of us. We both wanted children, and at that time we thought we wanted children with each other. That was so difficult, because you thought to yourself, Isn't this selfish, to be saying, "Well, it's not *convenient* for me now."

I once read that every woman who goes through this thinks in her heart of hearts that it's wrong, but when the time comes and you have to do it, you do it. It's like situational ethics. I can't say I felt guilt, but I can't imagine going into it and not feeling something, some compunction about doing it. I think it's just a very emotionally involved procedure.

What happened afterward? When were you allowed to take a bath and to have sex?

I don't remember being told anything about baths, and I think I was told to wait a week to have sex.

How soon afterward did you get your period?
It was about a month—it was just a regular cycle.
How did you get pregnant?
On the sponge. I had read about the sponge, and it sounded great. My doctor later told me the sponge was disastrous: the pregnancy rate with it is amazingly high. I went back to the diaphragm.

LAPAROSCOPY

L aparoscopy is a common procedure that allows gynecologists to look into the abdomen, either for diagnostic or therapeutic purposes, without inflicting major surgery on a woman.

A small incision is made under the belly button or sometimes in one of its folds. The surgeon feeds a hollow needle into the incision and pumps carbon monoxide to inflate the abdominal cavity—to create both visibility and space to maneuver. The needle is removed and replaced by the laparoscope, a long metal tube with a lens and light at one end and an eyepiece at the other (imagine a cross between a telescope and a miner's cap). If a procedure is to be performed, another instrument is inserted through an incision made above the pubic line.

Laparoscopy is performed under general anesthesia and, like a D&C, may be done on an outpatient basis. One woman, however, advised staying in the hospital overnight, "because you're tired and you'll want to be taken care of." There is some soreness following the surgery, described as "mild" or "tremendous" depending on the woman, but everyone was back to her normal schedule within a day or two.

———————

"I GUESS I WANTED TO TRUST MY DOCTOR AND LOVE HIM, AND I WANTED HIM TO TAKE CARE OF ME. I'M NOT GOING TO DO THAT ANYMORE."

A thirty-year-old stage manager, married, who had a laparoscopy to determine treatment for a cyst.

How did you discover that you needed medical attention?
It's really strange, and they still don't know what it was. I developed a ridge on one side of my pubic area. It hurt to touch it, and it hurt when I urinated.

So that got me to the doctor. I hadn't been in a long time. He

told me it was a pulled muscle, but while I was there he did a
Pap test. Then, during the time I was waiting for the results of
the test, I started developing a really dull pain on my right side. I
knew it was my ovary, because I'd had cysts on my ovary before.
The doctors had put me on the Pill, and the cysts had gone away.

My doctor called with the results of the Pap test and said I had
Class II cells—a II out of five possibilities. Class V is cancer; IV
is very bad; III is not great; and II, they don't know—it's just not
normal. He called it abnormal cell activity, "mild dysplasia." Apparently, a II on a Pap is fairly common. It's not a disease or
anything. People who have been sexually active, which I haven't
been except with one man for two years, are more prone to it.
And apparently it's more common in your twenties.

I made an appointment to see him and have another Pap test,
but I started getting these pains, so I asked to come in earlier. I'd
also missed a period, which is very unusual for me. The doctor
went into mild fits because he thought I had a tubal pregnancy.
He said he felt a lump the size of a small lemon or a huge cherry
—it's amazing how these fruits change; I guess he wasn't sure
what size it was. The pregnancy test came back negative, so that
was a relief. Then he said, "Well, it could be a non-hormone-
producing pregnancy, so don't think you're out of the woods yet."
And the second Pap result came back, again with a Class II. A
few days later he sent me for a sonogram. They found a cyst big
enough, he said, that he needed to go in and have a look. He said,
"Laparoscopy first, and if I see what I think is there, major surgery." They would open me up, take out the cysts, and do a biopsy
on my cervix to find out why the Pap smears weren't quite right.

Did you know what a laparoscopy was?
It's one incision in your belly button and another right at your
pubic hair line, very small, a third of an inch long. They put
something like a periscope in the belly button incision and blow
up your stomach with carbon dioxide gas so that it becomes like
a dome. They can see and prod everything—it's exploratory surgery; that's how they refer to it. Then they stitch it up: you have
two or three stitches, and they just dissolve. I still have a little
scar.

Were you nervous?
The doctor made one comment that freaked me out. Before I went
in for my sonogram, he said, "Well, you're a young woman. The-

oretically, this isn't cancer." That scared me—I felt like it was a possibility. And I'm not someone who gets cancer fits.

Did you go for a second opinion?
This is what I really hate myself for. I didn't insist on getting a second opinion. I didn't want to deal with it. I was in pain—I could feel this weight on one side, moving and hurting me. I was concerned about the Pap smear. The abnormal cell activity could be precancerous, he said, and I just trusted him, for some odd reason. My uncle, who is this nice, old-school doctor, looked up this guy's credentials, decided he was a top man, and said, "Why don't you just go with him?" And frankly, I had very little money and I just didn't want to spend it on a second opinion. So there I was, slapped in the hospital.

What's the preparation for a laparoscopy?
I went in the day before for tests: I gave them urine and blood and had an electrocardiogram. The next day, I checked in and found I was sharing a room with three other women who were exactly my age and had all been married a year. Really nice roommates. They were all exactly like me, and they were all recovering.

So anyway, they shlepped me to the operating room without giving me a sedative—something had gone wrong, and the doctor was mad at them. Luckily, I could meditate to calm myself.

What were the results of the surgery?
I woke up in the recovery room and the first thing I heard was, "Well, we didn't have to operate. It was just a laparoscopy." At first I was relieved, but then I got depressed thinking, So what the hell was this all about? Now that I'm in debt, he's very breezy. The doctor's very much like the guy on *Fantasy Island*, Ricardo Montalban. He's got this very great accent and a Mercedes, and he's very handsome. He said, "The cyst was a little smaller than we'd thought. We did a biopsy and the cells are fine, and good-bye." So then I proceeded to have four days of horrible depression. I'm not good with drugs: the anesthetic really threw me for a loop. And it was painful afterward. I walked really gingerly for five days and felt this tremendous soreness through the whole abdominal area. And you know, when you have any of these operations, you get gas really bad. Not gas pains like we know them. Sharp pains. I had that for a day or two.

I spent two days total in the hospital. When I left I still had a really bad pain on my right side. I called the doctor and he said maybe the cyst was exploding but not to worry about that. And he said he'd put me on the Pill for at least six months. Frankly, I don't know why he hadn't tried me on the Pill in the first place. The surgery cost me like $2,000. My medical insurance is minimal—they gave me $350, because they pay 80 percent of the 1982 figures of what they think a procedure should cost, and they think this operation should have cost $400. I'm really mad about that because I have been treated for cysts before with the Pill, and apparently it worked.

Why does the Pill help?
Your ovaries don't function when you're on the Pill. My cyst went right away. And you can't form cysts because you're not ovulating. At least, that's what I understand.* To this day, I don't get any information from my doctor that I don't specifically demand, and he doesn't take enough time to explain things, which is why I'm getting a new doctor.

Did you go back for a postoperative checkup?
Yes, about a month later. Then he decided he wanted to do a cervical biopsy, and he did that in the office. Without anesthetic —and it hurt. He pinched off a tiny bit of the cervix. That's what it seemed like he did.

When he got that result back, he said I had mild dysplasia and he did cryotherapy or cryosurgery—he used both words. That's freezing the entire cervix. They take off a layer of that tissue from the cervix. I passed a lot of water for a week, but there was no blood. Then you get better and have a brand-new cervix. That's the only good thing that happened out of this. Apparently the cervix can take a lot of abuse. I saw my cervix in the mirror. That's one good thing this guy does; he shows you your cervix in a mirror. And I saw it. Before, there was a small red line going down. Now it's cured. And that's the end of that.

What advice would you give women considering a laparoscopy?
I would definitely tell them, if they have a cyst, to ask their doctors why they couldn't try shrinking it with the Pill first. Running

---

* By suppressing the natural hormone cycle, the Pill can shrink existing cysts and prevent new ones from forming, according to the American College of Obstetricians and Gynecologists.

around with a cyst is very uncomfortable—very annoying, a heavy kind of dull pain—and it drains you, but surgery is a big thing, both financially and emotionally. Then, go to a second doctor, definitely. My doctor was really cavalier about it, I see in retrospect. I guess I wanted to trust him and love him, and I wanted him to take care of me. He's very charming. But I'm not going to do that anymore.

"HEARING THE NURSE DESCRIBE THE OPERATION WAS LIKE LISTENING TO A GOOD MECHANIC. SOME OF MY FRIENDS SAID, 'OH, I'D NEVER WANT TO KNOW ALL THAT,' BUT, TO ME, IT ALL SOUNDED VERY DO-ABLE."
A free-lance picture editor in her forties, married, who had a laparoscopy followed by abdominal surgery to remove tumors on her ovaries.

Why did you have a laparoscopy?
The idea was to find out why I couldn't get pregnant. I spent two nights in the hospital and had no pain except for a sore throat from the tube they put down your throat under anesthesia. It was not traumatic. I wasn't crazy about the scars—one near my pubic hair and one by the belly button—but since the abdominal surgery, I have a vertical scar that connects the two, so "Oh, what the hell" is my feeling now.

Serendipitously, during the laparoscopy, my doctor discovered a tumor on my ovary. When he came to give me the news, it was just like a Bette Davis movie. The lights were low, there wasn't anybody around. He sat at my bedside—he's a very nice man—and he said, "We've laparascoped and we found something else." My heart stopped. He said, "We've found a tumor on one of the ovaries." I felt, Oh, God. He said, "I'm sure, from the look of it, it's benign—it's very small, about one centimeter, and it's thick in nature—but we have to take it out immediately." I really freaked out about it.

Did you go for a second opinion?
Yes, and that doctor said the tumor absolutely was not palpable and suggested I have a sonogram. The sonogram showed up another tumor on the other ovary. The first doctor hadn't been able to see this tumor with the laparoscope because there was scar-

ring, either from some pelvic infection or an abortion I'd had or something like that. So now we knew there were two tumors, and I had to go right in for surgery.

What did you do to prepare for surgery?

I asked my doctor's nurse to schedule me as his last patient one day, so I wouldn't be interrupted, and I went in with a long list of questions. I also talked to everybody I knew who had had the operation, and I got books like *Women Care* and *Our Bodies, Ourselves.*

But what I really wanted to know was what the actual surgery was going to be like. My brother put me in touch with a gyneco-logical surgery nurse who was the head of her department. She was fantastic. She asked me, "How much do you want to know?" I said, "I want to know from the minute they start to the minute they stop." I had images of lying there naked, and blood spatter-ing. She told me there was very little blood, that they drape you and cut a hole in the cloth so you're not naked. She explained that the first cut is made with this instrument, and the second cut with that one. . . . I followed it all in my mind's eye, and it calmed me down. It was like listening to a good mechanic. Some of my friends said, "Oh, I'd never want to know all that," but when she explained the process, it all sounded very doable.

I wrote my will, because I was very, very nervous about the anesthesia—I had no control over who did the anesthesia. But when I saw the anesthesiologist, he looked so macho to me, I thought, This guy would never want to lose a conquest or a card game or a patient. Later, when I found out I had to have the tumors removed, I campaigned to get that same guy. I made my doctor operate on the day he was on.

Was this enthusiasm for the anesthesiologist purely visual, or did you talk to him as well?

I called him up on the phone. See, no one ever tells you you're going to be intubated—have a pipe for breathing put down your throat. The worst thing about the laparoscopy was my sore throat afterward. I was not going back for surgery unprepared. I asked the anesthesiologist if he could use a smaller tube; he said if it was medically safe, he would. I also asked if I could use Chloraceptine to spray my throat afterward. He said sure.

What did you bring to the hospital?
I had a little postsurgery kit of lozenges and Chloraceptine for my throat, though, as it turned out, I had no problem this time. Maybe he used a smaller tube.

I brought in my own flowered pillowcases, to make it a little bit more like home. I had books and also special tapes that calm you before surgery and help you heal afterward. They came from Planetree, which is a physical and mental health research group as well as a store. They do medical research for you, sort of holistically oriented. The presurgery tapes calm you with music and tell you to trust your doctor and that you are in good hands. The after-surgery tape talks about how all the antibodies are rushing to your scar now, like an army of soldiers, to help you heal. (In fact, a surgeon friend of mine says the antibody troops do march to the front after surgery.) The tapes were very helpful.

I even brought a special mattress, an "eggcrate," they call it. You get it in a surgical supply store. It's supposed to be more comfortable to lie on. It really wasn't necessary, but I wanted to be prepared. I bought new nightgowns, too.

The night before surgery . . .
A girlfriend of mine went to the hospital with me. She brought flowers for the room and dinner for us. I hung some pictures and we fixed up the room. I didn't feel that vulnerable the night before. I had a very, very nice nurse, and a private phone, and my best girlfriend said, "You can call me at three o'clock in the morning if you need me," and I did call her at one o'clock.

How did the surgery go?
My understanding with the doctor was that if he could save the ovaries, he would, and I had to sign a paper giving him permission to do a full hysterectomy. It turned out that he could save only half an ovary. I was already forty-two, and if I wasn't going to try to get pregnant, he might not have bothered to save the half. But he was able to do it, and women can have ten children with half an ovary.

And your recovery?
I had been anxious about the catheter—some women are bothered by it—but it turned out not to be a problem. I didn't even know that it was in, and then they just took it out. I also had been freaked out about having gas pains. Well, I never had one. Not one. And I'd worried about walking right after surgery, but I'll

tell you, the anticipation was much worse than the reality. Much worse—that's the truth! I think the books I read were very alarmist. It would be helpful to tell people, "You might have all these problems, but you might have none."

The interns come in and talk to you, and they ask you a million times, "Are you allergic to anything?" I think you have to be very patient with all that double-checking everything, because it's all for your own good.

I had put out such an alarm that I was going into the hospital that I had a cadre of people on call. My entire room was filled with gorgeous flowers. That was very good therapy: I would get up every day and prune, I would garden. It was great. And I tried to schedule people coming in to visit. It's a little funny in a hospital: people can walk in on you whenever they want, and I didn't like that. I'm a controlling type of person. Sometimes incompatible groups were there together. It was like holding court. But mostly it was really nice.

At home . . .

I tried to keep a certain romance alive with my husband, because we couldn't have sex for such a long time. So sometimes we watched dirty movies and fooled around a little bit. I didn't want him to feel distant from me—I was so self-absorbed at that point.

The surgical recuperation went very, very well, but I found my hair became lifeless. My beautician told me the anesthesia had affected my hair. No dermatologist could tell me what to do, but I found a product called KMS Finish—it's a tangle and medication remover, and it really has helped me a lot.

What was your emotional state?

My surgery was in January. In May I started getting depressed. I stopped menstruating, and I went into a horrible clinical depression. It made the surgery seem like a picnic. It was the worst thing that ever happened to me. My doctor thought perhaps I was in menopause and tested my FSH levels. FSH is the follicle stimulating hormone. When you go into menopause your FSH increases. Usually that's what causes the night sweats and everything. FSH stimulates the ovaries to produce estrogen; the release of estrogen is a cue to turn off production of FSH. As the level of estrogen drops, FSH levels rise.

My levels were normal, but something was definitely going wrong. My life stopped. You wouldn't know it was me. My voice was flat, I had to give up all my work, I couldn't leave the house.

I didn't want to go on antidepressants because my doctor said it might interfere with getting back my period, so I went to see a psychiatrist. My doctor twice gave me a hormone, Provera, and finally my period came back; and as it did, the depression started to lift.

I had my period again from September until this past June, and then I stopped menstruating. I went into hideous hot flashes, every hour on the hour. It was devastating. It was also humorous. I was in Alaska at the time, and everybody else was stuffed into parkas, freezing, and there I was, sweating. When I got home, I had my hormones tested again and they were starting to rise.

And how are you now?

I'm in menopause now, and because I'm in *early* menopause, I have to worry about osteoporosis—that's a whole new wrinkle. I've had to be tested for osteoporosis twice, and there is some bone loss. It's been advised that I go on hormone replacement therapy, except that I'm still producing some estrogen and have some bleeding as a result of taking Provera every two or three months to shed the uterine lining. Probably by next year, I'll be on hormone replacement therapy. I'm thinking of the transdermal patch, because I have intestinal problems, but I've learned that the absorption of estrogen is not even with the patch. And my endocrinologist is taking all his patients off the patch because it's causing a lot of irritation. Maybe they'll have worked out the kinks by the time I'm ready for it.

CONE BIOPSY

Conization, or cone biopsy, is recommended when repeated Pap tests find irregular or malignant cells on the cervix. Performed in a hospital, under general anesthesia, cone biopsy scoops out a wedge of cells from the mouth of the uterus (imagine cutting an eye out of a potato). The goal is to remove enough tissue to catch all the irregular cells as well as a margin of safety. The procedure is both diagnostic and, if all the irregular cells are eliminated, a means of treatment.

Whether the Pap results are described to you as Class I or II, if cone biopsy is the suggested treatment, then you don't have invasive cancer, according to Anthony Calanog, M.D., director and attending surgeon, gynecologic oncology, Lenox Hill Hospital, New York. "You do cone biopsies to prevent invasive cancer. With cone biopsy, you can cure what we call preinvasive lesions in about 90 percent of cases—everything is curable before it becomes invasive. It is also true that if the lesions are left untreated, 90 percent will become cancer in ten to fifteen years."

The traditional cone biopsy uses a scalpel to cut out the cells. An alternative method applies laser to vaporize the cells (see interview with J. Victor Reyniak, M.D., page 266). If laser is used, the hospital stay is shortened from a few days to a few hours. (With both scalpel and laser, there's no abdominal incision: the surgical approach is vaginal.)

There is a risk, with cone biopsy, of weakening the cervix—the door to the uterus—and increasing the chances of a miscarriage or premature delivery. This risk is thought to be lessened with laser.

"THIS EXPERIENCE MADE ME REALIZE MY HEALTH WAS IMPORTANT TO ME. BEFORE THIS, I DIDN'T CARE. I

LIVED IN THE FAST LANE, SMOKED A LOT, DRANK A
LOT, DIDN'T EXERCISE AT ALL."

*The owner/chef of a successful restaurant in Seattle who
had a cone biopsy two and a half years before this interview.
She is thirty-two years old and single.*

How did you discover you had a problem?
I've always done my yearly, good-little-girl Pap test. I went to a
gynecologist who is a very good friend. He was not real alarmed,
but he said, "Your Pap test has shown some bad signs of dysplasia."
What level was the dysplasia?
It was Class III. So he said, "We've got to do a biopsy right away."
That's where you go in and they cut out a little piece of cervical
tissue. He numbed the area, but it was still uncomfortable.
And what were the results of the biopsy?
It was cancer, and we had to decide quickly what kind of surgery
it was going to be—whether it would be a freezing method or an
actual cone biopsy. Of course, I went to all the books I could find
and read the pros and cons of both. Since my gynecologist has
been a friend of mine for ten years, I very much trusted his opinion.
*What surgery did your doctor recommend, and what did he
tell you about it?*
He wanted to do a cone biopsy. He drew a diagram of the incision
and described how he cuts out a piece of the cervix in the shape
of a cone or pyramid so the cancer cells won't grow in an invasive
way. He showed me how he could do a tiny cone or a larger one.
The idea is to do a small cone that's big enough to get all the
cancer cells but keep the cervix from scarring over too much.
  The only thing that alarmed me was that something like 35
percent of all women who have a cone biopsy have a hard time
carrying a child to term because of scar tissue in the cervix. So if
I wanted a kid, I was taking a chance by having a cone biopsy.
But he kept assuring me, "As a friend, and because I know you'd
make a great mother, I'm going to do such a great job on you that
you're not going to scar." And in fact every six months when he
checks me, he says, "That was a great job I did! The scar tissue
is healing so well, you can hardly tell it's there." So I feel good
about how well he did.

*How soon after the cancer cells were discovered did you
have surgery?*
It was probably within two months.
How long were you in the hospital?
I went in at nine in the morning, the surgery was around eleven,
and I went home about nine at night.
Did you have general anesthesia?
Yes. And the whole thing took about an hour.
How was your recovery at home?
My mother came down from Vancouver and took good care of
me. She was there for two weeks after the surgery because it was
a pretty intense time of healing. I couldn't get out of bed except
to go to the bathroom. They didn't want me to risk hemorrhaging.

There was no pain, but you know how, when you have your
period, you feel as if there's a gravitational pull on your uterus?
That was the feeling when I stood up. It felt right for me to be
lying down. By the second week, though, it was definitely, "I'm
ready to go, Mom, so you can get out of here. I've got to go back
to the restaurant." But I stayed home the rest of the week and
did all my business from the telephone. I saw this rest period as
perfect timing in my life. I had been going at such a fast pace, it
was almost as if I needed this to remind me to slow down and be
aware of how blessed I am with my life and with good health. It
just made everything, the pleasures of living, so much more intense.
Did life return to normal after your two-week rest?
Well, almost in a rebellious spirit, I got pregnant immediately.
The doctor had said, "No sex for two weeks," which I adhered to,
but right after that I really went to town. And I couldn't believe I
was pregnant. It was almost masochistic. Four weeks after the
surgery, I had to go in for another general anesthesia—it was a
full operation, a D&C. I felt very stupid. I had been very stupid
with my body.
Were you using any birth control?
In general, I do. But that night I didn't use my diaphragm.
Did your doctor recommend the diaphragm?
I decided it was the best form of birth control. I think that the
IUD has contributed to cervical cancer in women. The cervix is
not protected in any way with an IUD. And because this is a
promiscuous age we've been going through, every time a woman
makes love to a different man, it's a whole new set of flora and

fauna the body has to deal with. I think our immune system has a hard time adjusting to a new chemistry being introduced into our bodies by each new man. The diaphragm offers some protection. At least that's my theory.

And does your doctor agree with your theory?
I talked to him about my theories. I've asked him whether he thinks that the sexual revolution has anything to do with the number of cases of cervical cancer he sees—because it's one of the cancers women are getting most frequently right now. He said he agreed totally. Realistically, if you consider the kinds of sexual choices we all have, it's a hard time for all of us. The consequences of the fact that we're sexually active seem to be coming down on us in certain forms of cervical cancer, AIDS, herpes, all that stuff. I think it's making us more conscious about what we're doing. I *know* the people I date. I may not have relationships that lead to walking down the aisle, but I do know they will be honest with me if I ask whether they have any sexual diseases or whether they're promiscuous. And that kind of relationship is only possible after knowing someone for a long time.

*Has this experience with cancer caused you to change
your life in any way?*
It's made me realize my health was important to me. Before this, I didn't care. I lived in the fast lane, smoked a lot, drank a lot, didn't exercise at all. I've just started exercising, and I like it a lot. So I think that the operation actually helped me enjoy life more. I think it's going to help me live longer, or at least live healthier.

So you feel you have completely recovered from surgery?
The operation was perfect. Well, we'll see how perfect it is when I do decide to have a baby. Because I'm pretty sure I'm going to. I have heard of a woman who had the same kind of operation I had with Class III dysplasia. She has been trying to get pregnant, and has miscarried three times now. So that's a risk you take with this method of surgery.

Are you afraid that the atypical cells will return?
No, although once in a while I've wondered about it. But I figure as long as I keep my Pap tests going—for the first two years, I had a Pap test every three months, and now I have one every six months—with a doctor I really trust, who sincerely cares about my health, we should be able to catch it if something else happens.

*Does your doctor feel it's important for you to get pregnant
within the next few years?*

No. He says I'm so healthy I can have a baby when I'm fifty. He
thinks there is no such thing as the right time for a woman as
long as she's fertile.

*What advice would you offer to women who have been told
they have cervical cancer?*

To do as much self-education as possible, and not to put all their
trust in one person's opinion. Even though I educated myself a
lot during the process, I learned even more after the operation,
and I'm wondering now whether I would have been better off
with the freezing method. I'm not completely sure that the cone
biopsy was the right thing for me to do. I am now reading statistics that seem to confirm that women who have cone biopsies are
finding it difficult to carry babies to term. But it's Russian rou-
lette, and I won't know if I did the right thing until I get pregnant.

So I would advise a woman to be completely informed. I would
also get a second opinion. I got a second opinion even though I
trusted my doctor completely. I went to a cancer specialist in
Seattle, and she told me that he was doing the perfect thing.

"MY GYNECOLOGIST WAS VERY FATHERLY—THAT WAS
HIS GREATEST GIFT—BUT UNFORTUNATELY, HE WASN'T
INFORMATIVE. THE DOCTOR I GO TO NOW TREATS ME
LIKE AN EQUAL, AND I KNOW WHERE I STAND WITH
HIM."

*A thirty-two-year-old free-lance illustrator who had a cone
biopsy after a Class III Pap smear. She has been married for
two years.*

Was that the first irregular Pap smear you ever had?

No. Right before I got married I had a Class II Pap. The gynecologist didn't feel it was too serious. But I was a little concerned,
so just to make sure I called up my mother's obstetrician who is
retired and a family friend. At the time I had very serious acne
and was taking a medication called Accutane that had dried out
my face and lips. He explained that the Accutane could have
caused the appearance of irregular cells in the cervix because

the tissue in the cervix is the same as on the lips. So I just wrote off the irregular Pap as a side effect of Accutane.

When did you have another Pap?

I waited a year, and this time it was a Class IIIA. My gynecologist said, "This is pretty serious," and at the end of October 1986 he scheduled me for a colposcopy.

Can you describe a colposcopy?

It's a more conclusive test than the Pap. It's done in the office, and you're in the stirrups as with a regular pelvic. The doctor puts in a speculum and then uses the colposcope—which is essentially a microscope—to look at the cervix. The cervix is first swabbed with a special solution and with the help of a powerful light shows up white spots on any abnormal areas. He took snips of tissue from around my cervix at one o'clock, two o'clock, three o'clock—I think there were twelve snips in all. It isn't painful, but it's uncomfortable because you're up in the stirrups for such a long time—over an hour. I was very depressed afterward. I felt very violated.

The tissue samples are sent to the lab to be identified. I think 75 percent of all my snips had carcinoma in them. Some areas were worse than others. He thought that we should act quickly even though it wouldn't turn into cervical cancer for probably fourteen years.

Was the cone biopsy your first surgery?

Yes. And I was a little bit nervous because, the night before the operation, a resident came into my room and said he was working with my doctor. Maybe I overreacted, but I completely panicked. I thought, Oh, no. I don't want a resident to perform the operation. I called my brother-in-law, a doctor in Louisiana, and asked him if the resident could possibly perform the operation. He said, "Yes. That's the risk you take when you go into a teaching hospital." The waiver you sign explains that the hospital is a teaching institution and that residents can perform surgery. Well, when my doctor came in the next morning before surgery, I said, "I want *you* to do it. I don't want the resident. I trust you, and I pay *you*." He said, "Don't worry, I'll do it." But still I put a little note on myself before they took me to the operating room that said, "Please make sure you perform this operation."

After the surgery the doctor told me he had done a D&C as well as a cone biopsy. When they do any extensive surgery during a cone biopsy, a D&C is done as a matter of course to scrape the uterine walls, in case there might be some irregular cells there.

How did you feel after surgery?

Everyone told me that having a cone biopsy would be really easy, that it wouldn't hurt. I was in incredible pain—it was like the worst cramps you could ever imagine.

Why were you in so much pain?

I didn't know. And the frustrating thing in the hospital was that the nurses said, "You're not supposed to be in this kind of pain." They were really hesitant to give me Demerol. They said I didn't need it because a cone biopsy isn't very painful. My mother was with me and she used to be a nurse, so she insisted they call the doctor, and sure enough, he said, "Give her anything she wants." It was five hours before the Demerol took effect, and they had to give me two injections. It was a nightmare.

I didn't find out the reason for the excruciating pain until months later when another doctor I went to for a second opinion explained that a very deep cut had to be made in my cervix to remove precancerous cells in the glands.

Did you have much bleeding?

Yes. I think that was from the D&C. I was in the hospital for five days because my gynecologist wanted to keep an eye on me in case I hemorrhaged. He did all the right things. And he was very fatherly—that was his greatest gift. But unfortunately, he wasn't very informative. He never told me what he was doing.

Did the intense pain subside after a couple of days?

Yes, but I was pretty sore for at least five days after the surgery. They gave me some Tylenol and codeine after the Demerol, and I took those regularly. I was still very weak when I was discharged.

How much did the surgery cost you?

The insurance covered most of the surgery, but it didn't cover the private room I had. That was around $120 a day. The doctor's fee was $1,500 and the anesthesiologist was $350. Lab tests amounted to about $100.

How was your recovery at home?

My mother arranged for me to say in a hotel in New York for a couple of days so I could have room service. On the third day I went home and my husband took care of me. I was in bed until Christmas Eve, when we went down to Pittsburgh where my husband's family lives to spend the holidays. A really embarrassing thing happened there. The doctor had inserted a cold pack in me to hold the stitches intact while the cervix healed, but the cold pack dissolves and produces this horrible-smelling discharge. It's probably a combination of blood and body fluids and the pack. It was so bad that I would wrap the used sanitary napkins in four plastic bags and they would still smell. And we were sharing a bathroom with my husband's sister! It wasn't until the middle of January—a month later—that the discharge completely stopped.

Did the doctor tell you what to expect with the cold pack?
He told me to expect a discharge, but he didn't say anything about the odor.

How long was it before you were back to normal activity?
I took it easy for a full month. My husband and I had intercourse after that, but it hurt. I was a little worried about that, but I wasn't scheduled to go back to the gynecologist for three months so I thought the discomfort must be a normal part of the healing after surgery. Even though I didn't have invasive cervical cancer, I was still a little concerned about the possibility of cancer somewhere else in my body. So to ease my anxiety I decided to get a complete physical. Around the ninth of January, I went to a hospital that specializes in cancer detection and had an exam. All they discovered was that I was anemic—not seriously anemic, but I had to take iron and eat a lot of iron-rich food.

So then you went for your three-month checkup?
My gynecologist said I had irregular cells on my cervix and needed to have another cone biopsy. He said, "It often happens that I have to perform two or three cone biopsies to get all the cells." The idea of going through all that pain again was very upsetting, so I was determined to get another opinion.

And what was the second opinion?
The doctor said, "It doesn't look as if the cervix healed properly. The reason you may be getting an irregular Pap is because of healing exfoliation." He said, "Let me take another Pap and we'll see what happens." The Pap he did came out normal, so I guess that must have been the problem. Also, for two weeks previous to the Pap I hadn't had intercourse, so my cervix was probably less stressed—maybe that had something to do with the result. Anyway, I was so relieved that I didn't need another cone biopsy. He said it looked like the precancerous lesions were gone, but he said I'd have to have three or four more normal Paps before I

could be sure all the cells had been removed. And to this day, my husband and I are very moderate about sex. If we do it every day, the area gets really sore.

Did you go back to the gynecologist who performed your surgery?

No. But I did go to an oncologist for a third opinion. He didn't do a Pap, but after his examination and after looking at my record, he recommended another colposcopy and another cone biopsy. He did make an interesting suggestion—that I try cryosurgery [freezing the tissue off with liquid nitrogen]. He said, "Normally, cryosurgery doesn't work in cases like yours, where there's carcinoma in situ as well as precancerous cells in the glandular area, but there's a 50 percent chance it could work. It isn't painful, so why not try it? If we can't get all the cells, we can do a cone."

I liked the oncologist, but I decided to go with the doctor who gave me the second opinion, even before I had the results of the Pap he did. I liked his directness. He treats you exactly as an equal. He might not be as comforting and gentle as my original doctor, but you know where you stand with him. Based on that experience I switched to him, and he's my regular gynecologist now. Another thing that made him attractive to me was that he told me he works with a woman gynecological oncologist at his hospital. If I ever needed another colposcopy, she would do it for me, and I think I'd feel more comfortable with a woman doing that procedure on me.

OVARIAN SURGERY

A woman may discover that she has an ovarian cyst either during the routine gynecological exam, after having no symptoms, or more dramatically, when she is taken suddenly by pain that is like menstrual cramps but usually more intense.

A cyst is a fluid-filled sac. There are over two hundred kinds of ovarian cysts, one of the most common being a very strange construction called a dermoid cyst that may contain teeth, fatty tissue, strands of hair—the result of genetic information gone awry. Functional cysts are formed during ovulation if an egg is not released from its follicle (an envelope of cells that "hatches" eggs). These cysts generally collapse within a few months and should be treated conservatively. The Pill suppresses the menstrual cycle, and without hormonal support, the cyst should vanish. "Another way to handle the cyst," says Anthony Calanog, M.D., "is just to leave it alone. If the patient has no symptoms, examine her after six weeks. If the cyst hasn't disappeared, you keep following up on it. Most likely it's a neoplasm—neoplasm means new growth—and it's either benign or malignant. Prior to menopause, there's a 90 percent chance the cyst is functional and a 10 percent chance that it's neoplastic. If the patient is postmenopausal, however, every cyst has to be considered malignant or neoplastic because the patient no longer ovulates."

The ovaries may also develop solid benign tumors. Medical wisdom advises removal of any persistent growth, cystic or solid. If the growth turns out to be malignant, the surgeon will remove both ovaries as well as the uterus and fallopian tubes (see pages 216–229).

Assuming that the growth is benign, the surgery consists of removing the growth and repairing the ovary. It's considered major surgery and is performed under general anesthesia, with a hospital stay of from four days to a week.

From our interviews, we've learned that it's possible to become pregnant on half an ovary—which also means that half an ovary is enough to ward off surgical menopause.

We've also learned that a woman, assuming the cyst or tumor is benign, should discuss the scope of her surgery with her doctor. As we said in the introduction, if you've had children or are past forty, your doctor may very well be planning simply to remove your ovaries rather than try to save them. If you are at high risk for ovarian cancer, you might happily seize this opportunity to rid yourself of a danger. If you want everything to be done to save the ovaries, you must make your desires known to your surgeon.

Recovery from surgery restricted to the ovaries is considerably easier than from hysterectomy. For more discussion of the ovary debate, see the interviews with Drs. Blanchard (page 189) and Reyniak (page 266).

"HOWEVER TRIVIAL THE QUESTIONS SEEM IN THE DOC-TOR'S OFFICE, THEY MAY NOT BE TRIVIAL WHEN YOU'RE LYING IN YOUR HOSPITAL BED."

A senior manager for a nonprofit advocacy group. In 1984, at age thirty-six, she suddenly required emergency surgery for two ovarian cysts. After the surgery, she learned that she had endometriosis.

Did you know you had cysts?
No. I had some relatively minor pain maybe six weeks before. The day before, I was on my way to a meeting and started to get really uncomfortable. I got into a cab anyway, but the pains became so bad that I asked the driver to take me home. I called my internist, whom I'd been using as my gynecologist, and he said, "Get in a cab and come here immediately." He examined me and said he thought it was probably an ovarian cyst. He was wonderful. He said, "I want you to be seen by somebody really good—a friend of mine who is an expert in this—and I'm calling her right now. She'll meet you in the emergency room."

So I called friends and they took me to the emergency room. Then I had to wait for the doctor to show up. I think she was delivering a baby. And while I was sitting and waiting, the hospital people kept trying to push some intern on me, saying, "It's hospital rules." But being relatively assertive about these things,

I refused. I just didn't want to go through another pelvic exam when I was in such bad pain. I've been through enough gynecological procedures to know that if you don't put your foot down, people will do things to you that don't need to be done. They relaxed after a while, and eventually the doctor showed up.

What kind of pain were you in?
It's the kind of cramp that makes you double over. It's like menstrual cramps to the power of ten. The pain is near your abdomen, on the side. You could think it was peritonitis or appendicitis. The diagnosis is tricky.

Cysts can grow to huge sizes in a short time. The surgeon said that those cramps I'd had a month and a half before were a warning signal, and somebody with a lower tolerance for pain might have acted on it. But I've had those kinds of things before and it's never meant anything. And I do get really bad menstrual cramps, so it's not as if cramps send me into a state of despair. And I had no reason to assume that I had developed cysts since my last examination, which was probably only six months before.

But I knew the minute I got the pains that day on the way to my office that something was seriously wrong with me, and I knew I had to see a doctor immediately.

So finally this lovely doctor, who happened to be Chinese, this woman surgeon, came and examined me, and she was very gentle. She said, "I'm quite certain that you have ovarian cysts." I think she used the plural.

What was the next step?
She kind of wanted me to check into the hospital. I don't know whether the pains were subsiding or whether I was getting used to the rhythm of them, but I seemed to be more in control, and I wanted to sleep in my own bed. She said, "If you promise that you won't be alone, I will let you go home tonight." She said, "I want you to come first thing tomorrow morning for a sonogram." It was already evening, so I don't think they could have done anything then. I mean, I wasn't asking questions like "Can't you do a sonogram now?" I sort of trusted this person. She seemed to be nice and to know what she was doing.

The next morning I called for a sonogram, and, as she'd warned me, I had to fight to get an early appointment. So I went in and had the sonogram, and I could see the little thing on the screen. A doctor came out and very clinically announced that I had two cysts and told me exactly how big each was and telephoned my doctor. She got on the phone with me and said, "I want you to walk over to the other end of the hospital and check yourself in immediately. Don't eat or drink anything. We're going to try to schedule surgery as soon as possible. One of your cysts is about to rupture, and both are very large." It was scary to be told that, but she was very matter-of-fact and gave me as much information as she had at that point.

Were you nervous about going into surgery without a second opinion, with a doctor you didn't know?

People kept coming in to me during the three or four hours that I was waiting for surgery and saying, "Oh, she's a wonderful doctor." And my internist had said she's the best. But honestly, I was totally out of it. I felt confident with her, and with the hospital—it's very bustling, very clean, new, a teaching hospital, which means there are a lot of people running in and out all the time, looking at you.

At one level that's reassuring, and at another it's very fatiguing because someone is constantly saying, "Hi, I'm so-and-so, and I'm a third-year student, and how are you today?" Even a pleasant request about how you're feeling, asked too many times, can be an imposition, especially when you're sick and tired. And because it is a teaching hospital, some of the people who are constantly taking blood from you or whatever haven't necessarily developed the best technique in the world. But I would say that most of the people who troop through, even though they were kind of annoying, were basically pretty nice—they ranged from being innocuous to pleasant. And they did come in and give me a full explanation of the anesthesia, and who would be in the operating room, and the rest of it.

I remember, when they wheeled me down to surgery, being left in a corridor for about five seconds and almost panicking. They had too many stretchers coming down all at once, and they were trying to clear up the traffic jam. It was a little touch of black humor. I was thinking, This is like something out of *Hospital*. And I remember that almost everybody in the operating room was female, and I found that tremendously reassuring. Although my internist was male, I have made an effort to have female gynecological care, and here the anesthesiologist, the surgeon, a couple of the nurses, and an intern were women. It was kind of nice.

What do you remember after surgery?

It was all downhill from there. Hospitals are run on very rigid time clocks. You have to be awakened at a certain time and fed and drugged at a certain time, and it doesn't seem to matter whether your body is conforming to those expectations. I felt awful after the surgery. It was a very long surgery, a couple of hours, and though they did not have to remove either ovary, I felt real sick afterward, as one will after surgery. I'm not scared of hospitals, but I don't like them. I didn't like the blood being taken constantly. I couldn't believe it—I mean, I was so weak and tired, and they'd waltz in to take more blood. It was certainly more than once a day.

The first night after surgery they give you Demerol, and whatever dose they gave me didn't last as long as they thought it should. I woke up in really bad pain, asking for more painkiller, and this Nazi-type nurse made me feel like a drug addict. But I think that was just one person being stupidly bureaucratic—it never happened again. After that, they were happy to let me take whatever medication I needed. And I didn't feel too terrific, so I was pretty out of it most of the time I was in the hospital. My attitude was, this is a disgusting and unpleasant experience; I saw no reason to have all my mental faculties about me. Should I be more alert so I could watch the game shows better?

Did you have a private room or private nurses?
No.

How long did you stay in the hospital?
Four days in all. They try to get you out as fast as possible if you're in pretty good shape—it's better for you. They get you off the IV as fast as they can and get you up walking.

Did you take any painkillers after you left the hospital?
Yes. They told me to take Tylenol if I needed any. I didn't take a lot, but I was sometimes in sufficient pain over the next couple of weeks that Tylenol was not really adequate.

How did your recovery go at home?
I got depressed that I still felt as much pain as I did and that I was still so weak. I kept thinking that there was something wrong with me. They said things like "Total bed rest," but after two days, I thought, Well, surely I can take a shower. I took a shower and was so exhausted that I realized that "Total bed rest" means "Don't get out of bed."

At one level I was very sophisticated about what had happened to me, but I didn't really understand that I was going to feel as sick as I had in the hospital; I would just be home in my own bed.

A friend finally asked me, "Are you still feeling the effects of the anesthesia?" I said, "What effects?" She said, "Well, it takes about three weeks for the anesthesia to wear off—it has a depressant effect."

Well, I didn't know that. I'm the kind of person who always sets standards for herself—even about recovering. I had to get out of the hospital at the first possible time; I had to recover as quickly as possible. I kept expecting that I would feel a little better every day, and that wasn't how it worked. How it worked was that I felt really shitty for a couple of weeks and then suddenly, in one big leap, I started to feel seriously better.

I don't think people like me have a good mechanism for dealing with a situation where we are dependent on other people to do things for us. Fortunately I had one friend who was a wonderful advocate, who would appear in my apartment every day and say things like, "You are recovering from major surgery. You're going to be okay, but you have to take care of yourself. You cannot worry. You are not going to talk to people from your office. Just because your vocal chords are functioning does not mean that they are allowed to call you up and bother you."

How did you feel when you went back to work?
I was certainly more rested than I had been in a long time. I went back full-time and full speed. I guess I had the resources to do that, because I didn't get sick or anything.

How much attention did you get from your surgeon?
I knew the honeymoon was over with her the day after the surgery. I felt very grateful to this woman and still do: I've talked to a lot of people who had elective surgery for ovarian cysts, and a lot of them ended up without an ovary. And some friends of mine who are physicians, when I explained to them what size cysts I had and where they were, said, "You had a very good surgeon."

But when she came to talk to me the next day, she told me that one of the cysts was "endometrial"—the magic word—and though the endometrial tissue seemed to be in one place, it was still the beginning of endometriosis. And she said, "I would advise you, if you're thinking about having children, to get pregnant as quickly as possible."

Well, I couldn't believe that she laid that on me one day after my surgery. Getting pregnant was the last thing I wanted to think about. Maybe I overreacted, but it seemed highly insensitive to me. It might have been a cultural thing—I mean, she's not a native English-speaking person—but she came on like gangbusters. Oh, she was good on a few issues. The next day she said, "You're recovering really well, and you're basically a very healthy, strong person. I advise you to stay in the hospital the minimum amount, even if you're very tired when you leave—it will be better for you to recuperate at home. You should have somebody stay with you for at least the first three weeks because you won't be able to do anything. You have to have total bed rest." She said, "Some people go back to work after four weeks. I don't really advise it. You have a high-stress job, which may very well have contributed to this in the first place, and I advise you to take a six-week recuperation. You'll feel basically like yourself for the last two weeks." And everything she said was exactly the case. She was very sensitive to my needs.

Did you have someone to help you at home?

Yes, I had somebody staying with me for the first three weeks. My friends were great about it. A few came in from out of town to take care of me, and it was nice for them, too, because they weren't hostages—they could run around and do things in the city, and it was a chance for us to play catch-up and visit. That really cheered me up.

What did you do about the endometriosis?

Here's where we get to the messy part. After six weeks, I went to see her. By this time, of course, I had talked to everybody I knew and come to the conclusion that they don't know a whole lot about endometriosis, and that I was not really a hardship case, even though I had a lot of the classic symptoms, like bad cramps and bleeding a lot.

What's "a lot" of bleeding?

Bleeding really heavily for six or seven days and getting your period every twenty-three to twenty-five days. My cycle is getting shorter now, but that's okay. Anyway, I went to see her, and she said, "Oh, you look great," and then she said she wanted to put me on birth control pills. And I said, "Oh, no, I've been through that. I hate them. They make me crazy. They make me fat." She said, "Look, are you thinking of having a child?" She was more delicate this time. "If you want to ensure your fertility," she said, "you can't just let this disease continue to accelerate. The best way to control it is to regularize your ovulation. I can put you on a really low dosage, and you can try it for a few months."

And I said to myself, "All right. If I'm seeing this doctor, and this is what she recommends, and there basically isn't any other course of treatment, this is the only thing I can do."

You agreed even though you still had objections.

Yes. The only other treatment, called Danazol, is horrible. A lot of people get very bad side effects from it—you get hair all over your body, and the same kind of blowing-up effects of cortisone. It's an experimental drug that they use for hardship endometriosis cases and fertility cases. And she did recommend against Danazol.

So I started taking the Pill. And right away—maybe it was my mind-set, maybe it was the Pill, maybe she didn't make the best choice of progesterone-to-estrogen ratio—I got so depressed that I was constantly bursting into tears for no reason. I am moody, but not that moody. I had back pains far worse and more sustained than any I had ever had and leg pains that started me thinking I was getting a blood clot and I was going to be one of the one-out-of-a-thousand people that dies from taking the Pill. And while I pay a fair amount of attention to my health, I'm not a hypochondriac. If I had been a hypochondriac, I would have been in the emergency room the first time I had a pain with this.

I thought maybe it would ease up. I ignored it for about three weeks, and then one of my friends said to me, "You've really been off the wall lately." I told her about taking the Pill, and she said, "I think you'd better call your doctor. This sounds like more than minor side effects." So I called her and she said, "I'm sure that the leg pains and back pains are stress-related, but if you are that physically uncomfortable and unhappy, stop taking the Pill."

So I stopped, and pretty much everything went away. She said, "Come see me in three months," and I did. She said, "Maybe we can play with the dosage and just watch you more closely." She hadn't given up the idea of the Pill.

At this point, I came to the decision that even though I felt grateful to this woman for saving my precious ovaries, we had a communication problem. I was one of those women who came in with a legal pad and a list of questions and had read every article that pertained to my health care, and it was hard for me to communicate with somebody who wasn't as verbal as I and who seemed to have a different perspective on the whole problem. And from what I had read, I was convinced that the Pill was not the only form of treatment. So I finally decided I would get another opinion, as they say.

How did you go about looking for a second opinion?
A friend of mine who is a DES baby, and has been through many gynecologists, really liked the one she was seeing. This was interesting because it was a male, an older man, and she said, "This guy is so easy to talk to, and so lovable." I went to see him, and right away it was just a great relief, because he is very open and very kindly, but not in a condescending way at all. And he seems to be very up-to-date with everything. I sat down and spilled out my sad little saga, and I'm sure I was crying by then—"What am I going to do?!" He listened very carefully and was very thoughtful, and said, "Well, it sounds as if your surgeon really dealt with your problem very well"—not undermining her—"but I really disagree that oral contraceptives are the best or the only form of treatment, especially in a situation that doesn't seem to be too out of control yet, and especially with somebody who has had problems with them."

Now, I had told her that I had problems when I took the Pill in my early twenties, and the fact that I hated them didn't seem to resonate for her. But for him, it had significance. Her theory was that if you take the Pill, you bleed less and that's good. His theory was that it isn't good to stop you artificially from ovulating the way the Pill does: if you're getting your period regularly, you should either stay the way you are or else you should stop having your period at all—stop any and all bleeding. What he liked to do was let people have their periods, watching them very carefully to see that things didn't progress too seriously, and if they did, he'd put them on a pill so they didn't bleed at all for a few months. Then he'd take them off that and they'd go back to being normal. This way you don't have the Pill's constant assault on your body.

Well, that made sense to me. He was equally adamant that Danazol is really horrible, and on the subject of fertility, he said that some people have more endometriosis than I do and they get pregnant without any problem. And I knew that was true because I had a very dear friend who was diagnosed as having endometriosis when she was thirty. She had surgery for ovarian cysts and lost one ovary, which hardly affects fertility, and the physician said to her, "If you're thinking about a kid, you'd better get working on it." She married the man she was living with and became pregnant in two months, long before she had any intention of doing so.

I've been seeing this doctor for eight months, and I like him and trust him. He was not at all put off by the fact that I was up on what was going on medically with endometriosis. He said, "I really prefer to have patients who do have opinions about their care and have thought about these issues. Ask me as many questions as you want." I was amazed, really—here's this man who is in his seventies, and he's more flexible and feminist than . . . I wouldn't say than my surgeon, because that's an apples and oranges kind of comparison. I think she's a marvelous surgeon, and with the passage of time, my annoyance with her—her difficulty in hearing me and persistence with certain forms of treatment—has kind of receded.

Would you have done anything differently if you had had the time before surgery?

Well, you can be sure I would have asked a whole lot of questions: Who is going to be seeing me besides my surgeon? How often? Why? Are they going to be asking me questions, or are they going to ask to look at me? Is this something I have options about? Let me tell you how I feel about that. How many times a day are you going to be taking blood? How long will I be on an IV? What kind of medication will I be offered after my surgery and for how long? If that isn't working for me, how do I change it? I would try to get as many answers as possible ahead of time. However trivial they may seem, they may not be trivial to you when you're lying in the hospital bed. That's what I would advise somebody who is going into elective surgery.

I would also say, Think about your friends—not necessarily the person you're closest to, but maybe the one who shares your attitudes about dealing with these kinds of issues—and see if you can get that person to hang out by your hospital bedside as much as possible. Family support is great, but that's different from having somebody to be your advocate.

And for all that, I have to say, I think I got pretty good care. Hospitals are crazy, weird places, and they definitely bother you a lot and do things to you that you don't feel are necessary, but by and large, I think the doctors are not so bad. I didn't run across anybody who was really awful, except for that first nurse who was like a Nazi. The rest of them were nice.

"MAKE YOURSELF AS HEALTHY AS POSSIBLE BEFORE THE SURGERY, AND HAVE SOMEONE THERE FOR YOU AFTER WHO CAN REALLY TAKE CARE OF THINGS."

A forty-one-year-old technical manager for a large computer company, she had surgery to remove an ovarian cyst in June 1984. She is single.

What made you realize something was wrong?
In November of 1983, I had been very sick—I thought it was food poisoning. I had a high fever, chills, stomach upset. About two months later, exactly the same thing happened. I went to see a gastroenterologist and ended up having a sonogram, and then a barium enema, processes that were very difficult to go through for me. The sonogram found a growth that looked like an ovarian cyst, and also some fluid outside the uterus. I'm confused about what it was, but the short of it is that I had to have the barium enema. My doctor decided that it was either appendicitis or an ovarian cyst.

What was so difficult for you about these two tests?
Oh, they're miserable. All of this stuff was worse to me than the operation. For the sonogram, they fill your bladder so you feel as though you have to go to the bathroom, and when you can't stand that feeling anymore, they take photographs of your abdomen. I had it done twice, and the first time, I drank what they told me to drink, about 8 eight-ounce glasses of water, and it was far too much. The second time I drank less. You can see you bladder on the screen, and the second time my bladder was not quite full—it was slightly flat on top—but it was fine for the test, and I felt fine.

For the enema, what you do is take more and more powerful laxatives all through the day. And the last ones make your intestines cramp so it's like giving yourself the flu. And then they put you on this table and start swinging you all over the place—up-side-down and all around—while they're taking X-rays. You have a gown over the front of you and this hose going up into your ass so you feel . . . [she grimaces]. There's a man behind the screen saying things like "Okay, now hold your breath" or "Move this leg here." The hardest part is that they're filling you up with barium so you feel as though you have to go to the bathroom.

I thought that this was going to be the most humiliating experience in the world, but I must say, there is someone who comes and talks to you, and whoever she was, she dealt with me so effectively that it didn't end up being unbearable. The whole thing lasts maybe ten or fifteen minutes. And they keep you very aware of how it's progressing. And because of that, you can handle it. They treat you well—which is essential in that setting. Otherwise, it would be torture.

How did you decide to have surgery?

I went to my gynecologist, who was sure that the growth was an ovarian cyst. She thought that my stomach illnesses hadn't been tied in with the cyst at all, but I'm sure they were because they haven't recurred. I think she didn't want me to link it to the cyst because the cyst might have been around in late October when she had done a checkup, and if so, she missed it. The gastroenterologist did a much more thorough internal exam than she had —I could tell from the feeling of it. Of course, he was definitely going for something, while she was just doing her standard six months' exam.

She sent me back for another sonogram and, as a result, recommended surgery. I called the gastroenterologist, hoping he'd see a way around surgery, but when I said, "She thinks I have to have surgery," he said, "As well she should." And when I asked why, he said, "You obviously have a growth of some kind. I think it's a cyst, but there's a possibility it's your appendix or a tumor." The way he said it, there was no implication of its being cancer, but I did decide to just go ahead and have the surgery.

You felt two opinions were enough?

Yes. I dealt with the two of them and felt as though I had done it pretty thoroughly. I didn't want to fight it at that time. I thought, I'm just going to have it done. And that's pretty much in my nature: if something's wrong, let's make it right and then go on. And I had faith in my gynecologist as a surgeon. She was the first gynecologist I felt comfortable with after going to probably ten since I've been in New York. She's very businesslike. My one fear was that maybe she wasn't as thorough as I would have liked, but I decided to go with her. Also, the gastroenterologist wasn't a surgeon, so I would have had to start looking for another surgeon.

The thing I was most concerned about was the humiliation of it. That is, being pretty much taken under control, and shaved . . . just all of it. Even the idea of having my stomach muscles cut, having my body damaged in some way, and then having to recover from it without really understanding what had happened.

Did you research the operation?

I got some basic information, but I don't think I got much from the surgeon. I think all I got was, "We do a bikini incision and remove the cyst and try not to remove the ovary." I didn't feel comfortable asking what all the stages of the procedure were—from going into the operation through recuperation. I eventually learned what I needed to learn from a friend of mine who's a doctor. I have two friends who are doctors, both women. One said, "Oh, boy, I'd hate to have something like that," and, "Thank God nothing's wrong with me." I thought, My gosh! She's just making me more nervous.

The other friend said, "Let me tell you exactly what they do. They don't cut your stomach muscles; they pull them apart to get to where they need to go, and you'll recover very quickly from that. You're in very good shape, so it won't be difficult to cut through your stomach." As a surgeon, she said, you like someone to be lean: if the patient's very fatty, it's just messy. I felt much better after talking to her. I also read *Our Bodies, Ourselves* and some biology texts I had. I wanted to understand how an ovarian cyst starts, but no one could explain it. I mean—it just happens. I thought about whether or not I could be killed off with anesthesia, and I just decided, Well, I probably won't be, and if I am, I won't know it.

I tend to have a pretty positive outlook. There were times when I got frightened, but I never really let that go very far. It was a matter of deciding that this is something I have to do, so I'm going to do it. And that there are worse operations, and I'm in a sense very fortunate that I have to go through this for something so simple.

What arrangements did you make for the hospital?

I was very involved at work and wanted to take as little time off as possible. I think I told them it would be three to four weeks. And I ended up taking off five weeks. The fifth week was not essential, but it was the one where I began to feel well. I wanted to enjoy that week of feeling well before I went back to work.

For the hospital, I wanted a semiprivate room. That ended up being three other people instead of only one other, and I was upset. Also, I went to the hospital by myself, which was a lonely thing to do. It was a work day, and it was pointless for anyone to take a day off work. But it was difficult, going alone.

I signed in around two o'clock and ended up getting to my room by six, after registering and having tests. I just sort of sat on my bed, discovered there were all these people in the room, two of whom had just been operated on, and waited for the next thing to happen. The next thing to happen was an enema. They were totally screwed up in terms of nursing—the person who was supposed to prepare me for each succeeding thing never got to me before the person who was doing the thing. But again, I just thought . . . [she shrugs].

I was upset about being shaved between my legs. I had had a leg operation once and this guy had come in with a razor and shaved my leg completely, and then it became inflamed because he had shaved it too closely. It turned out, with this operation, that they shave you after you're under the anesthesia. I had also worried because a friend of mine who had been shaved was both in pain and itching terribly when the hair grew back. But none of that happened to me.

A couple of doctors (interns, I think) came in to see me, and one of them said, "You have the blood pressure of a plant," which I took as a compliment—I had been working out a lot at that point, running and using Nautilus equipment. Then a guy came in to give me a sleeping pill, and I wasn't going to take it because I don't like to take anything mind-altering. I was worried about control. I'd been able to keep myself from being anxious about this, and I didn't want to do anything that might take my guard down and make me frightened. I don't see tranquilizers as providing support; I see them as removing control. But eventually I did decide to take the pill, and boy, it put me to sleep in a snap. It was fine.

What do you remember of the morning of surgery?
It ended up being wonderful because I was supposed to be operated on around ten A.M. but they were able to take me early. They gave me a shot, then took me upstairs to what looked like an equipment room. And I thought, What a weird place for them to keep me! I remember feeling terrific and cracking jokes with the orderly or whoever the person was, and saying, "Now, just remember, I'm the ovarian cyst."

Then they wheeled me into the operating room—it was fascinating. The anesthesiologist introduced himself to me, with his mask on. It's funny, I can feel a little anxiety right now, just describing it. The anesthesiologist said, "Okay, I'm going to put this needle in your arm, and you're going to have the taste of garlic in your mouth, and that'll be it." And I remember that taste . . . so strong. And that *was* it.

I don't remember the recovery room at all. I woke up in my room, feeling cold. A friend of mine was there, and I said, "This is nothing. I feel great, I can't believe it's over. I've got to call my parents and tell them everything is fine." So I did. I remember saying to her, "It's so hard to dial the phone when you're a little out of it." But I actually did dial my parents and told them I was okay. Then another friend called, and I fell asleep talking to her.

I guess the next thing was becoming aware of all the tubes. Things in my arm and in my bladder. The catheter. That had been one of the things I was afraid of—I thought I was going to be embarrassed by it, and I wasn't. It ended up being uncomfortable, but not terribly, except when it was removed—that was painful.

I became more aware of things hurting: not the incision—the IV. I couldn't get up at all. The nurse was trying to get me up, and I felt sick and started to fall back, which made me worry— when was I going to be able to get up and get moving? But a friend of mine who was visiting was very encouraging and managed to get me walking.

The worst thing, I think, is not knowing what to expect, not knowing how you are, compared to how people normally are.

Is that said as an overachiever—seeing recovery as a competitive sport?

It's said by a person who wants to be in control, because if you're not, who knows? You'll just collapse and never be able to do anything again. And I was getting good feedback on how I was doing. That is, someone said to me he'd rarely seen someone in as good condition as I was in. That meant to me that I would be able to recover quickly. Some of the residents would make me feel good by giving me comments on how I was progressing, although I must say a lot of them came by and didn't pay attention to me because I wasn't an interesting case. And when they do pay attention to you, they tend to treat you as a case—"Let's take a look at this incision." I pretty much steeled myself for that kind of treatment. But I didn't like it.

How was the nursing care?
Terrible. I remember once I was on the bedpan and I asked the nurse who was taking my blood pressure if she could move the bedpan out from under me. She said, "I don't handle the bedpans." So there I lay. I just did it myself.

But the nice thing was, two of the other women in my room were there the whole time I was there, and we developed a very close relationship and looked out for each other.

How did your recovery go?
I felt better every day, and I could feel the pain changing. The hardest part—and someone had warned me about this—was the gas pains when your intestines start working again. That was just miserable. I remember walking with a friend and I was completely bent over. It was a pain I could tolerate, but it was miserable.

And the painkillers don't do anything for gas pains?
No, apparently they slow down the intestines—the contractions —so they work against the process of returning to normal.

Did you see much of your doctor after surgery?
You see your surgeon very briefly and probably only when she's just finished operating on someone else, so she's not at her best. She was very perfunctory. She spent very little time with me and certainly didn't offer any information at all, so the trick was to ask as many questions and talk as fast as I could to keep her there with me. I had told her, "If you have to take an ovary, okay, but if you don't have to, don't take it." She said she managed to remove the cyst—it was the diameter of a tennis ball—without taking my ovary. At one point she actually sat on the bed briefly and I just kept talking. I complimented her—I said, "I am feeling very good, and I think you did a good job." And she said, "Well, thanks," and got up and left. As though she were embarrassed.

How long were you in the hospital?
I was operated on Tuesday and went home Saturday. A friend and I decided the next morning that we would go to the country. She drove and I sat on a pillow with a pillow in front of me and one behind me—I didn't feel any bumps.

What surprised me was how long it took to recuperate. I had a friend who said she was running eight days after her abdominal operation. So I thought I should be able to do that. I was running, I think, in three weeks. Not far, just down my road about three-tenths of a mile. But I did start walking every day immediately, and I could begin to feel myself getting better and better. The hardest thing, actually, was trying to get up from a lying-down position.

How did the incision heal?

It's a nice scar. It's horizontal and not particularly noticeable. She did it with staples that just pinch the skin. And I'm getting the feeling back right below the incision.

Do you have any emotional ramifications from the surgery?

None that I can tell. The time in the hospital with these women was really wonderful. I felt uplifted in a strange way. I felt as though we all worked together to take care of each other, and there was a real feeling of generosity and caring. We dealt with each other in a way that insulated us from the medical establishment, which didn't handle us very well. I think my surgeon was very effective, but she certainly didn't show much warmth. Then again, I know what her schedule is; she's doing at least one operation a day, if not more, besides dealing with a practice and delivering babies and so on. I give her that. But I feel that there should be somebody who lends a human touch, and there wasn't. Occasionally someone would come by, maybe a night nurse, but there was no consistency in that.

How long was it before you felt you were back to normal?

I think it was a day in October. The operation was at the end of June, so that's four months. I have boundless energy usually, but after the operation and through the summer, I would run out of steam. But one day in October, I felt again as though I could go on forever, and I knew I was completely recovered.

Is there anything you would have done differently?

I would have asked the surgeon more questions. It was jarring when she said, "We'll have to operate, so let's set up a time to do it." I wasn't particularly frightened by it, but I was surprised. At that point I should have said, "Let me understand exactly what this operation is." I had many questions that I didn't think of at the time. And I would have liked to know about the catheter and the IV and about recovery time.

What advice would you give someone facing this kind of surgery?

For my type of operation, there isn't an emotional component, except in terms of being cut. The way I proceed most effectively —not that everyone does—is to understand what's happening and then do what you can to have it go well for you. That is: Make yourself as healthy as possible before the surgery; understand the operation and be prepared to address problems that might come up, like bad nursing care or a bad room. And have someone there for you who can really take care of things like bringing in a private nurse or changing rooms.

"DIAGNOSIS IS A TWO-WAY PROCESS. IF PATIENTS WERE TRUSTED AND ENCOURAGED TO ARTICULATE WHAT IS WRONG WITH THEM, A LOT OF THE MEDICAL HORROR STORIES YOU HEAR WOULDN'T HAVE HAPPENED."

A twenty-nine-year-old single woman, daughter of a medical malpractice attorney, who works in an art gallery. She had surgery two years before.

When did this begin?
It was the spring of 1985. I came home one night and all of a sudden I had a sharp pain, so sharp I couldn't move. The pain was in the general area of my abdomen. My first thought was that something was wrong with my stomach, because my stomach was distended, or perhaps it was constipation or gas. I called my father and he said, "Just get to the closest emergency room and I'll meet you there." So I went, with a friend. Really, I have a very high threshold for pain, and I've never experienced anything like this in my life.

When we got there—and of course, the cab got lost—a nurse said, "Have a seat, the doctor will be right with you." I said, "I'm not having a seat—I've been in emergency rooms before. I'm dying and I want to see a doctor right now." I was very aggressive because I didn't trust anyone to take me seriously. One of the interns took me down for X-rays. He said, "Well, the X-rays don't show anything. It's constipation." And he gave me a liquid laxative and an enema and instructions not to take any painkillers because they're constipating. And then he released me. I said to him, "I'm not a doctor, but I'm telling you that you shouldn't let me go like this."

My father and brother had arrived, and they took me back to my parents' house. It was now about two in the morning on

Friday. And I spent the next day and a half in bed, in a kind of semicoma. My father was calling his internist, he was calling everybody he knew, and nobody knew what to do. Finally, Saturday morning, I said that I had to go back to the hospital. I couldn't stand up straight, I couldn't move.

Why didn't you call your gynecologist?
I didn't think it was gynecological because I have chronic stomach trouble. And my doctor wasn't around—it was Memorial Day weekend. No one was around. So we went to the hospital near my parents, and the same thing happened. They kept us waiting, then they wanted to take X-rays. I said, "I don't need X-rays, they just took X-rays," but no one listened. I should mention that not one full-fledged doctor was present in the emergency room. Everyone was either an intern or a resident.

They decided they'd give me a barium enema so they could X-ray that part of me. You have to keep the stuff in you for an hour, and then they have to turn you around in all sorts of ways. And no one had really talked to me yet. No one had examined me.

Finally, when they didn't find anything with the barium enema, somebody started asking me questions. He asked me if I had an IUD, and I said yes. And he said, "Well, that's funny, because the IUD didn't show up in the X-rays." They got a gynecological intern or resident in there to give me a pelvic. He said, "Oh, my God, not only don't I feel the IUD, but I don't feel your uterus, your fallopian tubes—I don't feel anything."

What had happened was that I had an ovarian cyst that had blown up to the size of a grapefruit. One of my fallopian tubes was wrapped around the ovary, and the ovary and the uterus had receded.

It was now about eight o'clock at night. This had been going on for about ten hours. They called their gynecological surgeon. It took him however long it took him to get to the hospital. I was delirious. He examined me and said, "You guys are nuts. Get her under. She's got to go for surgery."

I remember being prepped, and right before they put me under anesthesia, they wanted me to sign a form saying that they could remove anything they had to. I refused to sign. The point is, they thought they'd have to do a hysterectomy on me. But what happened was, they cut me open and there was a huge cyst, with "weird particles," as he put it. He found part of a tooth in it, hairs . . .

That's called a dermoid cyst.

It had all these strange substances. And the fallopian tube was wrapped around it. He said that the cyst was about to burst and that I was very lucky—I could have died if it had burst. He removed one ovary and one fallopian tube. And the IUD. The uterus was fine, and so was the other ovary and fallopian tube. He made a vertical incision because he couldn't get to the cyst with a horizontal incision, and closed me up with staples. Then I had an amazing recovery, and I've never had a problem since. I recuperated in the hospital, pain-free, for four days.

Really? You had no pain?

I took Tylenol the first night, and that was it.

So you do have a high pain threshold.

I do, I really do. And by that time I was so sick of feeling half there, it was better to have a little bit of pain. I stayed out of work maybe for a week. I was very tired when I went back to the office, but I was also very tired of lying around.

Another woman we interviewed went to an emergency room with acute pain caused by an ovarian cyst. She was kept waiting, as you were, but the fact that a doctor was meeting her seemed to protect her from the kind of ineptitude you encountered.

I would never go to an emergency room now without my own personal physician. And I would never live anywhere again without having my own personal physician. At one point, I was in a room with my mother, with a sheet over me. They had given me the barium enema and I wasn't allowed to move. All of a sudden the room began to fill up with interns. They were coming in as though it were a coffee shop, and they were talking about me as I was lying there as though I were deaf or dead. Not concerned for me, just telling the story. They didn't even say, "Who's this?" It was more like "What's this case?" It was really humiliating. I mean, no one is trying to heal you—it's voyeurism. I finally said, "Just get out of here!" And for all that, I think I got better treatment than most people do because my father was there and he's a medical malpractice lawyer. He was screaming his head off and going up to the desk every five minutes. As bad as it was for me, that's how it was when he was there. You get the feeling you could just lie there and rot, that you're just a piece of meat.

*Have you ever had any other consequences from the
surgery?*

No. I go to that surgeon for an annual checkup, and every time I
ask him the same question: "Will it be a problem for me to have
children? I'm asking because it seems to me that I probably won't
want to have a child for at least another four or five years."

Once he said, "Isn't that a little late?" I said, "Well, Doctor, I
think the world has changed, and thirty-three or thirty-four isn't
too old." He said, "Well, after you've had surgery, there's scar
tissue in there. It might become more difficult to become pregnant." That was crushing. I said I understood that, but would it
be more difficult to carry the baby to term? He said no, but the
longer you wait, the harder it will be to conceive.

I felt he was moralizing—saying I wasn't doing what I should
be doing now, which is getting married and having babies. I
think that's the price you pay for having the kind of doctor who
acts like your father. They talk to you like you're a child, even to
the words they use, the metaphors—"the cyst was like a grapefruit"—these colorful, childlike words that make things seem benign when they're really not. I don't think I would have been
talked to in quite that way had I been a male patient with a male
problem.

In the emergency room, I felt that not one doctor took me seriously. I was looked at as not understanding my own body, not
capable of diagnosing it. And so I didn't take the pain seriously.
That was a very stupid thing to do: the pain was an indication of
how severe the situation was. Had I had enough faith in myself,
I wouldn't have stayed in bed for two days with it. And I don't
take responsibility for my lack of faith in myself—that comes out
of a physician-patient relationship, with a doctor who takes you
seriously, who listens to you. Diagnosis is a two-way process. If
patients were trusted and encouraged to articulate what is wrong
with them, thereby facilitating a diagnosis, then a lot of the medical horror stories you hear wouldn't have happened. Patients
need help with this—the right questions posed—because the experience of pain can be so overwhelming that you may not be
able to tell somebody where it hurts.

When you're sick, there can't be a question as to whether or not
you're going to be taken seriously. That's not for doctors to decide.
First, they have to take you seriously. Then, if they don't find
anything, they can psychologize you.

TUBAL LIGATION

Tubal ligation is surgical sterilization, and it is considered an irreversible form of birth control. Its purpose is to prevent the egg from meeting up with sperm. One or the other of the fallopian tubes catches the egg as it bursts out of the ovary and guides it to the uterus; the tubes act as a conduit for sperm to the egg—fertilization usually occurs in the tubes. To prevent the possibility of pregnancy, the surgeon creates an impasse in the tubes: tying them off and cauterizing them, usually in conjunction with laparoscopy.

The women we interviewed planned to have the tubal right after giving birth to their last child, so they would not have to return to the hospital for another stay. Most women had some discomfort after the procedure, but light painkillers were sufficient. One woman who, by mistake, received no painkillers described the pain as stronger than heavy cramps, lasting about seven hours and then subsiding completely.

Often, in making the decision to have tubal ligation, the woman and her husband discuss the possibility of his having a vasectomy (male sterilization). "There are many psychological facts that enter into a male having a vasectomy, strangely enough," says Dr. Louis Lapid of Mount Sinai Hospital in New York City. "The male feels castrated. Women are more realistic about sterilization."

Even some male doctors, we found, were not as "realistic" as one might expect. One woman was told by her (male) gynecologist that a tubal was preferable to a vasectomy because it was a "simpler" operation. Yet, comparing the two procedures—tubal ligation and vasectomy—a sourcebook published under the auspices of the American Medical Association finds that "vasectomy . . . is a simpler operation than that required for female sterilization and, because it does not require an abdominal incision, carries fewer risks."

Though both procedures are billed as irreversible, in some

cases reconstructive surgery has returned fertility: interestingly enough, vasectomy is more likely to be reversible. According to a leading textbook in the field, *Gynecology: Essentials of Clinical Practice,* by Thomas H. Green, Jr., M.D., "roughly 20 percent of women and 35 percent of men undergoing surgical sterilization can be rendered fertile again." Green goes on to weigh the potential dangers of vasectomy and finds that though sperm antibodies frequently develop after the procedure, and an immune reaction occurs in one-fifth of the men, neither possibility "appears to have any hazardous effects." In addition, "There are no adverse hormonal changes whatsoever." The real issue in vasectomy is emotional, as Dr. Lapid suggests. "Possible psychological complications," Green writes, "must always be borne in mind and discussed carefully."

Though tubal ligation requires general anesthesia and an extended stay in the hospital, the women we interviewed were all happy with their decision in favor of sterilization and enjoy particularly their freedom from the constraints and discipline of contraception.

"I DECIDED THERE WASN'T ANY METHOD OF BIRTH CONTROL I WANTED TO RELY ON."
A married nurse in her early thirties who had a tubal after the birth of her second child, two weeks before this interview.

What prompted you to have a tubal ligation?
I had decided that two children were all I wanted. I had various problems with each of my pregnancies. The first was a twin pregnancy, and I lost them at about four and a half months. Then my first child was excessively large; he was ten pounds fourteen ounces. And the baby I had two weeks ago was premature. So, with different things going wrong each time, I thought, That's enough. But what really made the decision for me was the fact that they took the IUD off the market, and that's the birth control I'd been using for the last eight years or so. I decided there wasn't any other method of birth control I wanted to rely on.

Did your husband ever consider having a vasectomy?
We had discussed that. As a matter of fact, he had decided to do

it, but then my obstetrician—a male obstetrician—talked him out of it. He had about an hour's discussion with my husband telling him all the pros and cons on the newest research into vasectomies. He said that after so many years of a male body absorbing its own sperm, the body might begin producing antibodies against sperm. It's not at all conclusive—I mean, at this stage we're talking about experiments with rats—but the reasoning was effective enough to convince my husband not to have a vasectomy.

The doctor went on to say that it's easier to interfere with a woman's production of one egg per month than the male's production of twenty million sperm per ejaculation. It sounded very chauvinistic to me. He prefaced it all by saying he was not a sexist and told an anecdote about a woman who made her husband get a vasectomy. The woman goes to a party and has intercourse with somebody and she gets pregnant. I said, "What in the world does that have to do with anything?" His point, he said, was, "It's the woman's body, so why shouldn't the woman take care of the problem?"

Were you bothered by his attitude?
Well, I found him to be the most gentle, considerate gynecologist I've ever been to, man or woman. His attitudes, I guess, are those of his generation. He's in his mid-fifties, pushing sixty. He made a sexist comment when I was on the delivery table with my first son. They had made a small episiotomy, but the baby ripped past that. He was such a big child. The stitching took the better part of an hour. I was, naturally, upset, and I was shaking on the table and crying. My husband asked what was wrong, and the doctor said something like "Oh, she's just happy." I thought at the time that was a very stupid thing to say. He also said he was going to sew me up so my husband wouldn't know the difference when I got home. I said, "Oh, brother." That was terrible. I guess, though, it's just his way. Anyway, I finally decided that since it *was* my body, I should do the tubal. If something happened to my husband or we split up, I'd still have to face birth control. And under no circumstances do I want any more children.

Is there a consent form to be signed before having a tubal?
The preliminary consent form is signed in the doctor's office. It's not binding; it's just so they know you're thinking about it. Then, the night before the tubal, I had to sign another consent form.

*Did you plan to have the tubal done in conjunction with
the birth of the baby?*

Yes. And we discussed all the different options. If it happened to
be a cesarean, they would do the tubal right away. After a normal
birth you could choose to have it done a few days later or you
could be readmitted to the hospital six weeks later. I thought if I
didn't have it done while I was in the hospital, I probably
wouldn't come back after six weeks—I mean because of the pres-
sures of time and the whole process of being admitted.

How long after the birth of your baby was it done?

As it happened, the baby was born by natural childbirth on a
Monday, and they did the tubal ligation on Wednesday and there
was no problem. Just the usual discomfort from the stitches from
the episiotomy.

*Did your gynecologist discuss the surgical procedure with
you?*

He told me he would make a very small incision, maybe an inch
long, just under the navel. They go in, locate the tubes, then tie
them off surgically. It takes about twenty minutes under general
anesthesia.

Is a tubal ligation permanent?

Yes. For all purposes, this is irreversible.

What do you remember about the procedure?

They gave me two Valium before I went up to surgery, for relaxation; then an IV was inserted, and medication to knock me out
was put into the IV. I was intubated—they put a breathing tube
down my throat. I didn't feel anything because I was out by that
time. Then they put the mask on for the gas. It seemed like a lot
of anesthesia for twenty minutes.

And when you awakened in the recovery room?

I went in about nine, and when I woke up it was about a quarter
to ten. The pain was a little bit more intense than I had anticipated. I thought because it was such a short surgery that it would
be nothing. The pain lasted all afternoon and half the night.

Were you given any painkillers?

Unfortunately, my doctors had neglected to write post-op orders,
and I couldn't get any pain medication. So all afternoon, while
they were looking for the doctor, I was in pain.

How strong was the pain without drugs?

Well, stronger than heavy cramps. It didn't hurt on the outside.
It was abdominal pain, all inside. I had difficulty trying to sit up

and more difficulty getting out of bed on my own and walking. By the time they found someone to write the prescription, the worst was over. It was early evening and I said, "Forget it," because I didn't want to be knocked out all night. The pain really subsided after six P.M. So we're talking about seven hours of discomfort and pain, from eleven A.M. to six P.M.

Could you eat after the operation?

Right after the operation, it was clear fluids. Jell-O and tea for both lunch and dinner. After that, just a regular diet.

How about problems with gas?

There was no problem, none at all.

When did you go home, and how did you feel?

Usually, they tell me, you can be discharged the next day. But because my baby was premature and in intensive care, the doctor let me stay one more day. So I was discharged on Friday, though by Thursday I was fine.

If you had known how easy it was, would you have done this earlier?

I don't think I was ready sooner. It was still a big decision, because it's irreversible. I felt a lot better about the whole thing after it was over. Before, I was wondering if I was doing the right thing; after it was over, I had no questions at all. The only thing I really had to think about was whether the baby would survive. He was such a high-risk baby, and a few days were touch and go. I had the tubal before I really knew he was going to be okay, but, considering his weight, and what they were telling me about him, I figured that he would survive, that he was a survival baby.

How did your husband feel about your having the tubal?

He resisted the tubal, I think, to the very end. He didn't want me to have it because he felt if something happened to him, I would then destroy my chances of meeting someone else and having another crop of children. We discussed this, but I decided that no matter what happened, I wasn't going to have a second group of children at the age of forty or forty-five.

"THE WHOLE TIME I WAS IN LABOR, I THOUGHT, THIS IS THE VERY LAST TIME YOU'LL HAVE TO GO THROUGH THIS."

A woman who had a tubal ligation when she was thirty-two after the birth of her second child.

What prompted you to have a tubal ligation?
I knew I didn't want more than two children. And even though other forms of contraception all worked fine—I'd used the Pill, the diaphragm, and the IUD—I really didn't want to bother using anything. The tubal was the only alternative. So when I became pregnant with my second child, we had a decision to make.
How did your husband feel about it?
He wasn't thrilled about it at first, but since we had time to decide, I thought, I'm not going to push it now. Of course, while I was pregnant, my husband said, "What if we have another boy? Maybe then we should try for a girl." I said, "I really think two will be enough." Finally he said okay.
Did your husband consider having a vasectomy?
When I told my doctor I wanted a tubal, he asked me if my husband would consider a vasectomy. I knew my husband wouldn't even want to hear of it. And of course I was right. That annoyed me a little. I told my husband that the only reason I asked him was because it was a much easier procedure for a man. The doctor can do a vasectomy in the office, in a few minutes, but for a tubal, they have to put me to sleep. My husband had a whole line of "buts," so I knew I was going to have to do it.
And you didn't have any second thoughts about the decision?
No. I didn't want any more kids, I didn't want to use contraceptives, and my husband wouldn't have a vasectomy. Even if, God forbid, something happened to my family now, do you think I would start from scratch, having babies and raising children again? There's no way I would want to do that.
Did you get a second opinion on the surgery?
I didn't feel any real need to. I'd been seeing my gynecologist since before I had my first son—he's six now. I've never had any problems with this doctor. When I call with a question he explains everything, and if he can't, he'll call back with an answer. He's been very good. I knew I wanted this done and didn't need to see a second doctor.
So the surgery was performed after the birth of your baby?
Yes. The doctor was able to do the tubal a day and a half later. Altogether I was in the hospital for five days.

What was the procedure?

In the morning, they gave me something to relax me. The doctor came in and asked if I still wanted to do this, I said, "Yes." And he said, "I'll see you inside." They took me into surgery, and it went really quickly. I went to sleep, and all of a sudden I was in the recovery room and everything was finished.

What kind of incision was made?

A small one. You know how your belly button has all these little tucks and folds? He made the incision right inside one of the folds. That's why I have no scar.

How did you feel after the surgery?

I was very glad it was over. When you're in the recovery room, you're just kind of in a daze. I had some discomfort, but they gave me Darvon. I took painkillers the whole next day. I would ask for them every four hours, and they gave them to me. I think I had some extra pain because the baby had been born at home just as we were on our way to the hospital. The paramedics delivered him. And you know, the whole time I was in labor, I thought, This is the very last time you'll have to go through this.

The only other problem I had was gas. It's terrible, because there's nothing you can do about it. My mother brought me some warm ginger ale, and that seemed to help move the gas down.

How was your recovery?

I was up the day after the surgery. I didn't walk far. I went to the nursery and back to my room, and then I sat in the chair. I really wanted to seem okay because they have sibling hours at the hospital and my mother was bringing my other son to visit me. I didn't want him to be scared by seeing me in pain. I took a painkiller just before he came, so I was kind of out of it, but I could sit and talk to him.

Did your stitches have to be removed?

No. The doctor gave me stitches that dissolved. There was a little knot where he sewed up the incision, but he said it would just drop off, and it did. For a long time the area was very hard, but he said that it would soften as it healed.

Is there anything else women considering this surgery should know?

Just that it's an irreversible procedure and there's no changing your mind. But once you're positive you don't want any more children, it's good not to have to use contraception. Everything can be very spontaneous. That's the best part, I think.

TUBOPLASTY

Tuboplasty is microsurgery to open and repair fallopian tubes: the ultimate purpose is to enable a woman to conceive.

The tubes look something like calla lilies. The stems are rooted in the uterus, and the flowery heads cup the ovaries, ready to catch the eggs after ovulation. If the stems are blocked, if the head is twisted away from the ovary, or if the petals are closed, conception becomes impossible; the egg can't reach the sperm. When infertility is due to blocked tubes, tuboplasty is a woman's hope for becoming pregnant.

Recovery from tuboplasty is comparable to recovery from any abdominal surgery. It's a delicate operation and may take from three to five hours. Hospital stays are usually five to six days. Getting back to normal takes approximately two months.

"I HAD MULTIPLE ADHESIONS ON MY TUBES. AND THE DOCTOR SAID, 'I WON'T SAY THERE'S A 100 PERCENT CHANCE YOU CAN'T GET PREGNANT, BUT LET'S SAY IT'S A 99.999 PERCENT CHANCE.' "

A thirty-five-year-old advertising executive, who had a tuboplasty five weeks before this interview.

What were the circumstances leading up to the surgery?
My husband and I had lived together for six years before getting married a year ago. I had stopped using contraception about three years before that, and one day, about a year and a half ago, my husband said, "You know, something must be wrong, because you should be pregnant by now." And I said, "I think you're right. I should find out what's going on." Even though I wasn't sure I was ready to have children, we called the doctor and I told him, "I just want to know if I *can* get pregnant or not, so I can deal with facts."

83

What did the doctor recommend?

He said, "Well, why don't we do all of the easy things." That's sperm count, the blood test, blood analysis. They also dilate your cervix and take a little nip out of the lining of your uterus to see if it can hold and nourish a fertilized egg—a painful procedure called endometrial biopsy. He gave me some kind of local anesthetic and a muscle relaxant because I have a very tight cervix and whenever it's dilated I cramp.

And after all that, the test results were marginal. Nothing said I couldn't get pregnant, but it wasn't the strongest showing. My doctor said some women's bodies produce spermicide when sperm is present. I'm one of those women. But when I want to get pregnant, he said, we could try using condoms at all times except during my fertile periods to get my body to relax chemically—there would be no sperm to trigger the spermicide. Then during the fertile period the body could be fooled into not producing spermicide, and I might get pregnant.

I realized that nothing was guaranteed. He couldn't say for sure that I *would* get pregnant using this method or, conversely, that we could make love whenever we wanted and *not* get pregnant.

Then he said, "There are two other options you can consider, if you really want to know if you can get pregnant. We can inject a dye through the cervix and then X-ray it." That way they can see any blockages. "Or," he said, "we can do a laparoscopy." He said that of the two, he would prefer, when we were ready, to do the laparoscopy because he could see the tubes and the ovaries and would be able to assess the problems more accurately. But he left it up to us.

Did you choose to have the laparoscopy?

Yes, in June of this year. For six months we'd been living temporarily in New York, but we decided to stay here permanently even though I quit the job that brought us here. By this time we were consciously thinking about having kids, and it seemed the ideal time to go back to Los Angeles where my doctor was, have the laparoscopy, and arrange our move to New York at the same time.

What was the surgery like?

It was my first experience in a hospital, so it was a bit frightening. A wonderful anesthesiologist explained the procedure to me. He told me he would give me something to relax me and then give me the anesthetic through an IV. I had no pain with the IV, and the next thing I remember is waking up and my husband looking at me. I was hoping he was going to say, "Nothing's wrong." Instead he said, "It'll be fine." So I said, "What's wrong?" He said, "We'll talk about it. It's fixable. Just relax." My throat felt like razor blades because of the tube down my throat during surgery. I drank a ton of water, and we got out of the hospital as soon as I possibly could. I'd gone in about 9:30 A.M., and I was out by 1:30 in the afternoon.

How did you feel?

I was depressed that I wasn't really all right. And physically, I felt sore. I didn't want anything on my stomach—no belt, tight waistbands, or anything like that. I was also obsessing over this tiny little cut above my pubic hair.

What did the doctor say the surgery revealed?

He said, "You're in excellent shape, and there's no reason why you couldn't get pregnant in terms of the health of your body. But your reproductive organs are a mess. You have all kinds of scar tissue." I had multiple adhesions on my tubes. He said it could have been from an infection, a high fever, a variety of things. And he said, "I won't say there's a 100 percent chance you can't get pregnant, but let's say it's a 99.999 percent chance." The adhesions had completely closed up my tubes, and there was just no way for the sperm to get to the egg.

What did he recommend?

A tuboplasty—opening the tubes with microsurgery. We decided to do it quickly, while I wasn't working and still had medical insurance.

What did he tell you about the procedure?

He explained what the tubes are like, how delicate they are—they're about the width of the stem of a fine flower. The ends of your tubes should be like the open petals of a flower. Mine were both closed. The surgery would try to duplicate nature and not only open the tubes, but get the ends to float naturally and reach out to catch the egg.

What is the success rate for conception after a tuboplasty?

He said he had a very high success rate. We said, "What's very high?" He didn't use his own record: he used the statistics for the profession and said there was a 95 percent chance that a woman would be able to conceive after this surgery. However, when we asked specifically about *my* being able to conceive, he said, "Listen, these are the percentages. I am as sure as I can be without misleading you that I can open your tubes. And if I can, then you have a 70 percent chance of conceiving." So we said okay.

Did you talk with any of your friends about the surgery before you had it?

I did, but, in fact, after a while I stopped talking to anyone. People's fears come across. One woman was worried about my having this operation because a friend of hers had the same operation, and she told me the friend had to hurry up and get pregnant because the tubes can close up again after only six months and then you have to go through it all again. I called the doctor and he said, "Of course there's a possibility the tubes can scar again, but who said anything about six months? It's during the *second* year after the surgery that there is the highest incidence of conception." Someone else said, "Boy, when you make love for the first time after surgery, you're going to be on the ceiling. It hurts so much you'll be screaming."

How was your second hospital stay?

I had the choice between a two-hundred-bed hospital and a two-thousand-bed hospital. My doctor recommended I go to the smaller one, which turned out to be really good. My husband was allowed to stay with me. We checked in together in the evening because surgery was scheduled for seven-thirty the following morning. They woke me very early. The nurse came to put in the IV. She struggled with it for about five minutes, and I finally yelped. I later found out she was using a larger-gauge needle than usual because they anticipated the surgery would be long. She said, "I'll get my supervisor." We tried to stay calm. The supervisor came in and said my blood vessels were too small. A second nurse couldn't get the IV in, either. My husband turned to me and said, "If you want to leave right now, we can leave." And I really thought about it. Finally a doctor came in, and he was very agitated with the nurses. He put the IV in, in one second, and apologized profusely. We sort of relaxed then.

One of the nurses came back to take me to surgery. She said, "You have to take your panties off." I started to explain to her that the doctor wanted me to wear them. He had said to me the night before, "If you wear low panties, wear them into surgery because people's hips are uneven. I would like to make the incision straight and what looks straight to us on the table may not be straight for you." He said he would make the incision below my panty line, which I thought was considerate of him. The nurse said, "I can't take you up to surgery with your panties on." I said, "Well, then, I guess you're not taking me up to surgery." And there was nothing the nurse could do about it. I went up with my panties on.

I think it must have been my spirit establishing itself and saying, "I am not powerless"—even though you *are* completely powerless. That was one of the most terrible things about this whole thing: once you're in the hospital, you feel you have no power. You must have complete trust, and you go on blind faith, but you know everyone can make a mistake. It's very frightening. I handled it by being very even-keeled during the whole thing. Very tranquil, very quiet. I just did not allow myself to think of the full scope of what was going to happen, or I could never have gone to the hospital.

But I remember my doctor lifting me off the gurney as if I were the figure in the *Pietà*. There was this sense of tenderness. He was very gentle and very nurturing. Maybe that doesn't have anything to do with his surgical prowess, but I felt very good about it. The next thing I knew, I was out of surgery, I was in bed, and my husband was sitting there.

How long was the surgery?
It lasted three hours.

What was your recovery like?
A lot of people told me they get you out of bed and get you walking from the first day, but the nurses were not like that. I stayed in bed the first day, and they said I didn't have to move around. I had a catheter for the first two days. And they gave me Demerol every four hours for the first two days. I had been very freaked out about the possibility of scarring and forming keloids, because I don't heal well, so my doctor had injected the incision with cortisone while I was still under anesthesia. He also prescribed antiinflammatory shots every four hours, to promote healing and keep me from scarring. I did seem to heal fast. The fourth day, they took the dressing off. I had staples in me that made my stomach look like a bad version of Frankenstein. But the incision was closed very flat except for one point that was bleeding a little bit. That point has just sealed over now—it's been over a month. I was really upset about it. It looked as if one staple were missing: that small part didn't come together like the rest of the incision.

What did the doctor say about your surgery?
He explained there was an incredible amount of scar tissue on the tubes, and one of my ovaries was almost completely covered. When he cut it away the ovary was perfect underneath it. They also found a fibroid about three inches in diameter, which they couldn't see when they did the laparoscopy because it, too, was underneath the scarring. They took that out as well. He was obviously pleased with the surgery. I said, "Well, what do you think the chances are now? Do we still have a 70 percent chance?" He said, "I would say you have an 85 percent chance. You look like a picture book inside."

How long was your hospital stay?
We checked into the hospital on a Monday night, and we left on Saturday.

Since you were away from home, where did you recover?
We had a bungalow in Los Angeles for a week, and then we went to stay with my husband's parents. All I did for the first week was stay in bed. He cooked three meals a day, and I would just get up and go to the bathroom. I don't have a very high pain threshold, but it wasn't painful. I just had the fear I could tear something, and I was uncomfortable. One day we walked three street blocks, very slowly. I had to lie down on someone's lawn at the end. Later that day, I started to feel like something was tearing, and I got very frantic. My husband called the doctor. The doctor said, "She's probably overdoing it. She has to tune in to her body." I got on the phone with him, and he said, "Take a warm bath, not too hot, or have a glass of brandy, or do both and relax. Do deep breathing or whatever you want to do, but you have to calm down." And I did.

But somewhere during that week I got very depressed. I'm not used to relying on other people to do things for me. I deal with that professionally much better than I do personally. Professionally, I can understand that it's good to delegate tasks, and that's how teams work. For myself, because I'm not a dependent, retiring sort of person, I tend not to allow people to do things for me. My husband and I have worked intermittently on it. It's something I would like to change, so I keep working on it when it comes up. This was a perfect situation to practice on because I couldn't do *anything*. It drove me crazy. It made me feel very apologetic and very insecure. My husband wanted to take care of me, and he couldn't read my mind. I was sort of suffering through it and being a pain in the ass. But once I figured out what I was doing, I just started crying. We talked about it. My body was traumatized. Until the operation was over, I hadn't allowed myself to think about what I had been through, because it was too scary.

Did your recovery proceed normally once you came back east?

Well, not normally, no. When we returned to New York, a friend met us at the airport. On the drive home, I was suddenly covered with a warm fluid. I freaked out. I just got very quiet, and I said, "Stop the car." We were on the Palisades, and we pulled into a rest station. My husband came into the ladies' room with me, apologizing to all the women in there. We went into a stall, and there was a yellow liquid all over me. It had no scent. He immediately called the doctor in Los Angeles—it was Sunday, I guess —and he said, "Don't worry, it's okay. It's like when you get a splinter or blister—the body naturally forms water around the wounded area." If I didn't have that hole in my incision, my body would have eliminated the water, internally. But when I pushed against this little opening, the fluid was released. I honestly thought I was dying. The doctor warned that it might happen again, which it did—three times. All because the staple wasn't there.

But it's been a little more than a month, and I have lots of energy. I can stand up straight. I can walk around. I don't feel comfortable walking quickly yet, and there's a soreness around the abdomen that wasn't there before. But I've gotten much more of my body sensation back.

Did you ever confront the doctor about the missing staple?

No. And we saw it right away, too, after the bandage was removed. But because we didn't say anything then, it seemed too awkward to bring it up later. And besides, he's taken such good care of me otherwise. I have to admit, though, that by the third time that yellow fluid came through the opening, I was very depressed. But it's healing very well now.

Do you have any advice to women considering a tuboplasty?

More important than anything else is to find a doctor you really trust, one you feel comfortable asking questions of and who gives you the kinds of answers that don't discourage you from asking more questions. I also think it's important to find out beforehand if the doctor will be accessible by phone. We called the doctor four or five times a week during the first two weeks out of the hospital with one little emergency after another. And he took the calls every time. If he hadn't, it would have been very traumatic.

FOLLOW-UP: Five months after surgery, she became pregnant, which proved to her that she could now conceive. Unfortunately, she miscarried within the first month. Her doctor told her it was not uncommon for women to miscarry within the first month of any pregnancy and, in fact, said that he had been quite surprised she had conceived so quickly. He assured her that it was too early to be concerned; if she is not pregnant after two years, they will investigate further.

———————

"IF YOU KNOW THE SURGEON IS TECHNICALLY GOOD, GO WITH HIM. PERSONALITY IS NOT THE MOST IMPORTANT THING—SKILL IS."

A thirty-four-year-old medical secretary who had her surgery eight years ago. She works in a hospital in a suburb of New York City and now has two children.

Why did you need surgery?
When I was twenty years old and got married, I went and had a Dalkon shield IUD inserted. That was the beginning of my problem. As a result of the IUD, I developed pelvic inflammatory disease (PID). Early on, I had chronic cervicitis [infection of the cervix] and had to have cryotherapy on the cervix—they freeze it. That was just an office procedure. Eight years later, in November 1980, after three years of trying to have a child, I decided to ask a doctor what was going on. He did some infertility testing, an endometrial biopsy, and then a hysterosalpingogram, an X-ray of reproductive organs, which showed that my fallopian tubes were blocked. I had a D&C and then a laparoscopy so my doctor could determine if tubal plastic surgery was called for.
When did you have the Dalkon shield removed?
Even before the cervicitis was diagnosed, when I first started having problems. I replaced it with another kind of IUD—I can't use the Pill because I have phlebitis [inflammation of a vein that is aggravated by estrogen] in my left leg—and I didn't know that

the cervicitis was related to the IUD. I had the second IUD taken out when I developed cysts on my ovary. The doctor I was seeing then decided that we shouldn't mess around—just take the damn thing out.

How did you decide to have the surgery? Microsurgery was still a relatively new procedure at the time.

My options were not to have children or to have the tuboplasty. My left fallopian tube was pointed away from my ovary—which means an egg could never find its way to the uterus. And on my right side, the fimbria were closed like the petals of a dead flower: the fimbria are fingerlike projections at the end of the tube that draw the egg from the ovary to the mouth of the tube. That's the way the surgeon described it to me at the time. And as a result of this chronic PID, my tubes were filled with fluid because they were blocked up.

I really had no choice. I wanted to have children, we both did. We didn't feel that we were ready for it when we got married—we were both twenty years old. So we put it off, and that's why I had the IUD! But I did very much want children, and I wanted them a thousand times more when I found that I couldn't have them. All of a sudden, it started to really hurt when I saw other children around.

My doctor told me that they were going to remove the adhesions surgically through microsurgery. They would open the fimbria [the "fringe" at the end of the tubes] by cutting the adhesions between each on the right; and on the left, they would remove the adhesions that twisted the tube and turn it back toward the ovary. And because it was such delicate surgery, they told me that afterward, I would have to stay in bed for two weeks and do absolutely nothing for another six weeks.

How did you find the right doctor?

My old doctor seemed all right at the time—the way he spoke to me was fine, and he kept trying to solve my problem—but he was having no success with me. When I started working at a hospital, I switched to the group of four rotating OB/GYN doctors in the hospital itself. My doctor came into the group just before I had the surgery. I was very lucky to know doctors, and be able to get their opinions about their colleagues, and to have this doctor join the staff. He had done a fellowship particularly in this type of surgery and had an excellent success rate—a lot of the infertility specialists in Manhattan don't have as good a rate as he does.

How did you feel before the surgery?

I was petrified. I remember the night before, I felt fine, there was nothing wrong with me—and I knew that the next morning I was going to feel miserable. Plus, they only gave me a 40 percent chance of being able to become pregnant after the surgery. I cried all night long, as a matter of fact.

I was also miserable because I was in a semiprivate room, and the woman in the next bed was on her way out—she was dying. She had gastrointestinal cancer, she was very old, they had all sorts of machines going, and the room smelled like vitamins, and she just lay there and moaned a lot. I'm shaking now, remembering the night before.

The morning of surgery . . .

I was scheduled for 7:30 A.M. They usually offer you one last trip to the bathroom. Then they give you a shot of something—I think Valium—and put the bars up on your bed. And then they come with the gurney and wheel you through the hallways.

Very soon after I entered the operating room, they put me under. I was grateful for that, because I didn't want to listen to them talking about the ball game or whatever—that's what they talk about. They discuss the surgery only when it becomes critical.

I was under for five hours. I remember in the recovery room a man on a stretcher got off and tried to walk out, stark naked! I found out later I tried to do the same thing!

Everything hurts when you wake up, your whole body hurts. I didn't know that I was able to ask for pain medication yet—I thought that I had a lot of pain medication in my body, what with the anesthesia and all. But the nurse asked if I was ready for pain medication, and I was grateful that she asked. She gave me Demerol. Wonderful stuff. And I slept most of that day. My mother, who's a nurse, was there with me.

I should also tell you that during the surgery they administered something called Hyskon intraabdominally. It's a high-density glucose solution that prevents adhesions and scarring. Later they gave me other drugs intramuscularly to help with adhesions and inflammation. I remember when I came home from the hospital I counted: I'd had 112 injections, including the IV and the blood they took—I had rainbows of black-and-blue marks on my hips.

The days after surgery . . .

I slept very soundly the first night because they gave me Demerol every four hours. I had shoulder pain all the next day. Lots of times you'll have shoulder pain after abdominal surgery. It's referred pain from having gas in your belly, and it got worse each time I used the ventilator—you have to blow into it and inhale deeply to keep the lungs open so you don't get pneumonia. The third day I was pretty much better because that pain had subsided. Even though they advised against, it, I tried to get a lot of exercise. I think they thought I did more than I should.

I had another complication, I guess on the fifth day, a strange sensation as though my throat were closing and my mouth were swelling. The next day, I started itching all over my neck and my trunk and arms. My surgeon decided that it was a fungal infection, thrush. The normal body flora would have restrained the fungus from growing too much, but because of all the antibiotics, I didn't have any natural flora. So I had this fungal infection in my mouth, on my face, neck, and arms, and also vaginally, but I didn't actually know about that, because everything down there was sort of weird anyway. They gave me Monistat-Derm [antifungal cream] and Mycostatin [antifungal antibiotic]. I was also still taking oral antibiotics when I left the hospital. They offered me some painkillers, but I wasn't taking them any longer. I still have the thrush—it comes and goes, and every month, when I get my period, I get a yeast infection.

Did you have any help when you got home?
My mother stayed for the first four or five days. After she left, the days were long. I wasn't used to being at home alone. I was able to move around enough to get to the refrigerator, I could stand at the sink and wash a couple of dishes, and I could manage to cook a very simple meal. I sat a lot. I did lots of jigsaw puzzles those six weeks and read a lot of books. It was a little lonely, but each day was better. I was very, very glad that the surgery was in the past. I had had to wait a long time for my surgery—thirteen weeks from the time I decided to do it—because the OR [operating room] schedule was heavy. Those thirteen weeks were very trying.

How soon after surgery did you have sex?
Six weeks.

And how soon did you conceive?
Seven months after I had the surgery.

Were you nervous, waiting to see if you could become pregnant?

No, because I had decided that I was going to try not to get pregnant for the first six months. I had a lot of drugs in me, and I wanted to give my body a chance to heal, to have the strength to carry a baby. My surgeon didn't think the wait was necessary, but I did. We used rhythm and coitus interruptus for six months, and the first month after we stopped practicing birth control we conceived.

Was your pregnancy normal?

For the first sixteen weeks of pregnancy, I couldn't have sex because I wasn't supposed to have an orgasm—it causes the uterus to contract, my doctor said, so why take a chance?

I was a high-risk pregnancy, because having had this kind of surgery, there's a greater danger of an ectopic pregnancy [the fertilized egg falls into the abdominal cavity and grows there instead of in the uterus]. You can die from that. In the beginning of the pregnancy I was very apprehensive because I had some left-sided pain. But I had a blood test, and an abdominal sonogram, and everything was fine.

What would you advise a woman considering this surgery?

First of all, I would advise you to do it. If you have the surgery, you have hope. It's miserable knowing that you're not able to have a child. It's very demeaning—you don't feel like a worthwhile human being. You're not able to fulfill your function as a woman. When you marry and plan to have a family, if you find you can't, it takes away from your whole future! So anyone who has a problem with this, I say—do it.

The other thing is, if you know the surgeon is technically good, go with him. A surgeon you can relate to on an emotional level is not always easy to find. When I started seeing my doctor, he didn't treat me badly, but he talked down to me. I really kind of resented it: he knew I was a medical secretary, I had worked in the hospital for years, I had some knowledge. But when I had the laparoscopy, my boss, who is a cardiologist, came in and held my hand and stroked my head. After that, my surgeon treated me totally differently. He said, "I didn't know you were such an important person here." All of a sudden he's talking to me like I'm a real human being, you know? Knowing him better now, I think he's shy. Doctors are human beings, too. They have all sorts of personality quirks.

But in the end, personality is not the most important thing. The skill of a surgeon is most important. You only have to deal with him a little bit, before and after you have surgery. It seems to me, after knowing quite a few doctors, that the best surgeons are the most arrogant sons of bitches you ever want to meet. I almost understand why they feel that way about themselves! The future of your whole family is in their hands.

CESAREAN SECTION

Cesarean section is the surgical delivery of a baby through an abdominal incision, performed after the gynecologist decides that the health of the mother or child will be endangered by normal vaginal delivery. It's done under general anesthesia or with an epidural. Recovery seems to be easier than from other procedures that involve opening the belly. The incision has to heal, of course, and the women spoke of feeling fatigue and discomfort in the weeks following the surgery, but as one woman put it, "You don't think much about the pain once you have the baby."

Though pregnant women now routinely prepare for natural childbirth through classes in the Lamaze method, just over 20 percent end up having a C-section instead. Typically, they go through an arduous labor, and then, suddenly, comes the decision to do a section and the rush to surgery. Given the statistics —one in five—we think it makes sense for all pregnant women to discuss a C-section scenario with their doctors: not only what would happen, but under what circumstances the doctor would decide to operate. (This discussion is particularly important for women who've already had a C-section. Doctors used to assume that once a woman has had a section, all subsequent deliveries will have to be surgical: this is no longer true. A 1986 study estimated that two-thirds of such women could avoid surgery.)

Being prepared not only reduces fear; it allows the patient an opportunity to express a preference for the kind of anesthesia she would receive if surgery became necessary. The women we interviewed suggest that an epidural is the method of choice: it blocks pain yet leaves you awake and aware of what's going on.

———————

"EVEN NOW, I'M MORE AFRAID OF HAVING NATURAL CHILDBIRTH THAN OF A CESAREAN. BUT I WAS JEALOUS AFTER THE OPERATION OF ALL THE WOMEN WHO HAD

96

DELIVERED THEIR BABIES NATURALLY AND WERE UP THE NEXT DAY, WALKING AROUND."

A married free-lance writer in her mid-twenties who gave birth to her first child by cesarean section.

What was the reason for a surgical delivery of your baby?
We saw, in the first sonogram at about four months, that the baby was breech. And every three weeks when I went in for my appointment, they would say, "The baby is still breech." I could see his head up here and his bottom down there. I decided that if I were going to have a cesarean, I'd rather do it like a lady, plan it and go in at the appointed time. They kept trying to convince me it wasn't a good idea because the baby might turn. But I knew he wasn't going to, and he didn't. As the due date came near, I got into this big fight with my doctor. I was crying, because you get very emotional when you're pregnant. We were using a group practice with three doctors, and they wouldn't answer my phone calls. Then one doctor said they were scheduling a cesarean, but he never did. That was really terrible. They were still trying to convince me to plan to do it naturally. Two weeks before I was due, they said, "We think you're going to be three weeks late." I went into labor that night, and they still hadn't made any plans for me. I must have done it just to prove them wrong.

How did you feel about having the cesarean?
I was so scared of the whole thing anyway that the cesarean didn't matter. I took all the classes in Lamaze, but early on, because the baby was breech, I thought I might have to have the cesarean. It took a while for me to psych myself into it, but by the time I had it, I was ready. If I was having a second child, I'd try for natural childbirth, though even now I'm more afraid of having natural childbirth than of a cesarean. But I was jealous after the operation of all the women who had delivered their babies naturally and were up the next day, walking around.

What was the labor like?
I was in labor for about six hours, so it wasn't really bad. But it was kind of traumatic. I mean, you're in pain and you're nervous and the woman next door is yelling. These two guys—residents, I think—came in to give me the epidural and made me lean over this table. I couldn't believe it, but first, they missed, and second, they forgot to ask if I was having a cesarean epidural or a regular epidural. They didn't give me the right dosage for a cesarean. Of

everything, that was the most painful. It was a shock to my system. Do you know that rather primal tune, "I Can't Stop My Legs?" Well, that's what happened to me. My leg was going up and down, and my whole body was shaking. Then they had to take the needle out and do it all over again. That was really horrible.

I began to feel numb all over, but I was totally awake and we went into the operating room.

What do you remember of the operation?
My husband was with me, and that made a big difference. Everyone was talking and joking. Then they said, "We're going to cut you now." They have a sheet, so you can't see anything. I'm sure that's a relief for many women, but I was sorry—I'm interested in that stuff.

My doctor, the one who operated on me, was a woman. She said, "You're going to feel a lot of pressure." And I did, a *lot* of pressure, but no pain. I felt like my body was a bag, and my organs were rocks. I could feel her moving the rocks around in me to find the baby. It was really bizarre, hands moving in there and everything being shoved around. And then, they pulled the baby up and out. I could feel that, too.

They gave me some Pitocin then, which starts the cramps, actually. They give it sometimes to induce labor, but for me it was so all the fluids and everything like that comes out.

They took the baby over to the side table and measured him and all that. I started to cry, it was very exciting, and my husband brought the baby so I could hold him for a few minutes.

They sutured me while they were cleaning the baby, and I think that actually took longer than they spent taking him out of me.

How did you feel in the recovery room?
They gave me some kind of drug, but after that they let me keep the baby. They put him on me. And I'll never forget that feeling. It was warm and wet, it was such a nice feeling. Then they took him away because they said they found with cesarean patients that they'll give the mother her baby and come back to find the baby hanging on, because the mother has fallen asleep. The next thing I knew I woke up in my room in the middle of flowers and my husband was there.

How was your first day after the surgery?
I was very tired. They had given me some new painkiller in the

recovery room because I guess the epidural wears off. I couldn't believe how hard it was to get up that first day. I was really thirsty, and they only gave me crushed ice to suck—they don't want you to drink anything because you're liable to be nauseated. I didn't have a private nurse, but the floor nurse was great. She said, "Now I'm going to make your bed and you've got to get into that chair." The chair was a foot away, but getting there was a major accomplishment. It was really painful.

It's hard to describe the pain, but it was worse than an extreme period. I mean, I have the worst periods in the world—I just have to go to bed. This kind of pain was the kind that pulled; everything was sewed up so tightly, it seemed, that to get up felt like it would really pull me apart.

They gave me Tylenol, and I finally was able to make it to the bathroom by myself. You really have to push yourself or have someone push you.

How were your second and third days in the hospital?
They'd bring the baby in to feed, though I had a fever for the first two days so I wasn't allowed to breast-feed him. But they brought him into the room, and he was allowed to stay the whole time, as long as I didn't have visitors.

Eventually, I could walk and hold the baby. But to lift him out of the crib was so hard for me. I remember shuffling around, hunched all the way over. I was very weak most of the time. By the third day I was learning to give him a bath. They'd leave me alone to change his diaper.

And the rest of your hospital stay?
I was in the hospital for seven days. I had the choice of going home a little earlier, but I decided to stay because I was so tired.

By the fourth day, I was eating solid food. The worst part of that was the first bowel movement. At least the gas pains disappeared with that, although I always have problems with gas so this was almost normal. By the time I went home, I was all right.

How did you manage at home?
I didn't want any live-in help, although I had someone come in during the day. The first week I didn't go out much. My husband would leave in the morning for work and I'd be on the bed breast-feeding, and when he'd come home, I was in the same position. I was just exhausted and didn't want to go anywhere or do anything.

My sister had a cesarean, too, but different people handle things differently. She left the hospital two days after giving birth. She'd climb the stairs holding the baby and took the baby out to lunch on her seventh day. I was never very strong, and she always was.

How did your recovery go?

I had a bikini cut. The incision was small, about three inches, right below my pubic line. My scar still itches, a year later. I mean, it's still red. I haven't gone back to exercising—I used to take aerobic dancing four times a week—but it's not because of the surgery. I work and I have the baby. I don't know where to fit it all in.

I don't think my concentration will ever get back to normal, not until he's eighteen or something. I'm a free-lance writer, and I really like writing. I used to be able to spend hours on it, but now I only have help from nine to five. And sometimes the writing doesn't happen in those hours. I used to be able to work all night if I had to or if I wanted to, but I can't do that anymore, because the baby's up, and if I don't get some sleep, I'll be a zombie.

When could you resume sex?

They tell you six weeks, but forget it. I don't think it had to do with the surgery—it's the breast-feeding. It dries you up; it's like you're a menopausal woman. It was so painful to make love. In fact, I have a friend who made it through regular childbirth with no drugs, and the most painful part of the experience for her was the first time she had sex afterward. For me, too. Now, thank God, it's back to normal. But it took a long time.

FOLLOW-UP: In February 1987, two years and a day after giving birth to her first son, she delivered a second boy through cesarean section. Again, her doctors—the same group practice she used during the first pregnancy—would not schedule a cesarean ahead of time, and again the baby was in an abnormal position for delivery—this time transverse [positioned across the uterus] instead of breech. The delivery was more difficult than the first and took longer, but she feels the entire experience was much easier. Though she was in labor for six hours, the epidural was administered correctly this time. And she was better prepared—she was physically stronger and knew what to expect.

―――――――――

"I FELT I'D LOST OUT—I MEAN, THAT I MISSED THE
EXPERIENCE OF HAVING THE BABY. IF I HAVE TO HAVE
ANOTHER CESAREAN, I'D GET AN EPIDURAL INSTEAD OF
GENERAL ANESTHESIA."

*A hospital lab technician in her mid-twenties who planned
to deliver her first child naturally until it was discovered
that her baby was in fetal distress.*

*Had you discussed the possibility of a cesarean with your
doctor before the delivery?*
I did bring it up because I was concerned that so many cesareans
were being done. Personally, I felt they were being done to make
it a little easier on the doctors. I wanted my doctor to know I was
aware of the issue, and I wanted him to try to avoid it if possible.
But it turned out to be an emergency situation. My baby was in
fetal distress, and they felt that if I didn't have a cesarean, I
might lose him.

What were the circumstances leading up to the delivery?
I had been in the labor room for approximately ten hours. I knew
something was going wrong. Because of my job, I'm kind of
aware of what happens in a hospital. The nurse couldn't get a
good reading of the baby's heartbeat with the fetal monitor. She
got someone else to come in, and then there were two of them
trying to figure out what the problem was. I had dilated to 9
centimeters, and I was pretty ready to go when they realized the
baby's heartbeat was dropping. They hooked me up to another
type of monitor that went around the baby's head, which they
could see at the time. The heart rate kept dropping, and at that
point they saw the baby had fecal matter in the fluid, a sign of
fetal distress.

*Did the doctors know why the baby went into fetal
distress?*
They told me the reason was because the cord was around his
neck.

*Once the decision was made to do a cesarean section, what
happened?*
Everything was rush-rush. I had at least six or seven people
working on me. They raced me into the delivery room, gave me

general anesthesia. They just capped my mouth with the oxygen or whatever they used. They had me count, and I counted to five and then I was out.

What kind of incision did you have?

When I went in for my six-week checkup, the nurse said the outside cut was vertical, but the uterine cut was horizontal. Now, I never really checked my records to find out if this is the case. She said that HIP [Hospital Insurance Plan] doctors do this on a routine basis because the crossed incision makes the abdominal closing stronger. Only now am I starting to think about checking, because later on, maybe I'll want to have another baby and I can try to deliver naturally, if I'm cut that way.

My incision is about two and a half inches, from right below my belly button to right above my hairline. With a pregnant stomach, it's a larger incision, but when your stomach shrinks back, it looks smaller.

The one thing that surprised me was they used staples to close the incision. It was amazing to me that you could actually see staples on your stomach. I had about six or seven. When they took them out four or five days later they used a staple remover. That was a little painful.

How did you feel after the surgery?

I wasn't feeling too much. I didn't see the baby until the next day. Back in my room, I just rested. It's a big operation, even though it's done often. The doctors felt I should get rest and make sure I didn't get any infection. But I developed a fever; I was in the hospital for about seven days, and for five of them I had the IV in.

What was the pain level?

I was sore. After my fever was gone I wanted to breast-feed the baby, but when you have a C-section you have to hold the baby by your side so it doesn't weigh on your stomach. It was also painful when I walked around. But you don't really think about pain once you have the baby.

And how was your recovery once you went home?

The only inconvenience was that I was used to doing a lot of exercise and sports. As soon as I had the C-section, I was worried about doing any sort of stressful exercise. They usually tell you to take it easy for six to eight weeks. They told me to be careful for an extra month so I'd heal without rupturing anything.

How soon were you back to normal?

After three months, I think. Then I could pretty much lift every-thing, and I felt that having the cesarean had been fairly easy. The only thing was, I felt I'd lost out—I mean, that I missed the experience of having the baby. If I have to have another cesar-ean, I'd get an epidural instead of general anesthesia, so I'd be awake and see what's happening. My husband should have been there, but they wouldn't let him because it was an emergency. Women should plan ahead to make sure having their husband there is okay with the doctors.

PELVIC REPAIR

A cystocele is a bulge in the front wall of the vagina resulting from childbirth. The muscle layer separating the vagina from the bladder has stretched out and weakened, allowing the bladder to sag into the vaginal canal. In a surgical procedure called an anterior colporrhaphy, that muscle wall is cut and then tightened to support the bladder. A rectocele is a similar condition involving the back wall of the vagina.

"I WISH I'D KNOWN IT WAS GOING TO BE SO EASY—I WOULD HAVE HAD IT DONE IMMEDIATELY."
A thirty-six-year-old administrator who had surgery to repair a cystocele after the birth of her second child.

How did you come to need this surgery?
Basically, what happened was I had a very fast birth of a very large baby—a nine-and-one-half-pound baby in about two hours. And, as you can see, I'm not that large [she's 5 feet, 6 inches, weighs 114 pounds, and had gained fifty pounds during the pregnancy]. Everybody thought I was so lucky to have labor over so soon. My first birth had taken twenty-four hours, was three and a half weeks late, with two tries in the hospital—so I was absolutely not expecting this at all.

About five or six days after I left the hospital, I was recovering, sitting at home, and I felt this tremendous weight in my vagina. I could feel an organ protruding there. I flew into a panic and called the doctor. Well, first I rummaged in all my women's health books to find out what it could be; I thought it was a prolapsed uterus, so I was panic-stricken. I called my doctor and said, "I have a prolapsed uterus, and you have to see me."

I was new to the area, and I was in one of those rotating practices with three doctors, which was not great. The woman who

104

delivered me examined me and said, "It's not a prolapsed uterus, it's the bladder in the vaginal canal." Basically, the vaginal wall had collapsed, allowing the bladder to fall directly into the vagina. She said that this could happen sometimes in older women —as I am classified in terms of childbirth—if you have a big baby and a very fast birth. It happens less frequently now because they do a lot of cesareans in cases where it might happen. And you can live with the condition, which many women of past generations did and many women still do. I later found out that an aunt of mine has had this all her adult life. Sometimes it repairs itself, or you can deal with it through surgery.

How did you decide what to do?
I was kind of angry. I felt that they should have discovered it in the hospital. I wasn't checked before I left. My first birth had been in another hospital, and there I was examined before being released. It's unclear to me how routine it is to do a postpartum examination, but I think it always should be done. I felt it shouldn't have been me discovering the problem.

And it took about six days to discover it.
Well, I'd been drugged up in the hospital and lying around. But I think it would have been evident by the time I was released, if they had checked me.

The other reason I was upset was, this doctor, whom I liked and who had seemed very competent in terms of the delivery, had never seen this before and had never operated on it. So I imagined it was something really terrible and weird—which, I later found out, it isn't. But she said she had a colleague who had done this operation before and could do it for me. Then she said, "Tell me, are you planning to have any more children?" I said no. She said, "Well, that's good because we can do a hysterectomy at the same time and that will give it more support."

I said, "Hold on a minute. I am not planning to have any more children, but that doesn't mean I'm ready to have a hysterectomy for no apparent reason." I thought, a) I don't want to be a guinea pig for this practice, and b), they're being incredibly cavalier about this hysterectomy. Nevertheless, we went ahead and scheduled the operation.

In the meantime, I ran to my old obstetrician to get another opinion. She said, "This thing is no big deal. It's very easy to repair, it's very common. And you could live with it as is. Give it time."

Then the cavalier doctor called me up, and said, "You know, I've been speaking with my colleagues and it's their opinion that you should wait. You've just gone through the trauma of childbirth. There's no reason to do surgery on top of it. And sometimes this will correct itself."

Was there anything you could do to help it correct itself?
I started doing Kegels exercise to strengthen the pelvic muscles that consist of repeatedly clenching the muscles as though trying to stop urination like crazy. And nothing happened. I just knew nothing was going to happen. And I knew I couldn't live with it as it was.

This condition isn't such a tragic thing, but any time you do any kind of athletic movement you'll become conscious of pressure, a heavy weight, and sometimes your bladder is literally hanging outside your body. I mean, this is not a pleasant thing to be running around with. Everybody says, "Oh, you can have sex, it's no problem." Well, you can have sex—but your bladder is in your vagina so you can only have sex lying on your back. Then I went to Paris in the fall and walked for miles every day. I'd come back to my hotel room with this situation. . . . That was it.

So I finally decided that I had to get a competent doctor in my hometown. I wanted to be operated on there because I have children and I wanted them to be able to come and see me. I kept postponing the operation because I had just been out on leave, but finally I did find a wonderful doctor who really speaks to you like an intelligent person.

How did you find this doctor?
Through word of mouth. He's a solo practitioner, and what impressed me was that, as an obstetrician, he's there in 99 percent of his births. He's a young guy, but he's smart, not condescending —which is very difficult to find, an obstetrician who's not paternalistic. He gives you choices and explains what the ramifications are for each of your options.

I went in as scheduled but with a terrible cold, and they sent me home. They said, "This is elective surgery—we can't do this in the state you're in." I knew that, but I was so desperate to get it done. . . . I went home with my tail between my legs. Three weeks later, they finally did it. And it was such a minor thing.

That's almost exactly a month ago today.
Yes, I'm on leave. That's why I'm here now, running around. I'm supposedly recovering.

You look recovered.
I was actually quite recovered the moment I came home from the hospital.

Did you check in the night before?
No, I came in that morning. They did blood and urine tests and checked blood pressure—they didn't do an EKG—and they put me on general anesthesia for an hour. I think the whole operation took about fifty minutes. It can last anywhere from forty-five minutes to an hour and a half, depending on the complexities of the case. And in fact, he found during the surgery that the cystocele was a lot more severe than had been indicated in office visits. I had kept saying, "It's really bad," but when you're under general anesthesia you're in full relaxation, and sometimes they can see things they can't see in an office visit.

How did you feel after the surgery?
I did not actually experience severe pain—it was really discomfort. But you are on an IV for a day or two, and you are on a catheter. You're in the hospital for four or five days because they literally have to retrain your bladder. They have to be sure you are fully emptying your bladder when they take you off the catheter. The longer you're on the catheter, the harder it may be to regain total control; you may think you've emptied your bladder but you haven't. So that became a huge goal for me in the hospital: Was I or was I not going to pass the catheter test so I could be released from the hospital?

Otherwise, I felt pretty good. It was just that being on the catheter is really awful. You've got this thing in you. . . . And having had a child, I always have a feeling of pressure on my bladder. So the whole time I was on the catheter, I felt like I had to go to the bathroom.

The other thing is, you've got this bag and you've got to carry it around. So there you are in your semiprivate room in a hospital gown with half your body hanging out of it, and on top of that you've got to carry your bag and your IV pole. It's degrading. And physically limiting. I remember saying that the thing that will make me feel good is to be able to wear my underpants!

What exactly was the catheter test?
They take out the catheter, you go to the bathroom. Then they put the catheter back in and measure how many ccs. of urine are left. If it's over 100 ccs., you've got to keep the catheter in and try

again. They ask you to drink a lot of liquid to create a sensation strong enough so you can feel it.

Had your doctor explained what the surgical procedure would be?

Yes. It's hard for me to explain, but basically he had to re-create that vaginal wall. What's amazing is how fast you heal. It rebuilds just as a bone would, just as strongly as it was before. So you're really 100 percent fine.

It was not a bad thing at all. You feel discomfort, but you ask for painkillers.

What did you take?

Percodan, my favorite—one of the pluses of being in the hospital. The other thing I did is get a sleeping pill. It took me three nights to ask for it because I am so against it philosophically, but the whole routine of being in a hospital is that they wake you every hour for one reason or another. And the nurses speak in very loud voices. The nurses come on night shift, and it's as if they forget people are trying to sleep, because this is their world—they're at work. One night there was a party going on right outside my room at one of the nurses' stations. It was wild. And the doctors come in at eleven at night, and will talk to your roommate in this *booming* voice. And then they take your temperature every two hours, they do your blood pressure. . . .

Did you have a private nurse?

No. I was in a semiprivate room, getting very routine care.

When you came home from the hospital, did you spend a few days in bed?

No. I thought I'd be napping every afternoon, but no. I put myself on a quiet routine. I did a lot of reading. I'd take short walks—no athletic activity—and I was basically back to normal. The problem was what to tell my office. A friend of mine said she had come back to work too soon after surgery and she had had a relapse. Everyone at the office rallies the first time you're out; they're not so sympathetic the second time. So I was very very conservative in everything I did. Also, I have full-time child care at home. All in all, I had a very luxurious situation, sitting and reading and doing very light stuff. And I took advantage of it.

What kind of follow-up care did you get?

They just said, take a good multivitamin and rest. I've just had my one and only checkup since the surgery, and I'm 100 percent fine.

And how do you feel now?

I feel great. People who've been through other gynecological surgery have told me, "You will feel weak. Two or three weeks later
you'll think you're fine, but you'll go on a walk and realize you're
not fine. . . . " I feel great. I feel great because my life has been
so restful this month—I never have a month of sitting in my
house. I never get to rest. You know, commuting—I'm up at 6
o'clock, I come home, I've got two children—my life is very crazy.
I've never been so healthy as I am right at this point.

How do you feel now in terms of bladder pressure?

That's repaired. Well, I'll never be perfect—I still have to get up
sometimes at night. I figured out that if I don't drink liquids after
eight I do a lot better. So that's my new regimen.

I wish I had known it was going to be so easy—I would have
had it done immediately. But you know, as someone who'd never
had surgery, the prospect was so frightening to me! That's why I
kept putting it off. I would come up with work excuses, but it was
partially that the idea of going into the hospital and putting myself under was so scary. Now I'm not that frightened. And it
made me realize that although I very often feel old beyond my
years—just tired, haggard—basically I'm a person in really good
health and I'm young and the body normally repairs really well.
You forget this because in the life-style that we have, you don't
feel great all the time.

What scared you most? Going under?

Yes. And pain. I'm not one of those brave souls.

And yet the Percodan does a good job of killing the pain.

Yes, this is truly a case where it's more discomfort than pain. You
don't feel sharp, stabbing pain. Even the first day, I dozed off a
lot, but I was up and about, sitting in my chair, reading, walking
around the ward.

When could you resume sex?

Now. After four weeks.

MYOMECTOMY

Myomectomy is a delicate operation to cut fibroids out of the uterus rather than simply removing the whole uterus, as in hysterectomy. The advantage of myomectomy over hysterectomy is that the woman preserves both her uterus and (if she is premenopausal) the possibility of having children. The disadvantages are that myomectomy is a longer, more painstaking operation than hysterectomy and not entirely reliable: in 15 percent of the cases, fibroids will grow back, and the woman, most likely, will then undergo hysterectomy. Fortunately, a few technical advances now make myomectomy an easier procedure and so a more sensible choice. Several of the women we interviewed discovered these new techniques and took a chance on them, to their great satisfaction.

The size of the fibroids determines whether the woman can have a myomectomy instead of a hysterectomy. How many fibroids she has means nothing, J. Victor Reyniak, M.D., said, "because they can be tiny, a quarter inch. Size is important. The bigger the size, the more difficult the case, the lesser the likelihood of preserving the uterus, and the smaller the chance for future pregnancy—because the whole physiology of the uterus has been disturbed by the fibroids." (See the interview with him on laser technology as it applies to myomectomy, page 266.)

Traditionally, the surgery is performed under general anesthesia with a scalpel. Using laser instead of the scalpel seems to offer significant advantages over the scalpel: it reduces blood loss and inflicts less damage on the surrounding tissue. One woman, whose fibroids had precipitated two miscarriages, underwent a myomectomy performed with laser. She was back to work in six weeks and delivered her first child just over a year after surgery.

A vaginal myomectomy is another option, made possible by the development of fiberoptic instruments—thin, flexible tubes, fitted with a lighting and lens system, that allow the surgeon to see into the body. One of the women had a vaginal myomectomy

performed with a hysteroscope—the fiberoptic tool used specifically for seeing into the uterus. To find out more about the technique, we interviewed the doctor who first described the use of
the hysteroscope, Robert S. Neuwirth, M.D. (see page 273).

The advantage of the vaginal approach over the abdominal is
a far shorter recovery period and the absence of a scar. Not everyone, however, is a candidate for this kind of surgery. Only fibroids
growing within the uterus are accessible through the vagina;
very large fibroids are more easily removed through an abdominal incision; and, Dr. Neuwirth says, a woman with large fibroids who wants to have children would be better off with the
abdominal approach—it gives her surgeon the greatest possible
visibility and so reduces the chances of damaging the uterus during surgery.

———————

"DON'T BE AFRAID OF MEDICAL ADVANCES! THE RISKS
CAN BE LESS THAN THE RISKS OF TRADITIONAL SUR-
GERY."

*A thirty-five-year-old newspaper editor who had a laser my-
omectomy after two miscarriages. She was interviewed several weeks before giving birth to a daughter.*

When did you first learn you had fibroids?
About five years ago during a regular internal exam I was told by
the midwife who assists my doctor that I had fibroid tumors about
the size of peas—and not to worry. She said that sometimes as
you get older they get bigger, that they are the leading cause of
hysterectomy in the United States, and that they would go away
at menopause. And—again—not to worry. She told me very little
about the possible growth of fibroids during pregnancy. I wasn't
even married then, and I don't know if I would have tried to get
pregnant sooner once I was married, but I guess I wish I had
known there was a connection between the growth of fibroids and
pregnancy hormones. They just told me that after thirty, fibroids
are very, very common. And that removing them is frequently
more troublesome and more dangerous than their side-effects. So
I decided to ignore them.

When did the fibroids become a problem?
When I was pregnant for the first time, which was in the summer

of 1983 when I was thirty-three years old. I was told that my fibroids were growing, one in particular, and very soon after that, at about seven weeks into the pregnancy, I had a miscarriage. Now, usually when a miscarriage is that early, you feel fine afterward. Sometimes you need a D&C, but, in fact, there are very few side effects. But I was in bed for a few days with pretty severe abdominal cramps—I felt terrible. The doctors tried to figure out what was going on. I was told that my uterus was still much bigger than it should have been, and that the pain was probably caused by the fibroid shrinking back to its normal size. But I wasn't told very much more than that. It was just suggested to me that early miscarriage—particularly in a first pregnancy—is so very common that I should wait a few months and then try to get pregnant again.

And so I was pregnant again the following summer, the summer of 1984, and the pregnancy seemed quite normal, except for the fact that my uterus was again bigger than it should have been. Other than that, everything seemed fine—I felt fine. And then I had a miscarriage at the beginning of the second trimester. And the doctors finally said it was because of multiple fibroids. [These tumors flourish in the presence of estrogen, and pregnancy raises the estrogen level.] The largest was described as somewhere between a lemon and a small orange.

When you became pregnant, your doctor didn't warn you
that you were in danger of a miscarriage?

No, and it is true that, in the contest between fibroid tumors and the fetus, frequently the fetus will win out. The fibroids will begin to shrink, allowing the fetus a normal blood and nutrition supply. I was told—I think by a girlfriend who had had fibroids during pregnancy—that the shrinking process was very painful but that it would just happen on its own. So by the time I hit the second trimester, I assumed that the pregnancy was going to be normal, and then it wasn't. When I went into the hospital after the miscarriage, there was much more bleeding than was normal, and my uterus was way too big, so there was talk about doing a cleaning-out procedure more complicated than a D&C—a D&E [dilation and evacuation]—which is more dangerous.

What's the significance of the uterus being larger than
normal?

They were afraid that I had the dates wrong, and if so, then I was further along in the pregnancy than we thought. They can't do a

D&C after a certain point. I was, at that point, out of town on vacation. I was being treated in an emergency room, and I was getting bad medical advice. The doctor was too slow to do the sonogram and other tests that would have convinced him that the size of the uterus was due to the fibroids and not to a miscalculation of date. So I spent a few unnecessary days in the hospital. I learned from that experience never to use a doctor assigned to you in an emergency room.

They were able to do the D&C after all, and everything seemed like it was back to normal. I was recuperating. I had some cramping, which my New York doctor told me was caused by the shrinking of the fibroids. I took another short vacation on Cape Cod and, again, was not at home when I was awakened by the most severe abdominal pain that I could imagine. Some paramedics came and thought it was appendicitis. I was taken to the hospital and told that the blood supply to the fibroids was being cut off and that the pain was comparable to a heart attack. When you have a heart attack, the blood is cut off to the heart, and that's the kind of pain I was feeling in my uterus. The doctor said that the only thing they could do was to give me narcotics for the pain or perform a hysterectomy, because, at that particular time, to try and remove the fibroids would be a dangerous and bloody operation.

Since I was only thirty-four and eager to become pregnant, a hysterectomy didn't strike me as a viable solution. So I took the narcotics for the pain and came back to New York, and then began the procedure of trying to find somebody who knew something about what had happened to me and what I might expect in the future. I was concerned about time slipping by. Normally they wait for you to have three miscarriages before they do any intervention, because having two miscarriages is not that abnormal. In my particular case, because the fibroids had been so large and because of the kind of pain I had, I wasn't satisfied with waiting and risking a repeat of the pain.

What choices did you have?
My own doctor suggested that a myomectomy was called for. I went through certain tests, the most important one being a hysterosalpingogram, which is an X-ray done after your uterus and fallopian tubes are flooded with a dye. It shows where the fibroids are in relation to the uterus—inside, outside, or in the wall of the uterus. Finally, the doctor suggested that I have a myomectomy,

done in the traditional way, which is with a scalpel. It's a very bloody operation, almost always necessitating a transfusion, and there's a very low fertility rate post-surgery.

My doctor was eager, I would say, to perform the surgery. I had the sense with her, as I did in conversations with other doctors, that surgeons like to do interesting surgery. When I began to find out more about myomectomy, I asked her whether or not it might be better to do the surgery with laser rather than a scalpel. She admitted that she couldn't do laser surgery, and that the hospital she was connected to didn't have the right equipment, but, she said, she didn't really know that laser would make that big a difference.

How did you find out about lasers?

My husband and I began to get recommendations of various doctors, and the idea of laser surgery was mentioned. And I read an article in *Self* magazine about breakthroughs in laser treatment: the removal of fibroids was mentioned in passing.

When I asked my doctor what she would do if she were in my situation, she said, when pushed, Well, maybe she would investigate laser. But there was a real hesitancy on her part to admit that this procedure, which she couldn't do, might be better for me. That's something that made me extremely angry, and makes me angry to this day.

Anyway, after searching around and having the benefit of living in New York, where much of this experimental surgery is being done, I got the names of several doctors who were doing myomectomies with lasers, and I went to see one whom I trusted immediately. He'd also come very highly recommended. He teaches in the city, and a lot of people who use laser learn from him. He also has a wonderful manner about him. And after looking at my X-rays and hearing my history, he did recommend a myomectomy with laser, which I then had.

Can you describe what you mean by a "wonderful manner"?

Yes. He took a tremendous amount of time. He included my husband in all of the discussions. He was enormously sympathetic to the pain as well as to the miscarriages. He was authoritative. He supplied us with medical reports as well as lay information about myomectomy.

And the other thing he did, which I really admired, was that he admitted to me that surgeons like to perform surgery, and that he was looking for candidates for myomectomies who were still in a fertile period. Women were coming to him for the operation as a substitute for hysterectomy, but many of them were, in fact, menopausal or very close to it and not interested in having children. For his study, he needed to have more women who were going to try to become pregnant after the surgery. I admired his honesty enormously.

What kind of arrangements did you make for surgery?
It had taken me about a month to get an appointment to see him, and it took about a month to get an appointment in his surgical schedule. One of the other things about myomectomy with laser is that there's a very low chance of transfusion and the recovery period is usually much faster than with scalpel myomectomy, where you can be laid up for four to six weeks. My doctor said that I should allow four weeks out of work, but, in fact, he didn't think I would feel bad much of that time—which turned out to be the case.

It was during the initial AIDS scare, so one of the things I did was to line up friends with the same blood type. My doctor also recommended that we get a private room—he felt that the hospital is an old and depressing plant, and he felt that state of mind was very important: if I could afford it, it would be worth the money to have the privacy and the slightly better room. (The difference in price was about $100 a night, which we had to pick up because the insurance company didn't pay for it.) He also suggested that the nursing care might be a little better in a private room.

Tell us about the night before surgery.
I checked in very late because I had preregistered. My memory is that I had a little dinner because the surgery wasn't until mid-morning—you just need twelve hours without food. And I was given something to put me to sleep.

Were you nervous?
Very. Terrified—that something would go wrong during the surgery, that I would end up without a uterus. Terrified that I would die. Terrified of the anesthesia. When I had the D&C after the second miscarriage, I had been knocked out, so I sort of knew what to expect. But I also knew that we were talking maybe three or four hours of general anesthesia as opposed to twenty minutes.

And my father is a doctor, and I can remember his one rule was never have general anesthesia unless you absolutely need to. I thought there must be a reason why he always said that.

What happened in the morning before surgery?

My doctor had made arrangements to get my husband into the room, so he waited with me. From the time I woke up until surgery, he was there. They checked blood pressure, they shaved my stomach, and I gave myself a Fleet enema—all that kind of thing. And then, maybe a half hour before they were going to take me down to the OR, they gave me a Valium.

My husband went with me when they started to wheel me down the hall. My doctor met me in a waiting room, and I remember his telling my husband where to sit, that he would come get him afterward, and that it might take as long as four hours. Then they took me into the OR. The anesthesiologist talked to me and told me that when they put the gas on your face, it smells like garlic.

The next thing I knew, I woke up in the recovery room about three hours later.

How did you feel?

I felt bad. I was in pain. But my doctor was there—he was the first person I saw. He told me that he had taken out fifteen fibroids, and that the uterus had never been cut. And that there had been no blood transfusion. He was very pleased with how the surgery had gone. He had also discovered other things wrong—I had a cyst on my ovaries, and also, there was so much scarring that my bladder was folded in on itself—they had used the laser to clean me up. And he said the prognosis was very good. He then told me I had been very funny under Valium—apparently I'd tried to make sure that the surgery did nothing to hurt my sex life. That made me laugh.

I was very scared by what was going on around me in the recovery room. It seemed to me that there were people who were maybe dying. I told him I was scared and that I didn't feel well, and they gave me some morphine. An hour or so later, I was allowed to take water. I remember very nice nurses and little else. I was pretty drugged up, and they took me to my room. I was on an IV for a couple of days and was receiving antibiotics through the IV.

After the surgery, they wait for your bowels to start moving again. You have gas pains, and that's fairly unpleasant. They finally gave me some milk of magnesia, I remember, and my bowels started to work, and then I was put on the standard regimen of clear liquids and semisolid food.

I was out of there in about six days. I was totally off all pain medication and feeling phenomenally well. Two days later, I was on a train to Baltimore for a vacation.

Did you take any painkillers once you'd left the hospital?
Nothing. While I was in the hospital, I took Demerol through the IV. As soon as I could take solids, I took Percocet. And I took it as frequently as they would give it to me, whenever I felt pain. I felt no moral compunction about it; I was not at all afraid of becoming a drug addict. It was my doctor who had suggested to me that being in pain was stupid. It means that I have very few memories of those days in the hospital, but I don't mind because it wasn't the most pleasant place to be hanging around. And once I left the hospital, I never even took an aspirin.

And the scar was beautiful. He had done a plastic surgeon's kind of suturing, stitching from the inside. So there's almost no scar at all.

I spent the four weeks recuperating. I slept a lot, I did a lot of walking and trying to build up my strength because you're very weak after abdominal surgery. I didn't do anything much around the house at first. My husband took care of me. I went back to work almost a month later, feeling—except for the fact that my abdominal muscles were weak where they had been cut—absolutely as well as I had before, if not better.

How soon afterward did you try to get pregnant?
When you have a scalpel myomectomy, you often have to wait nine to twelve months before you can attempt pregnancy, but with laser myomectomy, particularly one that doesn't cut into the wall of the uterus, you could attempt pregnancy after one normal menstrual cycle, according to my doctor. So I did. And I got pregnant. The surgery was in December, and I got pregnant in April. And it's been a normal pregnancy. And here I am, two weeks away from my delivery date. So the myomectomy seems to have been a success.

Is there any advice you would give someone who's considering this kind of surgery?
The only advice I have—and this is based on my own experience—is not to be afraid of medical advances. There was a sense of being terrified that I was going into the *Star Wars* age, trying

technology that hadn't been tested on enough people: the sample of people who had actually had laser myomectomy was quite small. But it seemed to me that the risk was less than the risk of doing the traditional kind of surgery.

And though I was very glad I got many opinions—I actually saw just three doctors, but I spoke to many others on the phone, I did research in magazines and books, and I had the benefit of my father's being a doctor—I ended up trusting my gut. I met somebody that I liked who engendered a feeling of confidence in me. And I went with him, and I'm glad that I did.

The other point is to ask more questions than I asked, even from the very beginning. I think any doctor would have suggested that I get pregnant the second time. But maybe if I had known more, they would have tracked that second pregnancy more closely to find out exactly at what point the fetus had died, so that there could have been more certainty about the fact that the fibroids were causing the problem. I would have gone to a more aggressive, more high-tech, less laid-back kind of obstetrical practice. For a younger woman who has no problems, a midwife-feminist practice may be appropriate. But I'm very glad that I'm not at such a place now.

Earlier, you said, "I learned never to use a doctor assigned to you in the emergency room." What should you do in that situation?

If you're lucky enough to have insurance, you do not have to let a resident examine you, and you do not have to let the doctor who's on call be your doctor. If you don't like him, you can say, "I don't want you," and they have to find somebody else for you. I didn't realize that. Now the problem is, if you're in a strange community, you have to find out who that other person might be. You could get a recommendation from a medical society, or by calling your own doctor. You can, in fact, be quite aggressive about that. It's hard—you're in pain, you're scared—but there are times when you know you don't like someone, and unless you're literally having a heart attack or you're unconscious, I think you can speak up.

You're not intimidated by doctors, are you?

No, and I will ask questions, and I will make it clear what I want. For instance, the obstetrician I see now, who I like very much, didn't return a phone call fast enough—I thought—at some point during my pregnancy, and I really let him have it. I'm not afraid to do that. There does come a point where I'm hesitant to learn more, where I think: Okay, I know enough—the doctor is the boss. I still want doctors to be authority figures. I want to rely on them. It's true they know more about it than I do or than I could learn through conversation.

―――――――――

"I CONSIDER PHYSICIANS TO BE TECHNICAL ADVISERS. I'M MAKING THE DECISIONS."

A medical writer, specializing in infectious diseases. She is single, in her early forties, with a history of fibroids. Although her gynecologist recommended a hysterectomy, she opted to have a myomectomy, using a new technique that avoids abdominal surgery.

What made you aware that you had a problem?
In my thirties, my doctor, who is a full professor in OB/GYN, discovered that I had fibroids. Over the years, I occasionally had sonography to test their size. All of a sudden, two years ago, I had some bleeding. I called the doctor for an appointment, and when I was on the examining table, I said, "Perhaps it's time we considered a D&C." And he said, "Well, I'll do a D&C, but if I think it's necessary, I'll do a hysterectomy."

I was shocked. It was outlandish to even think of having a hysterectomy that quickly. I mean, I work. I can't just go in and have a hysterectomy. I'd have to plan, get someone to cover my work, get a housekeeper. . . .

I was hustled into an office and asked to sign a release for major surgery. Like an idiot, I signed the papers. Later, after a long walk, which is when I think, I called him up. I said, "I want those papers torn up. You will only do a D&C, and if you find something that mandates a hysterectomy, you'll discuss it with me. This is not your decision, it's mine."

So you went ahead with the D&C?
Yes, but first I told my doctor that I wanted to give my blood in case I needed a transfusion—this was at the time when the AIDS virus was being discussed. He got very upset: "I've never had anyone bleed!" I said, "Bear with me. I'm a specialist in infectious diseases, and I want my blood to be there just in case. If you don't need it for me, give it to someone else with my bless-

ings." He fought me tooth and nail, but when I went to the hospital to give blood for an autotransfusion, the technicians said, "Wonderful! We've been writing letters to all of our doctors to ask their patients coming in for elective surgery to give blood."

Anyway, I had the D&C. He did it, I recovered; I was out of the hospital four hours later. But I knew I would not let the man do a hysterectomy on me.

How did you go about shopping for another doctor?
A medical writer told me about a doctor who performed myomectomies vaginally rather than abdominally, with fiberoptics. That's a technique using a long, flexible tube with light and telescope systems that allows visualization of a dark place. He did a hysteroscopic exam—the hysteroscope is the fiberoptics tube for looking into the uterus—to determine whether or not the fibroids were the kind he could scrape out.

Can you describe the hysteroscopy?
It's not a routine pelvic examination. You're given some Valium, but no anesthesia, and his assistant is holding your hand. You feel something going in—it's uncomfortable—and there's a little bit of bleeding. I thought I'd be able to walk home. As it turned out, I took a cab home and stayed in bed the rest of the day. [For more on the procedure, see interview with Robert Neuwirth, M.D., page 273.]

Afterward, the doctor said the fibroids were quite advanced, but yes, he could do a myomectomy with this technique. He told me everything that would and could happen. He said that sometimes the tumors that he couldn't remove become a problem, and ultimately, I might have to have a hysterectomy. He also said that if there was extensive bleeding during surgery that he might have to do a hysterectomy.

What does fiberoptic surgery entail?
It's considered intermediate surgery—between minor, like a D&C, and major, like a hysterectomy. He goes in vaginally, using the hysteroscope to see what he's doing and a "hot wire," an electrified loop that scrapes off the fibroids. He removed three large fibroids.

They gave me prophylactic antibiotics an hour prior to surgery: this is the correct way to get your tissue levels of antibiotics up. Then you're given more antibiotics right after surgery, in the IV, and once again a little later. The surgery goes through the vagina, where there's a lot of natural flora: it's easy to contract a postoperative infection.

After the surgery they put a balloon* in the uterus that stops the bleeding by pressing against the walls of the uterus. This is not the most comfortable situation in the world. I have never been so nauseated in my life—it lasted for about two days.

How was your recovery?

Miraculous. The pain is negligible—I don't remember taking even one painkiller. There was just a little bit of soreness. The third day, I walked out of the hospital. I started to wash the kitchen walls when I got home, which of course was a mistake. But from the day I got home, I could do business as usual on the phone. This is important for today's women—we work! Any gynecologist who thinks otherwise has a very narrow practice.

A week later, I walked a half mile to a pool, swam a mile, then walked a half mile back. Then I really had some bleeding. I was pretty scared. One of my neighbors, who is a nurse, put my feet up and took care of me. But a month after surgery, I was fully active.

What are you doing about the fibroids he didn't remove?

They've gotten larger, but I made the choice to have this surgery, and if necessary, I will have this surgery again rather than a hysterectomy. Fibroids are estrogen-fed tumors, and the hope is that, as I approach menopause, my estrogens will be reduced and the tumors will spontaneously regress. Menopause is a natural solution. Lopping out a uterus is not.

I have sonography fairly often. I want to see whether or not I'm ovulating and how my cycle is going, so I take my basal temperature, record it, and graph it.

The thing I like with my doctor is that I'm involved in this

---

* Note: According to Robert Neuwirth, M.D., "The balloon conforms to the uterine shape. It just *presses*. You can use air to inflate it, but for safety's sake we prefer a sterile saline solution. Then the pressure is raised to the mean arterial pressure or a little above it, and the bleeding stops because the vessels go into spasm, they clot. We usually keep up the pressure anywhere from six to twenty-four hours; then we gently release the pressure and peel away the balloon. We watch for a few more hours just to make sure the clot holds. If it doesn't, we reinflate the balloon. When the clot stays, we're home."

procedure. I'm making the decisions. I consider physicians to be technical advisers. They're supposed to give me their recommendations and as much information as possible in an understandable manner. And they provide the technical assistance. But it is ultimately my responsibility, as a patient, to make the choice.

I feel that malpractice, which has gotten out of hand, results from the fact that patients have been put into a subservient position—and women patients more than men, because women are not often considered peers of physicians, while men are. When a woman goes in with the attitude of, "We are working on this together. You are my peer; I am not your inferior, and I am not a child," it's better for the doctor as well as for the patient.

Is hysteroscopy still considered an experimental procedure?

To me it's not experimental. Enough patients have gone through the procedure, and more and more doctors are learning to do hysteroscopies. In fact, I think it's a far less risky procedure than a hysterectomy. The physician who did my operation is very well trained, has a very good reputation and a very good position in a very good hospital. He's training people across the country, but until women go in and say, "You don't do this procedure? Then let me consult someone who does," doctors won't be forced to learn the technique.

All I know is, I don't think it is appropriate in this day and age for a physician to jump from a D&C to a hysterectomy.

But your insurance company objected to the procedure just because it isn't a permanent solution—fibroids could grow back, requiring further surgery.

I have a private insurance company, and after the surgery, they wanted me to waive all rights to any future operations for female problems. This is illogical, unmedical, and untenable. Now they say they don't want to pay for anything—tumors of the ovary, whatever. So there are problems, and you're fighting tradition. You'd think that an insurance company would encourage women to have the least expensive, least invasive surgery. But insurance companies are companies. They don't pay for preventive medicine, which in the long run would be cost-effective for them. They should increase costs to people who smoke. They should encourage good health.

*Do you have any advice for women considering a
hysterectomy?*

I think women ought to understand that a hysterectomy is a
major surgical procedure, which has many hazards including a
long recovery period. It may be a minor procedure for the gynecologist, but it's not minor for the patient.

And never, ever sign anything in a physician's office.

HYSTERECTOMY

Hysterectomy is a confusing term because it's used colloquially to describe two different operations: one in which only the uterus is removed; and the other, in which the ovaries and fallopian tubes are removed as well as the uterus. We refer to the first as a "simple" hysterectomy and the second as "complete" or "total." (The medical term for the removal of ovaries is "oophorectomy" and for removal of fallopian tubes, "salpingectomy." The technical term for a "complete" hysterectomy is "hysterectomy with bilateral salpingo-oophorectomy.")

Whether simple or complete, hysterectomy is major surgery, usually requiring a week's stay in a hospital, four to six weeks' leave from work, and from two to six months (and in a few cases a year) to feel completely well. With oophorectomy, a woman who has not yet reached menopause will immediately go into "surgical" or "instant" menopause and may choose to begin hormone replacement therapy (see interview with Lila Nachtigall, M.D., page 257).

In some cases, the decision between a simple or complete hysterectomy is determined by the diagnosis. If a woman has invasive cervical cancer or ovarian cancer, current medical thinking insists that she have a complete to prevent spread of the cancer. With endometriosis, too, a complete may be necessary. But with fibroid tumors, which don't usually affect the ovaries or fallopian tubes, a woman will have a choice of surgeries. With uterine prolapse, in which the ligaments supporting the uterus stretch out, allowing the uterus to drop into the vagina, a woman may choose between surgery and a pessary (a plastic or rubber ring that catches the uterus at the top of the vagina, preventing it from slipping). In the interviews, you will see how women made the choices (also see discussion of the ovary dilemma in Is This Surgery Necessary?, page 9).

A hysterectomy is usually done by abdominal surgery, with a horizontal, or bikini, incision right above the pubic line. The alternative is a vertical incision, straight down from the navel to the pubic line, and is used only if the fibroids are enormous or if the surgeon wants the greatest possible visibility of the abdominal cavity because cancer is suspected.

A vaginal hysterectomy is a happy alternative to abdominal surgery. By avoiding an external incision, both the hospital stay and recovery time are shortened, and the risk of complications is lessened. Unfortunately, the procedure is rarely performed. It may be an option with prolapsed uterus, and with fibroids if the tumors are small enough and growing into the uterine cavity. What is "small enough"? According to New York gynecologist David Soper, M.D., if the fibroids have made the uterus too large to pass through the vagina (bigger than a navel orange, or about four inches in length), the vaginal approach is not possible. Neither is it possible if the uterus is not "relaxed" enough to enable the surgeon to reach and clamp the blood vessels that supply the uterus: this means that women who have not had children may be unable to have a vaginal procedure.

VAGINAL HYSTERECTOMY

"THE FIRST THING I ASKED HIM IN THE RECOVERY ROOM WAS WHETHER HE'D BEEN ABLE TO DO A VAGINAL HYSTERECTOMY. HE SAID, 'YES.' I SAID, 'TERRIFIC,' AND THEN SLEPT FOR A DAY."

The owner of a successful housewares store who had a vaginal hysterectomy because of fibroid tumors. She is single and forty-nine years old.

What first prompted you to consult a doctor?
Bleeding, just much too much bleeding. My periods had always been minimal, and when I was on the Pill from 1959 to 1982, I hardly bled at all—that is, until the last few months before I saw the doctor in October of 1982. The bleeding was slowly building up, and I was also in pain because, the doctor said, my cervix was dilated as a result of the blood clots. It was then that he noticed the fibroids and said, "We'll have to take them out eventually, but we can wait and see." He took me off the Pill, and I

had a D&C in the hospital, which helped both the pain and bleeding.

Why did the doctor delay the decision on surgery?

Well, the fibroids weren't terribly big. About four to five centimeters, and considering my age, then forty-five, I might have gone into menopause and there would have been no need to operate. But by May of the following year, 1983, the bleeding became a real problem. My periods lasted only about three or four days, but during the first two days I was using both Tampax and Kotex, and I'd have to change every hour.

Did your doctor schedule an operation then?

Yes, a month later.

How did you feel physically, during that time?

I didn't feel too badly—it was just a physical nuisance—but by the last two or three months I was exhausted. I was supposed to go to Europe on my last buying trip before the operation. I had gone out to the airport, but I was bleeding so much, I came home, called the doctor, and he gave me a prescription for Ergotrate to slow down the bleeding.

I was so weak that I had to wait a couple of days before I could leave the country. It was the kind of weak where you think you hear something in your eardrums. I was anemic, too. I had been a bit naughty. I was supposed to be taking iron, and I didn't because it made me constipated. The doctor was furious with me. Just before the operation I had to take a lot of iron.

Were you at all anxious about the operation?

Not really. My mother was a nurse, so operations and hospitals never worried me. The only time I was a little bit anxious was when the doctor thought I might need a transfusion because I hadn't been taking the iron. It turned out that I didn't. But for three weeks before the surgery, I ate everything with iron in it— liver, spinach, anything; I ate it all. And I took iron pills, and my blood built right up. I was obviously not so unhealthy.

Did your doctor discuss the surgical options with you?

Well, we talked about the possibility of a myomectomy. But I let him decide—whatever he felt he had to do. I had no particular desire to hang on to my uterus. Having children was not an issue. I was already much too old for that.

When did your doctor bring up the possibility of a vaginal hysterectomy?

I always presumed it would be abdominal surgery, but in the hospital before the operation, he said it might be possible to perform a vaginal hysterectomy. I said, "Oh, that would be just fantastic, if you could." He said he wouldn't know whether it was possible until he got into the operating room, but he would try.

Did your doctor explain why he felt he could do a vaginal procedure in your case?

Yes. He said that it took skill and that it depended on the size and location of the fibroids. My uterus was small enough to do a vaginal procedure. He said, "We can do vaginal hysterectomies on any uterus where we feel we can get to the uterine blood vessels. If I can safely clamp the uterine vessels, I can remove any size fibroid by a process called morcellation. This means I can cut the fibroid into little bits and remove them until the mass is small enough to be removed. Ovaries and fallopian tubes can also be removed vaginally."

The first thing I asked him when I woke up was whether he had been able to do a vaginal hysterectomy. He said, "Yes." I said, "Terrific," and then slept for a day.

Did you keep your ovaries?

Yes.

How long were you in the hospital?

I was in for three days after the surgery.

How was your recovery?

There was some discomfort around my vagina, so they gave me some painkillers for a couple of days. They got me up the day after the surgery, and I had an IV for the first day or so, but I could eat right away. I was in a six-bed ward with a couple of women who'd had abdominal hysterectomies. They had awful gas problems, but I had none of that.

The doctor said I shouldn't go back to work for three weeks, but I stayed out for just two weeks. The first week I stayed at home. I rested up. I was a little weak, but my doctor said I had to walk every day and I did. There wasn't any pain, but I didn't race around like I usually do. My body was tired, but I didn't mind. I was prepared to rest. I had planned a lovely holiday. Had it all organized, called out for food. It was great, fabulous. And then the second week I went down to the Bahamas with my boyfriend, and that was very easy, although I couldn't take a bath or swim for a month.

When could you resume sex?
I think it was one month. That and the bath came back at the same time.

And did you notice any particular physical difference in having sex after the surgery?
My vagina was a bit dryer, but I put that down to the fact that I hadn't done it for awhile.

How was your energy when you went back to work?
Oh, maybe I was a bit slower than usual. It was probably from not working for two weeks. But actually I could have gone back to work the second week because I was feeling very well.

"THERE'S SOMETHING PSYCHOLOGICALLY HELPFUL ABOUT HAVING NO VISIBLE SCAR. I HAD LITTLE DISCOMFORT AND NO PAIN."

A fifty-three-year-old advertising casting director; divorced, mother of a twenty-five-year-old son. She had a vaginal hysterectomy in 1981, at age forty-seven.

How did this begin?
It began with what I think is called dysmenhorrhea, which is very heavy bleeding at each period, more a gush than a flow. It accelerated over a period of about four years, so that it was uncontrollable and there were almost no days of the month when I wasn't bleeding. Very uncomfortable. I had a D&C to check out that it wasn't a malignant situation—and it wasn't.

My gynecologist of many years would periodically do hormone tests and say, "If you were quite a bit older and closer to menopause, these things would shrink." It's always a question of waiting to see what will happen first—menopause or the bleeding becoming impossible. In my case, I seemed to be quite far off from menopause, and the bleeding was draining me terribly. So we decided to do a hysterectomy.

He said, "If I can, I will remove the uterus vaginally." I had never heard about such a thing. I asked, "What's the up side and what's the down?" He said just that the recuperative period is much shorter with the vaginal, but he wouldn't know if he could do it until he got in there. As it turned out, he was able to do it. He also removed an ovary because he'd found cysts on it.

And, as he promised, the recuperation was very, very short. You have no exterior incision, which means that you don't walk around doubled over for several weeks, as most people do who have abdominal surgery.

There's also something psychologically helpful about having no visible scars. I had little discomfort and no pain.

I don't mean to idealize this. You do have to stay in the hospital for almost a week, being fed antibiotics through an IV for six days because the danger of infection is greater than with an abdominal incision. And you have a drain and a catheter, so the nursing care really has to be very good.

Was this your first time under general anesthesia?
No, I'd had an appendectomy. This was similar—you feel terrible, nauseated, drifting in and out of sleep. And thirsty—they give you that drug [Atropine] that dries your mucous membranes so that you won't vomit during the operation.

How did you feel the second day?
Better. Up and out of bed. I'd get weak and tired, but I had none of the pain of standing up that you do when you have an incision anywhere in your torso. I remember I was very pleased when they took out the drain, on maybe the fourth or fifth day.

When did you feel back to normal?
I would say within two or three weeks. One gets tired, but I was back at work, because my work is physically not very draining. I'd lost a tremendous amount of blood over the years, and it takes time to rebuild that. But when your strength comes back, you feel better than you have for years.

Did you notice any difference in sexual response after the hysterectomy?
None at all. In fact, happily, my marriage broke up soon after. When your marriage isn't too good, your sexual response isn't too good, either. But when the marriage ended, my normal libido came back with a vengeance.

"I KNEW A PROLAPSED UTERUS WASN'T LIFE-THREATENING, BUT I CAN TELL YOU IT DIDN'T HELP MY BODY IMAGE."

A sixty-seven-year-old housewife from upstate New York, mother of two grown sons with families of their own,

*who had a vaginal hysterectomy for a prolapsed uterus in
1986.*

When were you first aware of the prolapsed uterus?
For several years it felt as if my uterus were dropping and there
was some slight pressure on the vagina, but it wasn't uncomfortable. If I stood too long or walked a long distance, I would notice
more pressure, but when I lay down it seemed to be fine. I suspected it was a prolapsed uterus because some of my friends my
age had similar problems. When I went to my gynecologist he
confirmed it and recommended a vaginal hysterectomy, but he
didn't make it sound urgent and said it was elective surgery—so
I elected not to do it then.
Did the uterus drop further?
Actually, it did. It got to the point that when I stood up and
walked even for a little while the uterus dropped into the vagina
and I could feel it there all the time except when I was lying
down. I knew a prolapsed uterus wasn't life-threatening, but I
can tell you it didn't help my body image.
Even then I didn't want to have surgery. I guess I was afraid,
and because there wasn't any pain it was easy to put off thinking
about surgery. But I did consult another gynecologist, who was
against surgery. He suggested that a pessary might help. He said
many of his older patients used pessaries all their lives without
resorting to surgery. I was pleased about that, and I used mine
for several months.
What exactly is a pessary?
It's a doughnut-shaped device that comes in different sizes. It's
designed to fit around the cervix, and you insert it through the
vagina to keep the uterus from dropping down farther. It worked
fine at first, and then it began to slip, so I went back to the doctor,
and he suggested another size. I had him insert it, thinking it
might stay in place more firmly, but it didn't stay for even a day.
It hurt a little when I removed it, and I realized he had used a
much larger one than the original. I was really upset. I can't
prove it, but I think it stretched my vagina and allowed the uterus
to prolapse even further. So after that I stopped using the pessary
altogether.
Did the doctor tell you what caused your prolapse?
He said the muscles that hold the pelvic organs in place might
have been weakened during childbirth, or maybe I inherited the

tendency for weak muscles. He said it was often accompanied by a prolapsed bladder as well. When the uterus falls it puts pressure on the bladder, which is under the uterus.

Did you have bladder problems?

No real problems, but I had to urinate more often. The doctor did say one thing that made me very anxious. He said I should be aware that prolapse conditions like mine could cause bladder infections that might lead to kidney infections. Because the uterus had dropped into the vagina, it was so exposed that it could cause all kinds of infection in the area.

Was your sex life affected?

Not really. In the beginning there was no difference because when you're lying down you don't feel it. Even later on, having sex wasn't a problem, but I thought about the prolapse all the time, and it didn't make me feel very sexual.

What made you decide to have surgery?

The uterus finally dropped so far into the vagina that I could see the cervix at the vaginal opening. That really was very upsetting, and I knew if I waited any longer, my uterus would fall outside my body. So I called my gynecologist and asked him to schedule the surgery.

What was the surgery experience like?

After all the thinking about and putting it off, it turned out to be really easy. I went in for tests the day before, and the surgery was early the next morning. After they gave me the anesthesia, I don't remember anything until I woke up in my room and the operation was over. The only negative thing that happened was that I threw up a couple of hours after surgery. I think it was a reaction to the anesthesia, but no one seemed to be worried about it, and it happened only once, The nurse gave me some sleeping medication, and that day and the next were sort of a haze. I slept off and on for two days, and then I was fine.

Was there any pain?

No. I don't remember any pain at all. They took off the IV the day after surgery, and I remember walking to the bathroom, then back to my bed. I never took any painkillers after the original anesthesia wore off. I was very tired, though. I just wanted to sleep.

How many days were you in the hospital?

Counting the day I went in for tests, it was four days. I left the hospital on the morning of the fifth day.

How was your recovery?

It was very uneventful. I stayed with my sister for a week after the surgery, but I didn't stay in bed. The doctor told me not to lift anything or do any heavy work, so I took it easy. But by the time I went home I was back to normal—maybe I was more tired than usual, but that was all.

Do you have any advice for women considering this surgery for a prolapsed uterus?

I would say that unless the uterus has fallen deep into the vagina or unless it's very uncomfortable, there's probably no need for a hysterectomy. On the other hand, if you have to have a hysterectomy, I think there's no question a vaginal hysterectomy is the better option.

ABDOMINAL HYSTERECTOMY

"IT'S USEFUL FOR WOMEN WHO WORK TO HAVE A DOC-TOR WHO HAS A LOT OF PROFESSIONAL WOMEN IN HIS PRACTICE, WHO UNDERSTANDS THAT YOU, TOO, HAVE A SCHEDULE AND A BUSINESS."

A thirty-nine-year-old woman who had a simple hysterectomy six weeks before this interview. Married, with two sons, she is a producer on a TV news program and a model of organization.

Why did you need surgery?

I had fibroids that started to get very big very fast. In fact, when I walked out of the office of the second-opinion doctor, he was on the phone with the doctor who had done the sonogram, saying, "Are you sure they're just fibroids?" Because he had been convinced that it was cancer—an ovarian tumor. Everybody was really worried. So there was no question at all about having them out.

When were you first diagnosed?

I guess about two years ago. While my doctor was examining me, he asked, "Who in your family has fibroids?" I said, "My mother had them." He said, "Yeah? Well, so do you. Come every six months and let's check on their size." For a while they grew normally, and then, all of a sudden, they just took off. He sent me for the ultrasound and then said, "I really think you ought to do it soon."

It wasn't a hard decision. My second child had been born six years ago, and I was sick of birth control. My doctor made me get rid of my IUD when the fibroid was discovered, so I was using a diaphragm and sponges, both of which my husband and I hated. So I was planning to have surgery anyway, a tubal ligation.

I had also watched my mother go through nine years of cramps and floods from fibroids and finally have a hysterectomy, and I knew that I was going to have to do it sometime. Everyone who had been in a similar circumstance told me it was the greatest thing they ever did. I didn't see the point of waiting until I was forty-nine when I could do it at thirty-nine and have an easier time recovering.

How did you choose your doctor?

When I came to New York, I called a friend who's a tough critic, met her doctor, and he and I hit it off right away. He's very elegant and formal and treats you like a grown-up. Some women, who don't like my doctor, want to be a little bit taken care of. They want a doctor who's like a papa. But what I need is somebody who treats me like an adult.

I also needed somebody who understood my attitude. I mean, I was working the overnight shift during my first pregnancy, and when my ankles puffed out to here, my doctor said, "You know, you shouldn't feel guilty that you can't do the overnight anymore. In socialist countries it's illegal for pregnant women to do shift shit work. It's a disgrace that they're making you do it, and your discomfort is their fault." He's that kind of guy. So I would look for somebody who is temperamentally suited to what you want. I think it's very foolish to insist on a woman doctor. It's sexist. My neighbor, a woman who is a gynecologist, was the one who was pushing me to take my ovaries out because she'd seen so much ovarian cancer in her work that she expects to find it everywhere.

I also think that it's useful for women like us to have a doctor who has a lot of professional women in his practice and doesn't keep people waiting, who understands that you, too, have a schedule and a business. You can tell, if a doctor has a lot of women in suits in his office, that he's probably somebody who understands that kind of stuff.

Did you know what to expect from the surgery?

I sat there with the doctor and I said, "I want you to tell me what's going to happen every day." I had done a story on unnecessary hysterectomies years ago, and I guess I was suspicious. He told me about the catheter, the gas, how long I'd have the IV, how long I'd be asleep. He told me to cut down on my smoking— I was most scared about that because I really wasn't sure I could cut down. I asked him about doing the hysterectomy vaginally, which our friend in California, who is a very touchie-feelie, organic sort of doctor, had suggested. My doctor said that he wanted to *see* the ovaries because even though the ultrasound had showed them to be clear, the sudden growth of the fibroid had been such a scare that he wanted visual confirmation. That was reasonable to me.

I really recommend saying, "I want to know: What's day one like, what's day two, etc. In detail."

What did you decide to do about keeping or removing your ovaries?

That was the toughest decision I had to make because I'm almost forty. I don't think you should get ideological about it. You have to examine the information and make a decision based on that. My doctor said, "The odds are that you'll have a cyst sometime and you may have to go through this again. If you were forty-five I'd push you, but you're thirty-nine so I won't."

My mother left hers in. I called our gynecologist friend in California, who said, "If you were my wife, I'd tell you to leave your ovaries in. They're a very good drugstore. It isn't like you walk in and take Premarin [a brand of estrogen] the first time and get the right dose. It's a lot more complicated than that, and you're really taking a chance by having them out."

Then I talked to a woman in the building who's a gynecologist —a young pretty woman who just had a baby. She said 90 percent of the women at the hospital where she works have everything out, that she's seen so many women die of ovarian cancer that she really was pro take 'em out.

My husband brought home the *PDR* [*Physicians' Desk Reference*, a guide to drugs, their function, and their side effects]. He said, "Just read about Premarin and let that help you make your decision." Well, once I read it, it was clear to me. The possible side effects ranged from weight gain to heart attack. I told the doctor that if the ovaries looked funny, it was up to him; if they didn't look funny, I wanted to keep them. We decided that about every year I would go and have an ultrasound to make sure they're okay, since I would probably be paranoid about it.

What arrangements did you make for work and aftercare?
I'm very lucky with my work, because they give you three months of paid medical leave if the need for it is confirmed by a doctor. I'm taking seven weeks. My boss's wife had had a hysterectomy, so he understood what would go on and how I would feel afterward almost better than I did.

At home, I have a housekeeper, so I knew that the kids would be all right. She stayed the first weekend, and then I arranged for my mom to come one weekend and my sister another, because my husband works Saturday mornings. I also sent notes to both children's teachers so they would know what was going on at home. And I arranged with the school nurse that after the surgery, my husband would call him and he would tell the boys that I was okay. I also made a phone list so everybody would know who to call for whatever.

Were you anxious about the surgery itself?
Yes! It was absurd! I wasn't focused on dying—my fear was about leaving the children. And though the surgery itself didn't scare me, I was petrified about anesthesia. The night before surgery, I told the anesthesiologist how scared I was, but he wasn't much help. Anesthesiologists are not real reassuring. I think the reason they pick that specialty is they don't like to talk to people who are awake.

I was also petrified they might find cancer.

Even though you knew you had fibroids.
You never know until you know.

Checking into the hospital . . .
I went for pretests a week before—blood tests and a chest X-ray. I took my six-year-old son with me so that he could see the hospital; my big one had been in and out of the hospital because our pediatrician is there and because he came to visit me when the younger one was born. Which reminds me—if you can get on the OB/GYN floor instead of the general surgery floor, it makes a big difference. I think there's a different kind of nurse, and when you walk around you can go look at the babies. You're with a lot of happy people.

The day before, my husband and the kids took me out for a big lobster lunch and bought me a stuffed teddy bear, which everybody gave hugs to so that I could take the hugs with me. I also took makeup, some thrillers, and a nice bathrobe, though I wore the hospital nightgown the whole time: it was so much easier, and I didn't care how it looked—makeup was all it took to make me feel better. I had my Filofax in case I needed addresses and phone numbers. And stationery so I could write thank-you notes right away. I also brought an envelope of checks for the private nurses and all the insurance forms filled out. And only five dollars in cash—you don't want to leave anything around a city hospital. My husband brought my Walkman the second day, and somebody sent me a tape of all the back sides of Bruce Springsteen singles. That was the best present.

My biggest worry was that I wasn't going to have a television, because that's the way I could dork out—I'm a television person, and it was Sunday night when I went in so there was late news. But I got one—you pay for the TV, and for the phone, in advance.

Besides the anesthesiologist, a goofy first-year resident came by. I told him that my kids had given me the bear, and then the first question he asked me was, "Do you have kids?" But my doctor doesn't let residents near you very much—he's very strict. I had an enema, which I hated, and a douche, and they gave me two Valiums, which for me is like, forget it—I was out like a light.

The morning of surgery . . .

My husband was there, and because he's a doctor, I guess, he went with me all the way to the door of the OR. And the next thing I remember, I was back in my room. My husband sat there for days, and I kept falling asleep. The afternoon of the surgery, over my protests, my husband brought the kids—they were so relieved to see me. I asked the younger one later, "Did I look like you thought I would look?" And he said, "No, I thought you'd be all bloody." So it's good, if you can handle it, to let children see that you're okay.

How long did you have private nurses?

The first two days, I had nurses around the clock. The third day, from morning to midnight; and the fourth, just from morning to late afternoon. It was a lot of money, but my husband's insurance paid $135 a shift. And I want to tell you something: if you don't have enough money for both a private room and private nurses, the best thing is to have those nurses. Because they make you get up and walk. They give you a bath. They get stuff right when you need it. They give you pain medication when you need it. They pull out your makeup and say, "Come on, let's get up and wash your face." I can't stand to be taken care of—I *hate* when people do things for me—but I was so grateful! I wanted a private room because I didn't want to have to be nice to somebody; no insurance pays for that, and you can live without it. But private nurses are just invaluable.

What do you remember of your recovery in the hospital?
I was in Sunday through Sunday. I don't remember the day of surgery, Monday—I was so out of it. The second day, they took the catheter out, and I got to go to the bathroom and walk around the room. In the night, they make you blow up a balloon to make sure your lungs are working. That was the other thing I was dreading, and it was just as annoying as I thought it would be. Wednesday, I think, they took out the IV, or maybe it was Thursday, and gave me Jell-O and clear soup. I found my appetite was very small. A friend who's very smart showed up with rice pudding, saying, "I really believe in nursery food." Well, she was right. I didn't want Diet Coke or any of the oily or sweet things I usually eat—I just wanted calm food. They would bring soup and rice and chicken, and I would add the rice to the soup with a little bit of cut-up chicken.

I told everybody not to come until Thursday. Some people showed up before, and I was right—they shouldn't have. People think they're doing you a favor, and they're not. Also on Thursday, the doctor took the staples out, and then I knew I was much better.

I was never in terrible pain. The level of the pain was high only when going to the bathroom, especially peeing, because as your bladder empties, I think, everything moves a little bit. I think the gas was the most painful thing. My digestion was really freaky, and I had a lot of gas for weeks. It started just when they said it would, either Wednesday or Thursday. Friends of mine who had cesareans had told me to walk a lot and drink a lot of water, but my doctor wouldn't let me. He said, "It's too risky on your digestion because your bowels are still frozen. I'd prefer that you risk the gas instead." They give you a suppository, and some of the gas comes out, but part of it was that I was tight because I was uncomfortable. I was also very defensive. This was another thing I noticed, and it might have been from being so isolated. On Thursday, I went downstairs in my bathrobe with my nurse to buy stamps, and I was terrified that somebody was going to bump me. I felt like I was made of eggshells. I didn't want to be around people at all—which is not like me.

By the fifth day, Friday, I felt pretty good.

What are the best things visitors did for you?

Goofed around. Made me laugh. I don't think that people who make you feel you have to be on good behavior should come see you in the hospital. I told my mother, "Please don't come until I feel well enough so that I don't feel like I have to watch out for you. You can help me most by cooking for my family and playing with the boys." I loved getting all the flowers and that rice pudding. Funny cards. You do notice who bothers.

Going home . . .

My husband and I went to a coffeehouse and had an espresso, and then I came home and went to bed. I slept a lot and napped a lot. The first day, Monday, I went to the bank and waited in line. When I got home, I thought I was going to die. That was so stupid. I was very sore the next day and slept most of the time. The next weekend, we went out to dinner at a restaurant only a few blocks away, and I was exhausted even though I walked very slowly and cautiously. I tried to take little walks every day, thinking that if I got out, I'd be better off. But I think I probably did it too soon. Now I don't have as much energy as I want, and it's six weeks later. I'm annoyed that I don't feel altogether better and that I still am very sore and a little numb. My doctor said sometimes the retractor [a clamplike instrument that holds back skin during surgery] pushes on the nerve and it takes a while to heal completely.

What was your emotional state?

I had one day, right before I left the hospital, where I just dissolved. I think it was a release of tension. After the surgery, my mother asked me, "You don't have any feelings of depression or loss of femininity?" She said she'd heard other women talk about that. And I didn't, no. Having the children, I think, probably had a lot to do with that.

A million people have asked me how I felt "emotionally." First, if I wanted to tell them, I probably would have. And second, I don't exactly understand what the concern is. I had always hated having periods. I had terrible cramps before I had the kids, and I was real happy to have that over with. Though I think it's going to be hard to get used to missing periods, I sure won't mind that, and I don't mind not having to deal with contraception anymore.

Resuming sex . . .

It's not yet six weeks, and it's been hard for my husband, but I wanted to wait until it could be really nice. What I'm finding is that I'm still sore. Maybe I shouldn't bother waiting for the perfect moment . . . but I'm having a lot of sexual fantasies, which is kind of interesting.

Any other advice for women considering the surgery?

I think you shouldn't be surprised or embarrassed at how scared you are, because I don't know anybody who didn't feel like that. And I think you should probably listen to all your friends who tell you to rest and have as much help as you can afford. I was going to write three pieces during the seven weeks off from work. I was going to clean the closets, do our files. But I couldn't concentrate on anything. I read thrillers and watched soap operas for almost a month. I mean, I love soap operas under any condition, but the point is, don't expect to use the time at home for all the things you never have time to do, because you can't. And you can't concentrate. I think it's the anesthesia staying in your body a lot longer than anybody will admit. You're just discombobulated.

"I TAKE SUCH GOOD CARE OF MYSELF—HOW COULD THIS HAVE HAPPENED?"

A painter and illustrator in her late thirties, recently married, who had a simple hysterectomy.

Why did you need surgery?

I had a fibroid, but it was very small and apparently nothing to worry about. When I went in for an annual checkup, I found out it had grown very large and was pushing other organs near it. The doctor said I had to have a hysterectomy. The fact that it had grown so fast was what worried him.

How did you decide to go ahead with the operation?

After I was told I had to have a hysterectomy, I came home somewhat in shock—because I felt absolutely fine. I didn't have the pain or heavy bleeding usually associated with fibroids. The doctor gave me a couple of pamphlets, which gave no information at all, and I realized I had to see another doctor. I tried to get to one of the supposedly best doctors in town, but she couldn't see me for two months. Finally, through a friend, I was able to get an appointment with her. She said the surgery should be done immediately and for all the same reasons my doctor had mentioned. From what she could see, the fibroids hadn't yet affected the ovaries, but I should have the operation fast. She felt that the way the fibroids were growing and the rate of growth meant that the ovaries were in imminent danger of being pressured and harmed.

I also went to see my uncle, who had been head of gynecology at Albert Einstein Hospital in Philadelphia. Both he and his partner checked me and said the same thing. So that made four doctors saying, "Do this—the sooner the better." They apparently had some fears it was cancer. I had just spent years watching friends and relatives go through cancer. I wanted to get it over with. So I went in, in a matter of weeks, even though I felt fine.

What did you do to prepare for surgery?
I tried to find out about everything. And I made sure my body was as strong as possible. I've been a vegetarian for a long time, and I've always done some sort of exercise, but I exercised more than usual. I remember saying to the doctor, "I take care of myself so well—vitamins and diet and exercise. I want to know not only how this could have happened, but how it could have happened so fast." That was especially disturbing to me; that, and feeling so fine.

I was told that fibroids run in families, and since my mother and my aunts had had hysterectomies in their twenties, I obviously had been able to avoid it for a longer time.

Did you have any fears about going into a hospital?
My whole family is doctors, and I worked in hospitals for years. So I'm not scared of hospitals per se; I am very curious about it all. I do remember there were two big questions in my mind. One was, is it cancer? No one asked it aloud, but from my parents' and my uncle's concern, I knew there was a question. And then my mother had gone through early menopause because of her hysterectomy. I remember her physical discomfort all the while I was growing up. So the second big question was, am I going to go through menopause?

How did you feel after surgery?
That first day, I remember feeling like I had been hit by a truck. This was my first surgery, and I had no idea it would be so painful. I had brought books to read and some work to do. Everyone had said I'd be on my feet the day after surgery. I didn't know

that meant my feet would touch the ground with two people hold-ing me up. I was upset by that, but I was relieved that I didn't have cancer, that they didn't take out my ovaries, and that I wasn't going to be thrown into sudden menopause.

The second day, someone forgot to give me my painkiller, and that was terrible—waking from this half-sleep to this horrible pain. In the panic and pain, I had trouble breathing—that was really quite frightening. It didn't happen again.

Walking for the first time was very difficult. My uncle had said, "Get up every hour and try to walk the halls," so I was trying. I remember the nurse saying to me, "He doesn't know what it feels like, believe me. It's very hard, and you don't have to do it every hour."

I felt I was having terrible cramps all the time. Even though I was on painkillers, I was aware of the pain. The third day they gave me an enema, apparently to avoid days of gas pains, but that was absolutely excruciating. Maybe it helped, but it felt like torture.

After that, I was just on Motrin [a mild analgesic], and that was certainly enough to control the pain.

How was your first week home?
I was still taking extra-strength Motrin, which worked. And they gave me something to help me sleep at night. I was very de-pressed, because I hadn't realized how wrecked I was going to be. I was told how routine the surgery was, how easy. And I was told that I would be fine very shortly after.

What I realized was, not only are you exhausted afterward, but emotionally you're very fragile. The first week I was home, I would cry about things. Silly things would suddenly touch me. Something very romantic or tender, and suddenly there'd be tears.

By the six-week checkup, how did you feel?
I was still very weak. I remember I couldn't use the seat belt in the car because I was still very swollen. But I had started to move around.

I had a fright, though, at the checkup because they found an-other growth, a cyst on my ovary. That summer the doctor rec-ommended hot douches twice a day, and somehow that caused the growth to disappear so I didn't have to have surgery. Knowing I had the cyst weighed on me a lot. But by the end of summer, I was fairly active. I just needed a lot more sleep than usual—I never used to get more than six hours of sleep, and here I was needing nine or ten.

Although doctors say it's only a couple of months to return to normal, it took me up to a year. I never regained my old sleep patterns. Last year I even underwent a whole battery of tests to see if I was anemic or had thyroid problems, but they couldn't find anything. So the operation changed my life in that way.

When did you resume sex?
They say you can have sex after six weeks, but I would say it took another two or three months. There was not a lot of desire on my part, and there was a great deal of discomfort. The surgery depletes you so, on so many different levels, that I just wanted my body to be left alone. I felt very tender.

How did you feel about no longer being able to have children?
I don't know if I really ever wanted to *bear* my own children. As I got older I thought I might want to adopt them. But by the time my option to have children was taken away from me, I also realized we were both at an age where even adoption could be difficult. It's a little sad thinking we won't have a family. On the other hand, a great many friends my age are having children now and they're exhausted a lot of the time and their lives have changed dramatically. So, being realistic, I know I don't have the time to raise children as I would want to—I have two careers as it is now.

Any advice for women considering a hysterectomy?
I would have liked to be better prepared for how long the recovery was going to take. But I must say, there are benefits that have made my life much easier. I always had very heavy and painful periods, and every month there were a couple of days when I had to stay pretty close to home. I feel wonderfully free from that. And not having to use birth control is marvelous.

———————

"MY DOCTOR SAID, 'REMOVING THE OVARIES IS USUALLY ADVISED—BUT THEY'RE YOUR OVARIES, AND IF YOU WANT TO KEEP THEM, THAT'S UP TO YOU.'"
An advertising producer/film director who had a simple hysterectomy because of fibroids at age forty-six, a year and a

half before this interview. She is single, lives in Los Angeles, and maintains an apartment in New York City.

How long did you know you had fibroids?
About ten years ago, the only gynecologist I ever had discovered some very small fibroid tumors. He said, "We should watch these. They could stay the same size, or grow, or even disappear—anything's possible."

About three years ago I saw him, and he said, "You know, these things are getting much bigger. There's no emergency, but I want you to be aware that we may have to do something about them."

I noticed that I was getting a much heavier period flow, such that I had to change my super Tampax every hour the first day or two. But I've never been anemic, my blood pressure was fine, and other than very mild cramps, I didn't have any real pain.

At one point, I lost about five or six pounds on a diet, and I noticed I had a slight protuberance on one side of my belly that wasn't matched on the other side. It never occurred to me what it might be.

My gynecologist was killed in the Korean Air Line crash in 1984, which was very shocking. I didn't do anything about finding another doctor. His partner in New York examined me, and she said that there was a possibility I'd go into early menopause and avoid surgery.

Three or four months later, the woman who'd been giving me massages for a couple of years felt this lumpy area on one side and said, "I don't remember noticing this before. If I were you, I'd have this looked at." I really got scared. It seemed to me that the fibroid suddenly was much bigger. I was in California then, and a friend of mine called a friend who's an obstetrician to set up an appointment for me.

She was concerned about two things: that there seemed to have been sudden growth, and that the position of the tumor's growth might indicate pressure on the ureters, the two tubes linking the kidneys and bladder. In that case, I might have kidney damage. And I had noticed that I was beginning to urinate more at night than usual.

I went in for a sonogram immediately. I was pretty nervous. All the worst things go through your head, although it's almost unheard of for fibroid tumors to be malignant.

I had a terrific radiologist who stayed with me in the room during the sonogram. This doctor said he could see there was something very big in there and it was pressing on my ureters. The next day, I went for an IVP [intravenous pyelogram] and it showed everything was okay with my kidneys. Before the test, they told me to take Maalox and not to eat anything acidic, and they warned me about the possibility of getting nauseated from the dye, but I didn't. It was painless and over in ten minutes.

Meanwhile, I had given my California doctor the name of my New York doctor so they could compare the new sonogram with the old one. It turned out the fibroid wasn't that much larger than it had been six months ago. But we agreed that something should be done because it was pressing and could continue to grow over the next couple of years. My California doctor said I might not go into menopause for another five years or possibly longer. She said, "Even though it's not an emergency, you should think about it and get another opinion."

Did you get a second opinion?
The next time I came to New York I was examined again. The doctor said I should seriously consider a complete hysterectomy. I asked if that was absolutely necessary since my ovaries seemed to be healthy. I didn't want to deal with the thought of going through menopause at the age of forty-six. She said that removing the ovaries was standard procedure because a lot of scar tissue is created in doing this surgery, and should you develop any kind of cervical trouble or ovarian cancer, it would be a much more difficult surgery. I said I'd think about it.

How did you decide what to do?
I was feeling more and more comfortable with my California doctor. She was a feminist, as I am, and runs an all-female clinic, and I had heard so many wonderful things about her from so many women. When I went back to California, I told her, Let's pick a time and we'll just do it.

I also told her I had some feelings I'd like to talk to her about, and we spent a half hour in her office. I asked her if it was absolutely necessary to remove my ovaries if they seemed healthy, and she said, "No, it's usually advised, but they're your ovaries, and if you want to keep them, that's up to you."

I said, "Look, when you're in there, if you don't see evidence of disease, let's leave them alone." She said, "Fine." Then she asked me what I wanted to do about my appendix. Normally, they take it out.* And again I said, If it looks healthy, leave it alone.

Did you do anything to prepare for surgery?
My doctor suggested autologous transfusions. That means my own blood would be used if I needed blood during surgery. Usually they take a pint a week for three weeks, but I was going to be in New York so we could only do a pint. She felt it wasn't going to be necessary to use any blood at all, but the pint was a precaution.

I spent a lot of time right before the operation riding my exercise bicycle, doing calisthenics, watching my diet—just trying to get slim. I had the feeling that the more fat I had around the middle, the harder it might be for the surgeon, and the more possibility I had of scarring. It was just my personal theory.† My doctor put me on iron pills for a couple of weeks to build up my red blood cells. By the time I went into the hospital, my stamina was high. I was tight, lean, in good shape.

Anything we should know about checking into the hospital and registration?
One thing I didn't know until after the surgery was about unnecessary X-rays. When I was admitted, they took a chest X-ray. But I'd had one done recently as part of a general checkup. I found out later that if you have proof you had the X-ray within a year, you don't have to have another.

What arrangements did you make for your stay?
I requested a private room. In this hospital, the extra charge for a private room was $35. I chose that for several reasons. One,

---

* Note: According to Louis Lapid, M.D., surgeons no longer remove the appendix during a hysterectomy as a matter of course. "The appendix is always inspected, as you inspect everything in the abdomen. If you see there is a problem, then you might take it."

† Her theory is correct, according to Karen Blanchard, M.D. Operating on a fat person is "much more difficult, and the risks in the procedure are much higher, from complications in anesthesia as well as postoperative," she says. "There's more necrosis in the womb—more likelihood of a womb infection. There's usually poor aeration in the lungs and a greater likelihood of infections occurring in the lungs afterward. And there's more likelihood of bleeding problems. It's technically a much more difficult situation." So if someone is fit and doesn't smoke? "She's going to recover faster—that's just a fact."

I'm used to being alone. Two, I didn't want to deal with somebody I didn't know. What if the person was a smoker, what if she had a zillion visitors, what if I had a zillion visitors?

I didn't order private nurses because my doctor said that as far as she knew the nursing care at the hospital was so fabulous there was no real reason for it. And she was right, as it turned out.

What happened the night before surgery?
A few nurses came in to chat—one, a terrific Norwegian woman. The hospital is Catholic, and I'm not, and I made them take the Christ picture off the wall. They may have been a little upset about that. They showed me an audiovisual presentation about the procedure. I sort of got the feeling it was to remind me I was never going to be able to have children, but that may have been my liberal paranoia. They also gave me an illustrated orientation booklet about the procedure, which was very helpful.

When did they shave you?
When I was out, under anesthesia. I had said, "Please don't shave me any more than you absolutely have to because I've heard that sometimes it doesn't grow back the same way." And they just did the very, very top of my pubic hair.

What did you understand about anesthesia going into surgery?
I hadn't thought a lot about it, although I had heard it can be the most difficult part of the recuperation. I'd also heard it could be the most dangerous part of the surgery. So I'd been thinking maybe I'd have a spinal—you're not totally wiped out; you just don't feel anything below the waist.

The evening before surgery, the anesthesiologist came in, and the more I talked with him about a spinal, the more I felt he didn't want to do it. He said he was going to use a very, very light level of anesthesia, which is only in effect for two hours and is only used for office procedures. And I thought, If this guy doesn't want to do a spinal, I'm not going to tell him he should—I mean, maybe he didn't do them very well. I also realized that my gynecologist and anesthesiologist had never worked together before. That was the first time I really got nervous.

He and I agreed I'd think it over and let him know my decision in the morning. I called my doctor at home because she had said to call if anything came up. She reassured me that the anesthesiologist was one of the chief anesthesiologists at the hospital, and she agreed with my decision about the spinal. She didn't say he couldn't do it. She said, "If your instinct tells you not to push it, that's what I'd do."

I think I had this fear of being under. You just go into blackness and you come out of blackness and everything's going on but you don't know what happened in that hour. I'm too much of a control freak for that not to scare me. [For a comparison of the two anesthesias, see interview with anesthesiologist Marilyn Kritchman, M.D., page 249.]

How did you feel in the recovery room?
I was very cold. I felt very dry in the mouth, and I couldn't move because I was held down by sheets and blankets. I wasn't aware of pain, but something more like pressure and discomfort in my lower abdomen. My doctor was standing there looking at me. She said, "Hi, how're you doing?" And I said, "How *am* I doing?" And she said, "You're doing fine." They started putting ice in my mouth because you're dehydrated but they can't let you swallow anything—you might throw up.

This was the only time during the entire experience when I was really uncomfortable. A nurse came by and I said, "I'm very cold." And she started packing my body with heated bags of some kind of chemical, I guess. Most of the time I was lying there trying to get back to who I was, where I was, and what was going on. I think I was there maybe half an hour. They'd take my temperature, look in my eyes, and when they thought I was better, they took me back to my room, where my mother and a friend of hers were waiting. I had five minutes of feeling a little nauseated from the anesthesia, and I would say within two hours I was absolutely fine.

What were the results of the surgery?
They left my ovaries and appendix. The big concern was the biopsy and what the lab tests were going to show, and we weren't going to get that until the next day. My doctor said that as far as she could see, there was no sign of anything that looked the least bit abnormal to her.

When did you walk for the first time?
My doctor's philosophy is that you get out of bed as soon as you can. So that afternoon I stood up and went to the bathroom, all bent over. It's probably not true that you can't straighten up, but psychologically you think that if you straighten up, everything's going to open up.

Did you have gas pains?
That's the biggest problem. They tell you beforehand that you're going to have gas pains. They give you some kind of Maalox-type antigas medicine and give you food to stimulate your body, and every two hours they come in and ask if you've been to the bathroom.

How was your first day after surgery?
I was walking around. I didn't feel weak. I still felt that I couldn't walk as straight as I'd like to—I wasn't going to run anywhere. But it wasn't pain—it was achy discomfort. The gas pains began to subside. One of the nurses told me that if I lay on my right side and pulled up my knees, that would relieve the pressure on the colon. I was allowed to have visitors. My room was full of flowers, and I was getting phone calls. There was lots to keep me distracted. I found reading hard. The pain medication sort of made me drift off.

And the rest of your hospital stay?
By the second day I was on much lighter pain medication, and by the third day I had weaned myself off. I just didn't like it, and I didn't need it. I was antsy to get out of the hospital. My doctor was out of town, but her associate came in and took out the staples. That took all of about two seconds. On the fifth day, I went home.

What was the nursing care like?
What's really interesting is that you develop all these connections with these women. It was the first time in my life I had ever been in a situation where I was totally dependent on strangers. Fortunately, they were warm, loving women. I think a lot of them are a lot smarter than the doctors—they seem to know more about what patients need and how to respond to them. When you leave, you feel as though you're leaving your mommy—it was very healthy for me to be in a situation where I had to let people do things for me—I had no choice. It was wonderful.

How did your recovery go at home?
My doctor said, "Eat three meals a day and take it really easy for the next couple of weeks. Don't even attempt driving for three weeks." She said I'd be 100 percent recovered after six weeks.

I felt terrific the second day I was home. By the fourth day, I was out with friends and visiting people. I was the thinnest I've been since I had hepatitis. I looked gaunt. That didn't last long—I gained it all back in a month.

The thing that shocked me was how much muscle tone I'd lost. I started exercising, and at the two-week checkup, my doctor said I was healing very quickly and I could do whatever I was capable of doing, but I should just be careful about deep knee bends and arching my back. She even told me I could start driving if I wanted to.

I was interested to see if there would be any change in my hormones. I realized I was having the same premenstrual symptoms I'd had prior to surgery, and my breasts still got swollen. My doctor said, "Well, your ovaries don't know your uterus isn't there anymore."

When did you feel completely returned to normal?
My upper thighs were numb from the clamps that hold your legs in position during surgery. The numbness disappeared from one leg after a few months and after a year and a half from the other leg.

And I'm not thrilled with my scar. It developed keloids and was really pretty awful. It was about a half-inch thick and raised. My doctor was shocked. She asked if I had a tendency to keloid, and I said it had never happened before. But even if I had the tendency, there wasn't anything she could have done to prevent it. She said she'd be happy to put me under local anesthesia and stitch me up again, but the chances were the exact same thing would happen. My dermatologist gave me a series of cortisone shots over a couple of months and said the keloid should diminish in thickness. It's working. I've had two sets of shots. The first set really hurt. They're injecting it into scar tissue, and they have to use a high-pressure valve system to get more pressure behind the needle than you'd get from administering it by hand. The second set, because the scar was already much smoother, was not nearly as uncomfortable.

Did you have any emotional response to the surgery?
I had a sense of loss. A therapist was helping me with the meaning of all the different experiences—being dependent on those people in the hospital, the loss of a part of your body so heavily identified with your sexuality, the discomfort of feeling that your body is scarred now and not perfect. For me, because I'm very vain about my body, having a scar was a problem. The first time I went to bed with someone new after the surgery—nine months after, when the scar was really red and raw and thick and terrible—I remember being very self-conscious.

I'd never been hospitalized for anything. This was a reminder of the frailty of the body, how you never know from minute to minute what's going to happen. Even if you're a very healthy person, there's the possibility that something could happen, something could be wrong, and you wouldn't know about it. In my case, it was a very good lesson to know you have that kind of vulnerability. And that there's something you can do about it and you can allow yourself to be taken care of. I felt I took control by researching, talking to people, getting all the information. I've seen people who are passive in those situations, and I think that's very dangerous.

I think the fact that I trusted my doctor, that I was always going to get a straight answer, that if she didn't know she was going to say she didn't know, made it much easier for me. I wasn't frightened at all.

Any advice for women considering hysterectomy?
Make sure you're in really good condition so you don't feel weak and physically vulnerable. I think that helps you bounce back a lot faster.

Ask every single question you can think of because then you'll feel you're in control of your own life. The more information you have, the more comfortable you are. Ask: Why are you taking my blood now, what is this pill I'm taking, why do you need to know this? You can't be intimidated by the authority of the hospital.

Hysterectomy is a simple procedure, and if you've never had surgery, it seems traumatic, but in reality it's very common, and you're going to feel better when it's done. I don't miss bleeding like a stuck pig every month. I feel a heck of a lot better than when I dreaded bleeding through my clothes yet again, which always seemed to happen on a day when I was on the set. I could have risked seeing what would happen with these fibroids down the road—maybe I'd go into early menopause—but there was a risk of kidney damage. My doctor said, "You don't need your uterus, but you do need your kidneys."

"WHEN I HAD MY FIRST ORGASM AFTER THE SURGERY, I JUST BURST INTO TEARS—I WAS SO RELIEVED."
A literary agent in her mid-forties who underwent a simple

hysterectomy because of fibroid tumors. She is divorced with three children.

How long did you have fibroids before the surgery?
I had the fibroids for at least five or six years. They were within the walls of the uterus, so they couldn't be removed individually. The doctor was watching them. They were harmless, and I didn't have any pain. When they started getting much larger, they caused very heavy bleeding, sometimes even hemorrhaging, and constant periods. It was very unpleasant, but I didn't have any pain.

Was it difficult to make the decision to have surgery?
I was very reluctant to have surgery. I felt I wanted to keep what I had. Since I was in my forties, I felt if I could stick it out until menopause, the fibroids presumably would shrink and the problem would resolve itself. I had spoken to one woman who had waited, and she was glad she did. I mean, who wants major surgery? But I couldn't go anywhere.

I was the largest single purchaser of tampons and sanitary napkins. I never wore white clothing. I couldn't go to the beach. If I had to go to a football game or something that was outside where I would be far away from a bathroom for a whole day, I mean, forget it! It just got to the point where it was so intrusive in my life that it was a constant trauma.

I had had a doctor for a long time whose manner was always very curt. He had delivered two of my children. I felt he was a capable surgeon, he kept me in reasonably good health, but I really didn't like his attitude. He suggested I have surgery. I went to see a couple of other doctors. In fact, I saw a lot of other doctors, because I was looking for one who would say, "You don't need to have this surgery." Finally, I went to a doctor who said, "You're not going to find any reliable professional who isn't going to tell you the same thing. This is the course of action prescribed for this condition." So I talked with an author of mine who is a gynecologist. He's wonderful, and really likes women. He suggested I come to see him, and I said, "I can't come to see you because you're my client." So he suggested I see his partner, whom I really liked and trusted.

And he said the same thing, but he also said, "If you don't want to do it, don't do it. We'll wait. I'll wait with you. And when you decide, then I'll do it. But if you can hold out, fine."

I waited another two years, and every year I'd go and have all the tests. They could no longer feel my ovaries, so I had to get a sonogram. I mean, the whole thing really got out of hand. The fibroid had grown so much that it changed the shape of my body. It was the size of a four-month pregnancy, and I felt depressed about it. I think at one point he said, "Suppose you don't go into menopause until you're fifty-three? Are you going to do this for another eight years?" I finally said, "I can't wait anymore. Schedule it." I canceled it once, and then I said, "Schedule it again."

Do you think you made the right decision?
I am so happy I did it, I cannot tell you. Before, I had wanted to find somebody to write a book called *How to Avoid Hysterectomy*. After I'd done it, I told the doctor I couldn't believe how much better I felt about it. He is on the front line of New York gynecologists who are always being accused of doing unnecessary surgery. And he said, "It make me cross that people always refer to this as 'elective' surgery and say we do these things just to make money. When something is necessary for the quality of your life, it really is necessary." And it really has made a difference. I can't tell you how relieved I am.

How did you prepare for the surgery?
I read quite a lot about it. I discussed the matter of keeping my ovaries with the doctor. I said they could take one. They didn't take either one, as it turned out. They said they looked dandy and left them. I also asked him for a bikini cut, and he said it was going to be pretty tricky, because the fibroid was so big but he'd do his best. And he did.

Any problems checking into the hospital?
I really found it painless. The hospital staff was pleasant. They treated me nicely. They were attentive. The hospital I chose had a bad reputation for being big, dirty, and old, but it was wonderful.

Usually when you're in a hospital, fifty-five people come in to question you—first- and second-year students, interns. In this case, a woman who was in charge of asking questions and giving information came in. She told me she had two things for me to sign. One was permission for the surgery, and the other one was an acknowledgment that I understand that after this hysterectomy, I wouldn't be able to have any more children. I said, "Surely everybody knows that." She said, "You'd be surprised."

How was your hospital stay after surgery?
I woke up in the recovery room, not remembering anything. I was out for about twelve hours. When I woke up, a friend was sitting by my bed, which was the best thing anyone had done for me. She knew that sooner or later I'd wake up, and when I did, a friend would be here. I had a catheter in, which was very uncomfortable, but I was not ever in any pain after the surgery.

My recovery was very rapid. The worst thing is that all they feed you is what they call "clear fluids"—in my case, green Jell-O and chicken soup. And they say, "Did you have a bowel movement?" but that actually didn't turn out to be a problem.

I left the hospital after the fourth or maybe it was the fifth day. My doctor was annoyed because he felt it was too soon. But I felt so fine, and I was obviously a well person, so he said all right.

And your recuperation?
I was in bed for two weeks. I got up for meals and went downstairs, and came back upstairs, and that was a big effort. I'd go out every day and walk around. It was a huge effort to walk to the corner, but I did. I think after about ten days I went to the movies with my sister. I started to work again. I was on the phone. After two weeks, I actually came into the office one day. I shouldn't have done that. It was really too much. I was just tired. I wasn't up to doing anything. Like walking far or cooking meals or anything like that. But every day I felt stronger, and by the third week I felt fine. I'd say I really felt I could have a reasonably normal life in about four weeks.

What state were you in emotionally?
I would say it was positive. Because I felt all right, and I had this support system of family and friends. And I didn't want any more children—I already had three. My youngest is sixteen.

Was your concentration affected?
I found I was impatient with detail. I guess that's a way of not being able to concentrate. You know—"I can't be bothered thinking about this now. Put it in that pile." My assistant would tell me something that happened, and I'd say, "Oh, I don't want to think about that right now. Can you deal with it?" I think the exhaustion was the result of both the anesthesia and the surgery. Even if you don't have any pain at all, your body has been violated and chopped up, and it takes time to heal.

Did you have any concerns about resuming sex after surgery?

Before the surgery I was worried about sexual dysfunction, because a lot of books about hysterectomy refer to that. A lot of women complain that after they had a hysterectomy their sex life was ruined or they didn't have desire. I have not found that to be true.

I was very frightened and careful about resuming sex, but it was all right. In fact, when I had my first orgasm six weeks or so after the surgery, I just burst into tears—I was so relieved. After that it was fine.

I would say that there was a difference, and actually that's one of the reasons I was resisting the surgery. I had read that after hysterectomy, orgasms are different. I have found that they are. I guess part of the orgasm is the contraction of the uterus. When you don't have a uterus you don't get those contractions. So the orgasm may be slightly different—but it's still pretty nice.

"I DIDN'T ASK MY DOCTOR THE GOOD QUESTIONS. I COULD HAVE USED A SCRIPT: ASK THIS AND THIS."

A forty-four-year-old magazine editor, married with no children, who had a simple hysterectomy nine months before this interview. The experience was complicated for her because she believed there was a psychological component to her fibroid.

Why did you decide to have the surgery?
I had a fibroid they said was the size of a grapefruit. They describe it in different ways. In the record I saw that it was either six- or eight-week size. They see it as a baby's size, I guess, which is a little unnerving.

When did you first notice that something was wrong?
I'd had horrible cramps and periods for as long as I can remember. It was always upsetting, not only because it hurt so much, but because of the depression and tension that came with a bad period. I always thought the pain and the mood change was psychosomatic, that if I were really on top of my life, I wouldn't let this bother me. So every month there was this battle that I felt was a battle of character. And I tell you, since I've had that operation, and I no longer go through that struggle, I'm a much happier person.

How long did you know you had a fibroid?
For about five years. I would be examined and told I had fibroids,
and I never really knew what they were. I always thought of them
as something like the lint that gathers in the dryer. Of course,
they're nothing like that. I once talked to a therapist who deals
with the emotional components of illness and with the tensions
in the body. He asked me, "Did you ever see a fibroid? It's like a
very tightly wound spool of thread. You can imagine what tension
it takes, how much energy and intensity, for something like that
to come into being."

*He was implying that your fibroids were a symptom of
something emotional? Did that make you feel responsible
for them in some way?*
It depended on the day. One day, I would feel very passive and
sort of a victim of the fibroid—in the same way that sometimes,
when I would get depressed by my period or find the cramps
unbearable, I would think, I should be able to control this. Of
course, there were women who said their periods never bothered
them. That gave me the sense that they were handling it and I
wasn't.

How did you decide to have the surgery?
I had changed gynecologists a couple of times, and the most recent one said, "Look, you should know you have a fibroid, and we
should watch it." And he said, "Sometimes they shrink of their
own accord." He was wonderful. He had me go for a sonogram
regularly, and one day he said, "Well, this is growing, and I'm
concerned because your ovary is swollen. I think we should think
about having it out."

Well, I thought that meant a D&C. I said, "Then let's do it." I
asked if it was an overnight thing, and he said, "Oh, I guess you
don't understand." And I didn't say, "What do you mean? Give
me the goods right now." I said, "Oh?" He explained why he
wasn't going to do a myomectomy—that the fibroid was too big.
I went out of there caught up the way you sometimes get caught
up in the hysteria of a dream. I didn't really ask the good questions.

*Did you know the name of the operation he was talking
about?*
He said, "I'm going to write down 'simple hysterectomy,' but
don't get scared. We won't have to take your ovaries." He kind of
downplayed it. A friend of mine was surprised that I wasn't plan-

ning to go for a second opinion, but I trusted my doctor. On the other hand, I hated the hospital he was affiliated with, so, one thing leading to another, I got the name of a woman surgeon at another hospital. She said, "I don't think you need surgery now. I think we should watch it, but I'm not sure that surgery is necessary." It occurred to me later that she may have just wanted the business. She said, "Come back in six weeks." So I canceled the appointment for surgery with the first doctor. I'm not proud that I never wrote him a letter—I think I was angry with him for not explaining things to me better.

Six weeks later, the woman doctor sent me for a sonogram, and I could tell by the way the doctors were examining me that they were finding growth. I called her for the results, and she told me the fibroid had grown and there was a shadow on one ovary. The words were very nonspecific. It's almost as though doctors are deliberately vague so that you won't relate too much to what's going on.

Did you ask, "What does a shadow mean?"
She explained it, but not really. I don't think I wanted to know exactly what it was. She said she didn't think it was malignant, but if there was any indication that it was, they would take out both ovaries. She also said that she was able to do the surgery in a few days. I loved the idea of having it done fast—the anxiety of going into the operation would be worse than the pain of it.

What made you trust her?
Instinct, the fact that she was with a good hospital, and the fact that she was a real sergeant and struck me as very alert. She was very unwarm, and yet because of that, I felt that I could ask her questions. There wasn't any emotion in the room with her. She was very brittle and tight, and I felt that I could be that way a little bit with her.

I think you make it as abstract as possible so you don't focus on what's really going on. I felt that happen in the hospital, too. I remember just lying on the table. I mean, if I had cut my finger, I think I would have been more consciously upset. There's a sense of resignation. I felt the way you do at the major moments of life, in a crisis. You sort of play a role, suspend your own personality. I remember when I checked into the hospital, scores of other people were checking in, too, and we all behaved very civilly. Wouldn't you think somebody would get hysterical when they keep you waiting or don't call your number or can't find your file?

But you don't. I don't know what it is. I know that I gave up control. I decided to trust the surgeon. It didn't feel like being a child. It felt like I had made an executive decision—I'd hired this person.

Was there anything that surprised you about your
experience in the hospital?

My doctor wears a big gold ring with a lion crest on it. And when I saw her right before the surgery, she was wearing her ring on a big safety pin clipped to her surgical gown. When I woke up, the first thing I saw was that ring hanging from her gown, and her hand was on the inside of the rail around me. She said, "I never worked so hard in my life. It was four hours and you lost a lot of blood, but you have two beautiful ovaries left in there." And I kissed her hand. That was the number-one surprise to me, because I think what I did was pretty yucky, in retrospect, and because in some ways I hated her for being such a cold person. It must be what people feel at Lourdes. I felt she had all the power, and here I was powerless—I was just a person who had been healed.

Surprise number two is the way you feel when you wake up. Your mouth is dry, you can hardly see.

Do you wish you had done more research?

I almost feel like I could have used a script: Ask this and this and this. I went in finally with a list of questions, and the doctor said, "I don't have time for this." My husband, who was with me, said, "Look, she has a bunch of questions—why don't you answer them? It's important for her to know." He gave the extra push that was a big help to me.

I had to sign a form that said she could do anything she felt was necessary during surgery. But I wanted to know why she had to take both ovaries if there was a shadow on only one. And she said, "Look, my specialty is fertility. My specialty is to preserve in surgery. What I studied and what I specialized in was how not to do this surgery. But our data shows that if there is anything on one ovary, it makes more sense to take both." And I said, "Wait a minute. I don't want children, but I'm not ready to go into menopause. I'm forty-three years old and I've finally learned to be comfortable and happy sexually, and I don't want that snatched away." She said, in effect, "Too bad."

Not very sympathetic.

No, but I liked it. I was convinced by her—in contrast with that wonderful man that I liked very much before. When I would go in to talk to him in his office, he would have a cup of coffee and a cigarette. I didn't want a doctor who smoked and drank coffee on the job. I liked this bitchy woman who I felt was alert, and if something went wrong in the operation, she would not have to grab for a cigarette or ask the nurse for a cup of coffee. If there was a snap decision to be made, my sense was that she would do it right. I mean, I lost a lot of blood, but they didn't have to give me transfusions. So, as it turned out, I did make the right decision.

"I REALIZED HOW ANTISURGERY I WAS AND WENT ON A SEARCH FOR ALTERNATIVE WAYS TO TREAT FIBROIDS."
A forty-six-year-old writer living in New York City with her husband. They have no children. She resisted surgery for fibroids, trying several alternative therapies to reduce their size.

What made you finally decide to have a simple hysterectomy?
It was a ten-year-long process, beginning, I guess, when a doctor told me I should have a myomectomy for a small fibroid. It was only then that I realized how antisurgery I was. My reaction was, "I'll do anything not to have it." So, after seeing several other doctors who said they didn't think surgery was immediately necessary, I started looking for alternatives.

A friend told me about a doctor from India who treated patients with powdered herbs and diet and exercise. He was great. Although I had no idea what was in the herbs, they worked. My fibroids reduced in size, according to the sonograms I continued to have. I'm still on the diet—it's primarily vegetables with lots of grains, a few eggs a week, small portions of fish or maybe chicken a couple of times a week. No red meat, sugar, or dairy products except for a little yogurt. Nowadays I'm a little more relaxed about it all, I must admit. The exercise was yoga, which I did for about fifteen minutes a day. I felt very healthy, but to make a long story short, the herbal doctor died and his herbs went with him. My fibroids began growing again, and a gynecologist who was checking my sonograms every three months started talking about surgery, so I just stopped going to him.

In a way, it's too bad the herbal doctor *had* been effective—it kept me searching for another nonsurgical way of treating the fibroids. I went to an acupuncturist who said he could help me if I cut down on my activity, lay down for fifteen minutes every two hours, and took his herbs three times a day. I took the herbs—I never did ask what they were—but the rest of it I couldn't do.

The fibroids kept growing. And my periods were getting heavier. When even the acupuncturist said he thought I should consider surgery, I was really defeated. I began to be obsessive about my health, very strict about my diet—trying macrobiotics, which I think is terrific, but very hard to stay on. I was really getting crazy—focusing a lot of emotional and mental energy on avoiding the surgery. My stomach, which has always been very flat, was getting lumpy from the fibroids, and I started wearing looser clothes. I didn't feel like going up stairs or hills or running. I mean, I was acting like a sick person while frantically working at being healthy.

But eventually I stepped up the process of looking for a doctor, and when I found him, I made the decision immediately. I left his office with a date for surgery.

What made you choose this particular doctor?
I saw about nine or ten doctors over a period of months, and there was something not right about any of them. Some were too busy, others too laid back, and so on. My complaints had nothing to do with their competency; I was just being neurotic—I hadn't decided what to do. One was a doctor whose book I had read—he turned out to be the worst. I saw him for a total of fifteen minutes including the exam. He was perfunctory and arrogant. A doctor I wanted to see was booked for two months. One doctor said— during the internal, with his hand inside—"We'd better get this out as soon as possible. This is really big. Why did you wait so long?" The doctor I finally chose came through a friend's recommendation. He was direct and professional but sensitive. He wasn't authoritarian, but I trusted him. He worked quickly during the examination and didn't give me his diagnosis while I was being examined.

My doctor didn't say anything until I was dressed and in his office. He assumed I knew something about my body. In fact, he said, "You're a smart woman, and you know you have to do something about this condition." I am and I did know.

What questions did you ask him?

I wanted to know about the anesthesia. I was more scared of it than of the surgery. He told me that the anesthesiologist he worked with was very competent and that he trusted him. I believed him and was less scared.

I asked about saving my ovaries because I didn't want to go into menopause immediately. He agreed and said if they were not diseased—and he had no reason to believe they were—he always left the ovaries. I asked about the kind of incision he does and told him I wanted the horizontal or bikini incision because it was stronger-holding and mostly because it wouldn't show too much. After the surgery, I found out from the chief resident that it had been a tight squeeze because of the size of the mass—one fibroid had reached the size of a four- or five-month fetus—but the doctor was skillful enough to maneuver it. So I guess my trust was justified.

I asked about resuming sex after the operation and was told it would be six weeks of abstinence. I didn't ask about the surgery itself, what it consisted of, because it's an area over which I had no control. Once having decided on the surgeon, I figured I had to go with his expertise and not obsess about the details. I think, though, that women who have a more analytical mind might want to know what exactly happens and should ask and expect to be told.

What was important to me in asking specific questions was to see his reaction. I wanted someone who was willing to be honest with the answers.

Did you do anything to prepare for surgery?

I had a six-week wait. I talked to the doctor's nurse about other questions I had, and I wrote the doctor a letter. I restated what we had discussed about keeping my ovaries and the bikini incision. I told him I was consulting a nutritionist and that she had suggested taking some supplements to prepare for surgery. Some zinc, more calcium, vitamins C, A, B_6, and B_{12}. He called me when he received the letter and was really reassuring. He told me I was in good health, and that although the fibroids were very large, I was thin, which made the surgery easier. He thought the bikini incision would be no problem, and although he couldn't guarantee saving the ovaries until he was in surgery, he would make every effort to do it.

I don't know if the diet and supplements did any good, but doing *something* helped my head, so I guess it was worthwhile.

I was really anxious the whole six weeks, but the couple of days before going into the hospital were the worst. I was so psyched up that I confused the dates and was ready to go in a day early. That turned out to be a good thing. It broke the tension. My husband and I got hysterical laughing when we found out and went to dinner and a movie.

What did you take to the hospital?

My pillow and some fresh pillowcases, just like Linus. I also took cotton underpants that came up to the waist, the granny kind. Bikini pants hit you right on the incision.

I also took a long robe and several loose cotton nightgowns. I didn't want anything rubbing my skin that wasn't soft. I took my vitamins, body cream, makeup, magazines, stationery, shampoo, slippers—the kind you can slip into, because, honestly, you can't bend down very easily.

How was the night before surgery?

My husband and a dear friend were there. She brought juice and food, and we sat around trying not to be nervous.

My doctor came in and, again, was very reassuring, and said he'd see me in the morning before surgery. The anesthesiologist came in and explained the procedure. I asked him whether anyone had ever died under his anesthesia—you can see where I was. I wanted to focus him on how nervous I was; I figured he'd be a little more attentive. He assured me I would be very comfortable and wouldn't know anything until I woke up in recovery. He was right.

After everyone left, some nurses introduced themselves. One came in to give me an enema. She was very kind and explained what she wanted me to do—lie on my side—and we watched the water in the bag go down and into me. It wasn't bad.

I didn't think I'd be able to sleep, but that wasn't a problem. I read and watched television until I was tired.

When did they shave you?

When I was under anesthesia, and I was grateful for that. It seemed undignified to me, to be shaved, and it's just one more thing you don't have to experience awake.

Did you have a private room?

Yes, I wanted to be able to walk around, to use the john whenever

I wanted and all that. It's a luxury, but I certainly didn't plan to do this again, and it made me feel better. After saying all that, I don't think it was necessary. The recovery was quite straightforward.

What do you remember of the morning before surgery?
While I was still in my room, I was given an injection of something to relax me. I was very drowsy by the time I was wheeled into the operating room. They lifted me onto the table, and I was given another injection. I don't remember anything else until the recovery room.

I wasn't scared when I went into surgery. The most anxious time was the night before. Once the hospital procedures start—nurses, blood pressure, interns checking charts—it's easier.

How much pain did you have?
Right after the surgery, there was no pain. As the anesthesia wore off, I felt very, very uncomfortable. It was really hard to turn over in bed, and you didn't want to move too quickly. The first night was the worst, but I took painkillers and they *did* kill the pain. So I was okay. There was never *any* intolerable pain. But you know you can't jump around.

The next morning they removed the catheter. There's no pain connected to that. Then they get you up on your feet, and that's the closest you come to pain. It feels as though there's going to be a terrible pull if you stand up. But if you take a painkiller just before, you can actually straighten up. And every day after, until you leave the hospital, you get stronger by leaps and bounds. But it took at least six weeks before I was moving like a normal person. And, I have to tell you, it's a year now, and there is still tenderness sometimes. Up to three months ago, I was aware of the incision most of the time. But that's me. I have friends who weren't tender at all after the first four or five weeks. And for me, any discomfort was balanced by the fact that I no longer had to think about having the operation.

Did you have good nursing care?
I was very glad to have private nurses for the first twenty-four hours after surgery. They made me comfortable so I could sleep and gave me all the drugs I needed. But other people who didn't have private nurses told me the floor nurses are terrific. The only difference is that a private nurse does things for you right away. You might have to wait with a floor nurse.

How was your first day after surgery?

I walked to the door of the room, trailing my intravenous, with a little help from my nurse, and I walked to the bathroom. But mostly I was in bed. Friends came to visit. I was still a little druggy, but I talked with a lot of people and they said my voice was strong. I felt okay.

The second day?

It was much better. I walked down the hall. I read and could concentrate on television a bit. And I slept very well that night.

The third day?

I think I was allowed to start a liquid diet, so people brought me fresh juices and nice soup from outside. I was getting steadily stronger and walked around the halls.

The fourth day?

The IV came out, I took a shower (a friend told me that in hospitals on the West Coast, you can take a shower from the first day). And I was given real food. I wasn't very hungry at all, not while I was in the hospital nor for several weeks when I got home.

How much attention did your doctor give you?

He came in every day to visit, to check the incision. The chief resident in gynecology came several times as well. Even the anesthesiologist's assistant came in. They were quite nice, and I must say I never felt neglected or fearful once the operation was over.

Did you have gas pains?

No, I never did. It could be that I was being very careful about what I ate and drank. I ate only cooked vegetables, brown rice that my husband brought me, a poached egg or oatmeal in the morning, hot water with lemon. I didn't eat any meat, only a bite or two of chicken. And no dairy products. I kept my diet very bland, and that could have been why. Or I was just lucky.

How did your recovery go at home?

My ride home in the car was very rough. I couldn't believe how sensitive my abdomen was. I immediately went to bed and stayed there for a week. It was a little depressing. I felt sicker than when I was in the hospital, maybe because I had so many visitors in the hospital and they kept me occupied. And I'd look at the scar. It was bigger than I had imagined. I think the first week out of the hospital was the hardest.

The second week was lots better. I'd get up and make tea, but I was still very tired and couldn't lift anything. By the end of the second week we went to a dinner party in the country, and I think

I was halfway decent company. The recovery from then on was steady, but still slower than I expected. I got a little paranoid thinking I wasn't measuring up to a friend's recovery, especially since I'm so nuts about being healthy.

I really tried to take the first month very easy. The doctor said not to carry anything for a month. Of course I did, and of course I shouldn't have. The third week, I went to the store just to buy a couple of things for lunch, and while I was there, I saw something we needed, then something else. It was so little, maybe about six or seven pounds. Well, I could feel the pull, and the bag seemed to weigh a hundred pounds. I took a taxi for five blocks to get home.

By the following week, I went back to my office almost full time, and I was quite fine. I went out to lunch with friends and started back on a normal routine. We went out several evenings, and although at the end of the evening I was tired, I wasn't dragging.

How was the six-week checkup?

Fine. The stitches were healing, but he had to cauterize the incision on the inside, vaginally. There was some keloid formation— overhealing. He used something that looked like a torch to do the cauterization. That was a little creepy, but I didn't feel it at all. I could smell the burning skin, but it didn't hurt, and it took only a few minutes. Afterward there was a little bleeding. And I couldn't take a bath for a couple of days or have sex for a week.

How did your scar heal?

It didn't disappear into a faint white line as I was assured it would. It is still a rather angry raised scar about a sixteenth of an inch thick with a couple of perfectly healed portions along the incision line. I can only assume that any incision I have would keloid. The doctor said some women have tried plastic surgery. I think I'll live with the red line—my badge of what it took to be back to normal.

Any advice for women considering a hysterectomy?

Women should remember that even though hysterectomy is a very common operation, it is still major surgery. Your body is invaded, and you will need time to recover. I suggest you be self-indulgent, treat yourself well, rest, relax, allow other people to do things for you, and don't be in such a rush to get back to life. It'll be there when you're ready.

For women who do a lot of mental work, you should keep in

mind that there's a possibility your concentration will be affected. Everyone, obviously, is different, but my ability to concentrate was not back to normal for at least six months. It was very
frustrating. I could handle small things and read, but developing
ideas, any substantive conceptual thinking, I simply couldn't do
well. So if you find yourself drifting off, don't worry about it. It
does come back—one day you can do it.

I am one of those women who is very glad to have had the
surgery. Medically, I could have gone on as I was for a couple of
years, hoping for early menopause, because my bleeding wasn't
too heavy and I was in decent physical shape. But I put so much
time, effort, and energy into thinking about my body that it made
me self-obsessed in a way I didn't like. Not to mention what I
could have done with that time and energy. So, I guess I'm saying, if it becomes really overwhelming, mentally and psychologically, consider having the surgery even if it's not a medical
necessity. You also might not want to wait for it to *be* necessary.

"BEFORE SURGERY I PASTED A SIGN ON ME FOR THE
DOCTOR. IT SAID, 'GIVE ME A LOW BIKINI CUT.' "
*A deputy director of research for a multinational publish-
ing corporation. She is single, forty-five, and she was first
told she needed a hysterectomy in 1973. In 1983 a combination of fibroids and endometriosis made surgery essential.*

Is there a history of fibroids in your family?
Yes, but I didn't know it. I found out recently that my mother had
a large fibroid tumor that had to be removed before I could be
born. Women tend to follow their mother's medical history, and I
have very much followed her pattern. But not knowing about it,
I began taking birth control pills when I was in my early thirties.
I don't remember exactly how long I took them, but when I did
go for my regular gynecological exam, the doctor said, "My God,
you have a tumor. It's growing. I'm going to take you off the Pill
right away."
What size was the fibroid then?
It was the size of a grapefruit. The doctor said, "Really, you
should think of having a hysterectomy." This kind of broke my
heart even though I wasn't thinking about getting married or

having any children then. I was in my early thirties, and I didn't want to have it done. He said, "The problem is that your uterus is just full of little fibroids, and then you have this large one. I don't think you could get pregnant anyway, and if you did, the large one would definitely have to be removed, and I'm not even sure we could do it." He said, "We're going to have to watch this very carefully. The alternative is that you're going to have to spend a lot of time in my office because the tumor is growing." So we watched it, and then it stopped growing.

Did you seek a second opinion at that time?

No, I didn't. I had the highest regard for my doctor.

When did you begin to have problems again?

Things seemed to be fine for about ten years, but toward the end of that time I was having irregular periods with heavy bleeding and some pain with them as well. It was almost as though I were entering change. My mother went through a very early change, right after I was born. Anyway, prior to taking a ski trip out west, I had noticed that my tumor was moving around more. I skied very hard on the trip, and when I got back, I went to see the doctor. He took one look at me and said, "You are going to have to have a hysterectomy, and you're going to have to have it right away. The tumor is growing again. It's changed—it's soft, it's dangerous. You should have it done before it becomes gangrenous"—which, he said, could very easily happen.

How large was it by this time?

It was getting up to a five-month pregnancy, a little larger than a grapefruit. It was uncomfortable. I didn't feel very well, and I was tired a lot, but still, I was just panic-stricken at the idea of having a hysterectomy.

How soon did you have the surgery?

This all happened in March or April of 1983. I said, "Why don't we wait until September?" He said, "You can't. It must be done. You've got to make up your mind because it will take me a month to get you a bed. You have to decide in the next few days." I said, "I hope you won't mind, but I'm going to get a second opinion." So I went to another top gynecologist. He examined me and said, "Well, I've known your doctor for years, and I think I would go along with his opinion. It's a sizable tumor and should come out. But the one thing you should make clear is that you want to keep your ovaries."

Then he said, "You ought to have a sonogram. That will really give you a third opinion." So I went to have a sonogram that very day. The radiologist said it was a very large tumor and it definitely should come out. I said, "Does it have to be a hysterectomy?" And he said, "Yes." So then I called my regular gynecologist and told him to get the bed. But up until the day of the surgery I was still trying to get out of it. I'd call him up and ask, "Do you really think this is necessary?" He'd say, "Absolutely."

I also had a psychiatrist who was *very* supportive. He was pushing all the way to get me to do it because he felt it was obsessing me. I didn't even realize how much I was worrying about it until it was all over. I spent practically all my psychiatric sessions discussing whether it was going to ruin my sex life, and was I going to shrivel up and turn old overnight.

Did you ask your gynecologist these questions as well?

Yes. I had a long talk with him, too. And it was very good. But mostly it was my psychiatrist who helped me through the really difficult problems. I was a wreck as the day approached. My energy was being sapped by this thing.

*Was your physical condition interfering with your life in
any way?*

Well, the only thing I'll say is, sex was painful. It was not so painful that I didn't do it, but it just wasn't as much fun, because there was something in the way there.

So you checked into the hospital?

Yes. But in the hospital the night before the surgery, I told my mother—my mother came to help me, which was a godsend—that I was going to call and tell the doctor that I would not go through with it. I was terrified. One bad thing happened that night. My doctor's assistant came in to interview me. She was very brusque. She said, "Are you having a total hysterectomy?" And I said, "No, I am not." She said, "Well, most women your age have their ovaries out." I said, "I don't care what most women my age do. I'm not having my ovaries out." I said, "I've talked with my doctor about this, and if they're bad, out they go, but if they're okay, I want to keep them." She made me so angry that I said, "Anyway, I'm not sure I'm going to have the hysterectomy, and I don't want to talk to you anymore now." I called my doctor, and he calmed me down and I got through the night.

The day of the surgery . . .

Surgery was early the next morning. I pasted a sign on me for the doctor. It said, "GIVE ME A LOW BIKINI CUT."

And you awoke in the recovery room?

I was in recovery until six o'clock that night, because my blood pressure had fallen very low and they couldn't get it back up. And I was *so* thirsty. When I finally came to, I said, "Just get me a Dr Pepper and I'll get up and get out of here."

How long was the surgery?

It was very long. The surgery was much more complicated than the doctor had thought it would be. Even though he had talked about hysterectomy, he'd promised he'd do everything he could to save the uterus, but he couldn't. He said there was a huge vein that had grown to the tumor through the uterus, and that the tumor was positioned dangerously. It was pressing against the kidney and other organs. He also said, "You had a pretty bad case of endometriosis. That was the reason for the pain when you got your period. In fact, I am surprised you didn't complain more of pain." He said, "The reason it took me so long was because I had to do some very delicate cutting. You have to be careful now. There are lots and lots of stitches inside."

And he saved your ovaries?

Yes. He said, "Your ovaries are beautiful." So I was quite thrilled with that. And I got my bikini cut. My scar is almost gone. It will be three years in May.

How did you feel after the surgery?

I felt awful. I remember waking up at night in my room, with all these flowers around me, and I thought that I was dead or something. People called, but I couldn't talk to anybody. I was in very bad, knocked-out shape. I was on intravenous, and I couldn't have any water. And one nurse made me stand up right away, that first night. I said, "No way." But she said, "If you don't stand up now, you're going to be so bad tomorrow."

What painkillers were you taking?

Demerol by injection, then they put me on pills. They were going to give me morphine at one point, because the Demerol didn't seem enough. But then it began to work, and I was certainly floating around then, feeling pretty good. The hospital gave me almost as much as I wanted if I was in pain.

What were your hospital accommodations?

I was in a room with two other people. We had all had hysterectomies, so we were all in the same boat, moaning and carrying on.

And the rest of your hospital stay?
The first night, I slept mostly. But by the next day I was dying to get out of there and go home. The doctor said, "No, you've got to stay for ten days because there was a lot of cutting." For the first forty-eight hours I was on intravenous and had nurses around the clock. I panicked when the nurses were leaving. The surgery was on Thursday, and I was very uncomfortable until Sunday.

When did you get off intravenous?
On Sunday. The intravenous, the catheter—they finally took all this crap off and said I could wash my hair and take a shower as long as I covered the area.

Did you stay the full ten days?
I had to stay. But it became kind of a party. I had so many visitors, and everyone was so kind and understanding. I got so I really enjoyed it. It became very special because I wasn't used to having people doing things for me. My psychiatrist came to see me a couple of times. I remember I was trying to move the bed and I couldn't do it. He said, "Don't you want somebody to help you?" I said, "Yes," and I thought, That's pretty nice. I don't have to do everything myself.

Did your gynecologist come to see you?
Yes. Several times. He was the one who made a very special trip to tell me that everything was benign about three days after the surgery. I'll tell you one thing. I did exactly what my doctor told me to do. I walked a lot. They called me "the runner" in the hospital. I was up *all* the time. "You'll get out of here faster if you walk," they all said. So here I would come with all my armor and stuff and pace the floor, back and forth. I drank a lot of liquid. I used that little blower thing [incentive spirometer, used postsurgically to help aerate the lungs] to keep from getting pneumonia in my lungs and chest. And if he told me *not* to do something, I didn't.

And how was it back at home?
The taxi ride and the whole ordeal of getting home just wiped me out. I went right to bed and slept. Then I got up and had a nice bowl of soup. The doctor had told me that I could start off by walking around the block and increase it a little bit each day. It took me forever to walk around that block. I overdid it a couple of times. I walked around a department store, and on my way

home I had to stop and sit down. That's how much it hurt. I was sick to my stomach when I got home. I really paid for that trip.

My mother stayed with me for a couple of weeks, then she left, and a friend took me out to Southampton for two weeks. I read and walked on the beach. It was just wonderful.

How was your emotional state through your recovery?
I had dreams about not being able to have a child, and I discussed those with my psychiatrist. He got me through the whole thing very smoothly. I remember that when I went for my six-week checkup with the gynecologist and he gave me the go on sex in another five days, I was overjoyed—that is, until I saw pictures of little babies he had outside his office. It upset me a great deal that I couldn't conceive even if I wanted to; I found it hard to look at a baby carriage. If I saw a child in the park or anywhere, I would cry or turn away. But with the help of my psychiatrist, I finally was okay about it.

And when did you return to work?
I think the surgery was May 19, and I went back to work on July 5, so it was almost six weeks after surgery. But I was real tired. The first day I came in, I left early. The first week was hard. The second week I was a little better, the third week I was even better. But when I was fully able to resume my sexual activities at the end of July, it was great. I was very thrilled about that.

Were you anxious about sex?
I was very scared. First of all, I thought I was going to die sexually, that I would have no feeling. And it turned out that I was much more sensitive and much more alive than I had ever been. It was better than it ever was. I'm convinced it's because I didn't have to worry about getting pregnant. That's a big concern for a woman who is not married. I think I dwelled on it far more than I ever was aware consciously.

When did you begin swimming again?
It was several weeks after returning to work. I started off slowly and built back up to my mile in a very short time. In September, I went to Rancho La Puerta, a fitness farm out in Mexico, and I climbed mountains and did everything. I would say that by the end of the summer, I was 100 percent well.

So there were no setbacks in your recovery from surgery?
No. Except, what did happen to me—and the surgery, I think, had some bearing on it—was I had symptoms of going into

change. I started to suffer from depression even though I had my ovaries. Apparently, they weren't acting like they were supposed to. So I went on Premarin about a year after the surgery, and I've been on it ever since. My mother has osteoporosis, and estrogen is supposed to be very good for that.

Did your doctor determine that your ovaries were not functioning?

No. One of the reasons I got depressed, according to the doctor, is that even though the ovaries were functioning, the hormone balance was off. I've had some problems with Premarin—the dosages had to be changed several times—but basically I've felt great on the estrogen. I've felt like a million dollars since the surgery was done and I was on my feet again. I was back into everything I was doing much more quickly than I thought I would be, and I have more energy than before. The experience in the hospital gave me a greater appreciation of the people I have around me. It also made me realize that I could allow somebody to do something for me. It made me closer to my mother. So it was all a very warm and wonderful experience in the end. And I can live with the fact that I'm not having children.

"I WOULD ADVISE YOU TO BECOME A PARTNER IN YOUR OWN CASE AND APPROACH IT AS YOU WOULD ANY JOB. AS A TELEVISION PRODUCER, YOUR PHILOSOPHY IS: PREPARE FOR THE WORST AND HOPE FOR THE BEST."

A fifty-year-old television producer who had a hysterectomy three years before, at age forty-seven, because of fibroids. After resisting surgery for years, she had a remarkably pain-free experience, which she attributes to having had the surgery in California. A professional problem solver, she ran her operation as though it were a prime-time show.

When did you first realize you had a problem?

Six years before the surgery, I began to have very heavy bleeding during my normal, four-day period; gradually, the number of days increased. I was frantically busy at this time in my life. I was producing a television show that took me all over the world, and though the bleeding was an extreme inconvenience, I was never anywhere long enough to deal with it. And every time I would get ready to do something about it, the bleeding would become regular. So I just let it go. At one point I got tested for anemia because I was exhausted, but I was told nothing was wrong. I went on the Pritikin diet—essentially, it's low cholesterol, high carbohydrate, high fiber—and that did increase my energy level. I started to feel better, and the bleeding seemed to lessen.

Then it began again, really excessively. My doctor in New York gave me a D&C and said, "Let's keep an eye on it," and that was that. The next time I had a bad time, I was in Los Angeles. A doctor there gave me a shot of progesterone to stop the bleeding. It worked, but she said, "We really should check you out." Because of my work schedule, I didn't get back until several months later when she and I both felt that the continued bleeding was due to the IUD I was using. I'd had it much too long—eight or nine years—so we removed it, and that seemed to help for a few months. Ten months later I had another IUD put in, a more modern kind, but the bleeding started again, so again I had it taken out. I now had no IUD and the bleeding continued, appearing and disappearing.

When did the question of surgery arise?
Well, finally, in New York, I was verging on hemorrhaging, and I had a sonogram. The sonogram revealed that there was an enlargement of the uterus caused by multiple fibroids, one particularly large and several smaller. My New York doctor suggested we remove the fibroids.

Now, my orientation is to avoid surgery at all costs. At one time I was a documentary filmmaker and I spent a lot of time in hospitals, and the more involved you are in the hospital structure, the less eager you are to make yourself a part of it. Also, the mythology around hysterectomy is that it is a very painful procedure; that it will take six months before you get to feel like yourself again. I was producing a prime-time television show—there was simply no way I could take six months out of my life. I am single, I live up three flights of stairs, the logistics of getting someone to take care of me—it was simply more than I could deal with. I thought maybe I could make it to menopause, and the problem would go away. I asked if I was endangering my life by leaving the fibroids in, and I asked if there was a chance they would shrink. The doctor said, "Of course there's a chance they will shrink, but I don't think they will. And no, at this point, you're not endangering your life."

Did you take that as a license to ignore the fibroids?
No, I used alternative medicine to try to shrink the fibroids. I tried acupuncture and moxibation, which is a more intense form of acupuncture treatment using heat and herbs. And I kept up with the Pritikin diet. But I started developing classic premenstrual syndrome: I would have mood swings and a lot of difficulty sleeping. And between the bleeding, and the awareness that the fibroids were there, and the PMS symptoms, so much of my psychic life was involved with my period that it was really beginning to wear me down. And the bleeding was bringing me to the point of being severely anemic. I finally realized that I was either going to have to change my life and my career or deal with the problem of having the fibroids removed.

With a doctor on each coast, how did you decide where to have the surgery?
That was my first problem—logistics. In my experience, the East Coast is much more traditional and they want to do more radical surgery. The prevailing theory is, "Well, you're forty-seven years old, you're not going to have children, so as long as we're going in, let's do a complete hysterectomy." My New York doctor was willing to leave the ovaries if there was no reason to take them out. But I suspected there was a greater chance of my getting a complete hysterectomy in New York. I really didn't want to go through hormonal changes just because something might happen a few years down the line.

On the West Coast, my doctor, whom I like enormously, was not connected with a hospital that I felt was the most up-to-date in the treatment of cancer. And ultimately my real fear was: What if they open me up and find cancer? As a television producer, your philosophy is, "Hope for the best but prepare for the worst."

So this left me shopping around for a new doctor. I had pretty much decided to go to California, and a friend who had a hysterectomy in Los Angeles—who was back to normal inside of ten weeks—recommended that I see her doctor, who was an oncologist.

I flew out to California, and because I travel so much, I always carry duplicates of all my medical records—all the tests, all the sonograms. It's a procedure I strongly recommend—you just ask your doctor's office for copies. I also recommend keeping your first sonograms or X-rays that indicate fibroids: they might be useful to people evaluating your case later.

I was very impressed by the doctor. He felt that for a woman who was as physically active as I have been my whole life, the surgery wasn't going to be a big deal, that in six weeks I should be completely fine. He believes that you remove surgically only what is diseased and said that if, opening me up, he felt that one ovary should be removed and the other seemed healthy, he would leave the one. So here I found someone I liked, who assured me it was going to be no big deal.

How soon did you have the surgery?
Once the decision was made, I did not want to have a long wait where I'd go through anxiety. He said, "We can get you into the hospital in a few days." It so happened that I had inadvertently chosen the week that began on Passover and ended on Easter Sunday. And that was a very smart thing to do—a lot of female surgery is optional, and a lot of women chose not to go into the hospital at that time.

I went in, and it was a very loving, supportive environment. All the rooms are private. Mine was like a hotel room—with carpeting, a nice view, a little shower.

All the time this is going on, the doctor's nurse is a valuable ally. She wishes to be of help to you. She's very familiar with all the procedures, and you can call her up with all the questions you have that might seem too silly to bother the doctor with or that you think of when you're home. One thing she suggested was that even though I didn't have to register until 2 P.M. everyone tends to wait until the last minute to be admitted and it tends to get backed up. She suggested I go early.

How was the night before surgery?
During the testing, it was determined that there was some sort of irregularity in my heartbeat. So my doctor arranged for me to see a cardiologist immediately, who tested me on the spot and found that the irregularity is the kind of thing that many people show under stress, nothing to delay surgery.

The law in California is that the surgeon has to discuss the procedure with you in detail and tell you each thing that might go wrong and what he would do to correct it. So he came in and explained things like how the rectum might tear. That's easy— all they do is stitch it up. You have to sign a paper saying they can give you a complete hysterectomy if they find cancer. That made me nervous because so many people I know who went in for a partial hysterectomy ended up with a complete one. So I reiterated, "You must promise not to take out more than is diseased." He assured me that it is not his policy ever to do that.

That evening I had a very light supper and was allowed no liquids after 8 P.M. I had an enema, which was the single most uncomfortable thing in the entire surgery and postoperation situation. The anesthesiologist wanted me to take some sort of sleeping medication, saying that most people don't sleep well the night before surgery. I didn't want it, and didn't take it. I was tired out, calm, and I felt good, everything was under control. I felt I had done my job real well, that I had made a good choice of doctor, and I was relieved for the first time in years.

What do you remember of the morning of surgery?
I must have slept nine hours, and when they woke me, they told me I was going in for surgery at ten o'clock instead of twelve, which was wonderful. They give you a shot to calm you down, a combination of Vistaril [a tranquilizer] and Demerol [a strong painkiller]. I woke up in the post-op room and was back in my room at two in the afternoon. I had asked a girlfriend to be there to call my family—they live in the East—and tell them I was fine, because I thought, Why put them through a few extra hours of anxiety, waiting until I was lucid enough to call?

Within a half hour my doctor visited me and told me that everything had gone according to the book. The reason, however, that I'd been having such heavy bleeding was not due to the fibroids at all, but to endometriosis, which he found during surgery. It had never shown up in the sonogram or hysterogram. The cardiologist popped in to tell me that he had monitored the surgery and there were no problems. I was still pretty stupid from the anesthesia, and they told me I'd be on liquids until the next morning.

How was the pain?
I had no pain. In the first hours after surgery, they automatically give you painkillers. The first night, mostly you're tired—your body has been assaulted. I thought, How nice that my friend is here, but my God, I have to be entertaining when I just want to be left alone. How not to be rude was a big consideration, I remember. That night they gave me a Percodan to sleep, and I was on IV through the night. I remember nurses peeking in to see how I was doing, but I had a very good night's sleep.

What do you remember of the first day?
The hospital's philosophy is that you should return to normal activity as quickly as you feel able. In the morning, they want you on your feet right away. I felt no pain, but I was afraid of what might happen—even though this doctor tells you it's going to be real easy, you still have old wives' tales haunting you as to how bad it's going to be.

Well, I put my feet on the floor and walked, with the IV, the full length of the hall. I couldn't take big steps, but I still felt no pain. I was constantly encouraged by this medical system that said, "Do whatever you feel like doing." Obviously you're not supposed to lift a suitcase, but you're not going to feel like lifting a suitcase. I took a Demerol, which is very mild, and stayed completely awake. I felt great, watched TV, and just before noon, they said if I felt like it, I could have solid foods. I said fine. Now we're still only twenty-four hours away from surgery. I said, "I feel like taking a shower," and they said fine. They told me to cover the abdomen to keep the incision dry, so I used a towel. By now I'm off the IV, walking by myself, though very slowly—mostly out of fear of what might happen, and also because you can't swing your legs a lot.

I got back into bed, and they asked if I would like the next Demerol. I thought, This is silly, I'll wait till I feel the pain. I never took any more painkillers except for that night, when I took one more Demerol because I was afraid of not being able to sleep on my back. I slept through the night. By Thursday—surgery was on Tuesday—I was absolutely back to normal. I went for walks three times a day, and I was astounded at never feeling bad.

When did you go home?
I got out of the hospital on Monday morning, six days after surgery. I expected to get a whole list of prohibitions—what to do, what not to do. I was told not to drive a car because you don't know if you're going to get a spasm or something; I was told to eat what I want and do as much as I felt like doing. I said, "Can I walk up stairs?" and they said, "If you feel like it."

I was staying in a hotel that's all on the ground floor, and I could get room service whenever I wanted and not bother any of my friends. That first afternoon a friend picked me up in a car. We went for a half-hour walk in a shopping center, sat through a movie, and had supper. I came home and was tired enough to go right to bed. At one point when I was walking, I felt kind of a

twinge. So I called my doctor's nurse and asked, "Does that mean
I should stop, or should I walk through it?" She said, "Did it feel
like a real pain or as though you had injured yourself?" And I
said, "Absolutely not." She said, "Then just walk through it."
That alleviated my fears.

From then on, I did as much or as little as I felt like. I stayed
one week at the hotel as opposed to the three I'd planned, realiz-
ing that I could take care of myself completely. I moved to a
friend's apartment and lived a cautious normal life. I tired more
quickly than I normally do, but I never had pain and I felt normal,
not like a sick person. I listened to my body: when I was tired, I
rested; when I felt great, I went out. I think the thing to do is to
psych yourself into feeling normal and behave as if you are. If
you don't feel normal, behave the way you feel. Don't *not* do stuff
because of what might happen to you.

Two weeks after the surgery I went for a checkup. He said
everything was terrific. I said, "I can't believe it. I've been scared
about this for seven years. Am I unusual? Why was this so easy?"
He said, "Well, I don't want to take anything away from you, but
you are our typical patient." He took out the stitches. This was
the only surprise I had: there were little lumps along the incision.
That had made me really nervous, but they're part of the normal
healing process. It was the only thing I had not thought to ask
anyone, and no one had thought to tell me about. I also asked
him if I could go back to New York, but he said they don't like
their patients to fly until the stitches are completely healed—just
in case, I guess, there's some sudden turbulence that might
cause you to pull the incision.

Are you glad you had the surgery?
I felt healthier six weeks after my surgery than during the entire
five years before surgery. Two months after surgery, I resumed a
completely active, normal life. If I had known that surgery
wasn't going to be an ordeal, I probably would have had it sooner.
One of the reasons that I am not only willing but anxious to
participate in this book is to let people know that if you are
healthy and active, it should be easy for you. I think you should
take care of yourself before going into surgery: spend two months
sort of cleansing your system, eating right—doctors won't tell you
that because most doctors don't relate diet to health, but I do.
And I would advise you to become a partner in your own case and
approach it as you would any job that you were doing: get enough

information in order to be able to do the job well. Prepare for the
worst, and hope and know the best is going to happen.

"RELAX. IF YOU HAVE FAITH IN YOUR DOCTOR, RELAX.
IF YOU DON'T HAVE FAITH IN YOUR DOCTOR, SWITCH."
*A vigorous seventy-three-year-old woman who underwent a
complete hysterectomy—a former doctor's assistant who is
knowledgeable about hospital procedure as well as the best
kind of medical insurance.*

What made you realize you had a problem?
It started with the fact that I went to my doctor because, after
spending a lifetime trying to gain five pounds, I suddenly gained
seven, and for the first time in my life I had a belly and could fit
into only three garments. He sent me over for a sonogram, which
showed some sort of a growth. So I went back to my old gynecologist. He actually could feel something when he did the vaginal
examination. It was a seventeen-centimeter teratoma [one kind
of ovarian cyst] which had invaded the ovaries and uterus, hence
the need for a hysterectomy, which was done with a nine-inch
incision. And no problems.
*And you had no symptoms other than the weight gain? No
pain?*
No! None.
What about emotional symptoms?
None, I was premed in college and ran a doctor's office for many
years, and I know a great deal more about medicine than the
average person. So I tend not to get very emotional about surgery,
as long as they tell me in advance what they're going to do. The
only thing I did stipulate on the consent form was that I refused
to have a colostomy if they found that the intestines were involved. I wrote that in—"No colostomy permitted"—and initialed
it.
Did you go for a second opinion?
My doctor is the head of the department of the hospital, and I
consider him probably the best gynecologist in New York. That
was enough for me.
What kind of hospital arrangements did you make?
I always take a private room—I despise anybody near me when I

don't feel well. I took food in with me, knowing hospital food: sandwiches and butter and salt because they never give me enough of either. And I made arrangements for friends to keep bringing me food. I was in the hospital for precisely two weeks. The only complication was that at one point my hematocrit [a blood test to detect anemia—42 percent is an average reading for a woman] dropped to a ridiculous number, 28.5. They insisted that I have transfusions, and at one point in the night the needle came out, and I rang the bell. Do you know what a floater is? It's a nurse who comes in only over weekends. She came in, and I said, "This thing's pulled out." And she inspected it and said, no, it wasn't. Well, later, at three o'clock in the morning, some nurses came through with flashlights to check on me. And I was right, of course. The needle had disconnected, and I was lying in a pool of blood. Then they insisted that I had to have a hematocrit taken again on Sunday. I said, "I'm going home Sunday no matter what it shows. I'm fine." My internist happens to be my ex-boss, and the gynecologist knows me very well, too, and they know when I say I'm going home, I'm going home.

When they got the hematocrit report, my internist called me at home and said it was even lower than before. I said, "They're crazy. You can send Allied to check." Allied Chemical is a lab outfit that comes to the house. They sent this young girl up to take blood, and the owner of Allied called my internist and said, in so many words, "Are you crazy? We ran the test through twice —her hematocrit rate is 47.5!" That's very high for a woman. The point is, they had mixed my blood with somebody else's down in the hospital lab.

But I had no problems whatsoever, and still haven't. And I received excellent care from the hospital staff—except for that floater.

Did you have private nurses?
Yes, for three days, because I don't have the world's best lungs [she has smoked for all her adult life] so they had to put a breathing tube in. I also was catheterized. I had private nurses until they could get that tube out of my lungs, because I couldn't drink water and my mouth was parched so they were swabbing it with ice.

Did you have somebody to look after you when you came home?
No. My maid came in twice a week as usual. I was perfectly able

to get up and do my own cooking. I did my shopping by telephone or had somebody bring food in.

When did you feel you were back to normal in terms of energy and comfort?

Maybe about a week later. I have the world's greatest recuperative powers, which they tell me is due to the fact that I have always known how to relax. Which saves me a great deal of grief.

What would you advise someone going through surgery like this?

Relax. If you have faith in your doctor, relax. If you don't have faith in your doctor, switch.

How do you know if the faith is deserved?

Well, I always have the heads of departments of a major New York City hospital, and anybody who is the head of a department that big has to be good.

And I would also tell women to make very damn sure that they have medical insurance that is noncancelable for life. Most of them suddenly find themselves, at sixty-five, with no major medical, and now they can't get it because sixty-four is the deadline. And no one can afford hospital care. So I carry a great deal of insurance. I have AARP, the American Association of Retired Persons, which pays part of the nursing and so much per day in cash. And I carry a major medical, Equitable, which happens to be one of the ones that still pays for the difference in a private room. Equitable is the only one I know of, by the way, that is noncancelable for life.

What do you think makes a good patient—not one a doctor likes necessarily, but one to whom a doctor gives the best medical care?

Knowledge, first of all. Doctors want to know that the patient knows what she's talking about. They want to know that she's not an hysteric. That she is not a hypochondriac. They'll give her short shrift if she is. They'll simply discount practically anything she says. But if they know you're not a complainer, and that you know something about medicine, they pay attention. I mean, I'm not talking about *liking* you; I'm talking about listening to you.

A lot of women might think that the important thing is to be liked.

No, the important thing is to be taken seriously. And when they hand you a consent form, which of course they must for any procedure that can possibly endanger you, you are supposed to know what you're signing. And you not only have to consent for surgery, by the way, but for certain special procedures where there's a heavy dosage of radiation or anything of that sort.

What can you tell us about the consent form?
Learn how to read medicalese. If you don't understand the terminology, then for heaven's sake ask the doctor: What is the danger? What is the normal recovery period? Ask any questions that occur to you.

A friend of mind just came home from the hospital today. She had a lumpectomy. When the mammogram showed this growth, and they didn't know if it was cancerous or not, she told the doctor, "I will not have a mastectomy." And that's the way she signed it. And it was encapsulated—the cancer hasn't spread. They removed this very small growth, and a little of the tissue around it, and she's home and can do anything she feels up to doing.

As a matter of fact, you can elect not to have surgery at all. If a doctor recommends surgery, you can refuse it. You have a choice—you have a number of choices.

"PHYSICALLY, I FIND SEX VERY DIFFERENT SINCE THE SURGERY. MY DESIRE IS THERE, OUR RELATIONSHIP IS THERE, BUT SEX ISN'T AS GREAT AS IT USED TO BE."

A psychologist in her early fifties who had a complete hysterectomy in 1978, when she was forty-five. She is married and has grown children.

What was the reason for your surgery?
I had a fibroid tumor that suddenly became enormous. It grew to the size of a grapefruit or a four-month fetus. I could feel it. I started bleeding when we were on vacation in Martinique, and when I came home I went to my internist right away.

What did you decide to do?
My internist said I should get right over to the gynecologist, who said, "You have to remove this," and immediately arranged for a hospital bed. I wasn't concerned about the hysterectomy per se. I had my children, and I didn't feel this would be a devastation.

I didn't ask him any questions at the time, because I was so shocked at the suddenness of it. And there's a tremendous amount of cancer in my family—it's pervasive in the female line on my mother's side—and you live with the shadow. So I had no qualms about having the tumor out. You react to things like that very differently. It's sort of like, what's the bottom line—"Am I going to live, or am I going to die?" I was cool and calm with the doctor, but that night, when my husband came home, I told him and just burst into tears. It was all the tension of bleeding on the trip, rushing to the doctor. And I was suddenly, absolutely, hysterically anxious about the anesthesia. I was sure I wouldn't wake up from the operation. But somehow I got myself a little together.

Did you have an opportunity to ask the gynecologist about the upcoming surgery?

Yes, though my gynecologist is the kind you write articles about —condescending, patronizing. But he's also very, very good. The most important thing is that I trust his medical judgment, and I can live with all the rest. I had questions, but I didn't know how to ask him, so I called a friend of mine and she was wonderful. She told me all the things to ask: What kind of incision is he planning to do? Will it be a total or partial hysterectomy? I wouldn't have known to ask about that. And he told me everything. When it came to the question of the ovaries, he said, "I think we should remove them. They're silent organs and it's really dangerous to leave them for no reason. If there's any problem, like an ovarian cancer, it's generally found too late." Now, he happened to be saying this at a time when one of my closest friends was dying of exactly that. So I said, "Fine. Absolutely."

Was there any history of fibroids in your family?

My mother had had small fibroids when she was in her forties, but she never had surgery. When one doctor told my mother she had to have a hysterectomy, she went to another one, and when he also said she needed one, she went to a third. And he said forget it. That's the one she listened to, and she never needed it. She had a D&C, went through regular menopause, and that was it. But I had no choice.

Would you talk about being in the hospital?

My husband took me to lunch at the Carlyle, and then we went in for the preregistration—the blood tests and EKG and all that. Then we went up to the room and drank wine together, until cutoff time, when I couldn't take any more liquids or food.

They came in and did all the prep, the enema, and they shaved me. Also, I remember a resident coming in and asking if he could do an internal. I told him he had no right to do that. You don't have to allow anyone but your doctor to examine you. I also know that in a teaching hospital that's how residents learn, but it's not a requirement for you; it's your option.

The next day I had my surgery at two o'clock in the afternoon, so I was out of it that evening. I had private nurses for about twenty-four hours. They got me out of bed immediately. And I walked bent over like a little osteoparalytic. After three days, they stopped giving me all the painkillers, and I felt the pain.

Did you regain your strength quickly?

No! I couldn't believe it. I was tired. I didn't know that abdominal surgery could do that to you—it's such a trauma, an assault. For a few weeks it's very slow, and then you quickly feel better. After eight weeks, I was doing everything and I wasn't tired at all.

What were the aftereffects of having your ovaries removed?

I realized, intellectually, that complete hysterectomy meant instant menopause. But no one—not my friends, not my doctor—told me what it would mean. I don't know if my decision would have been different if I'd known.

Here's what happens. I'm fifty-three now. My body is like that of a woman of sixty, who had an ordinary menopause. It's shocking to me. It's the worst thing that's happened to me.

I look in the mirror. From the neck down I look like my mother. What happened to this body? It got flabby. You lose muscle tone. I have strength. I'm an exerciser. It doesn't matter. You get the pot belly that women get in their sixties. I never had a stomach. No matter what I eat now, I put weight on, and I can't get it off because the hormones aren't there. I mean, to lose five pounds can take a month instead of the week it used to take. And I really have no choice. I wouldn't take hormones, and my gynecologist wouldn't offer it, knowing my family history.

This all happened about four years after the surgery. My vaginal lining became so dry that I had to go back to the gynecologist. It just gets worse if you don't do something about it, because the lining gets thinner and thinner and thinner. He gave me a cream with minimal hormone content. It lubricates the vaginal tract and is absorbed by the body. And I also use plain, old-fashioned Vaseline.

I think it's a myth when people say sex is as great as ever after a hysterectomy. I don't know if it's our ages—my husband is seven years older than I am—but there's nothing great about getting older, including sex. Physically, I find it's very different since the surgery. My desire is there, our relationship is there, but sex isn't as great as it used to be. So the result is, you're not as crazy about it. We led a very active sex life, too. We've been monogamous for many years. It was important to us, and we enjoyed it.

"YOU DON'T HAVE TO DO WHAT THE DOCTOR SAYS RIGHT AWAY. YOU CAN SAY, 'LET ME THINK ABOUT IT, AND I'LL CALL YOU TOMORROW.'"

A package designer, specializing in cosmetics, who had a hysterectomy and oophorectomy in 1983 when she was forty-three.

When did this begin for you?
In 1972, when I was thirty-two, I had a myomectomy. My doctor said the fibroids might or might not grow back, but more than likely, they would. And I was happy with that. I was healthy, and I would go to the gynecologist every six months. And he'd say yes, they were growing back, but there was no need to take them out. Then, in 1982, I had excessive bleeding with my period. One day I thought I was really dying. I had no pain, but gobs and gobs of blood were coming out of me—so much so that I took one with me to the doctor. I was really white—this was definitely death. And the gynecologist said this is what happens when the fibroids get larger. They had grown to the point where they were dangerous and had to come out. And I was prepared for that.

What scared me was that in the last operation, they had strapped me onto the table before giving me the sodium pentothal. Since then I had developed acute claustrophobia. My doctor was wonderful. I discussed my fears with him, and he said, "I'll make sure they don't strap you in, I'll make sure you're comfortable."

Did you discuss whether or not he would remove your ovaries?
He suggested that I wasn't going to bear any children—at the time, I was forty-three. I conferred with my internist, and he also

suggested that both the ovaries and uterus come out. There could be a recurrence of fibroids if I left the uterus, and I could contract cancer of the ovaries. I definitely loved and trusted my internist, and he felt very strongly about it. I also felt, Who needs another operation?

Then there was the discussion of hormones—what I would have to take, and that if I was going to take estrogen, there were very few risks.

Were there any changes in hospital procedures since your last surgery?

They had a much better preregistration this time. Now you can have all the tests a day or two before you go in. You don't have to wait for the tests to clear so when you check in you can almost go right up to your room. The other advantage is that the day you go in for surgery, the hospital isn't strange to you. And this time, I knew what information I had to give the anesthesiologist and why. And I wasn't surprised by being shaved, though I've since learned that you can ask not to be shaved until you're under anesthesia.

What information did you have to give the anesthesiologist?

If I was allergic to any drugs—if I'd had any reactions to any drugs.

What did you do after checking in?

You go upstairs and, it's funny, because even if it's the middle of the day you take your clothes off and put on your nightgown or whatever robe they provide. And they just check you all over again, which makes you feel like you're sick. There are no flowers in the room yet. You're waiting. You're also arranging for private nurses if you want them. I ordered nurses for three days—nine eight-hour shifts—which my major medical paid for (it was $130 for each shift).

Why did you feel it was necessary to have private nurses?

I'm just spoiled that way. I really just wanted somebody by my side to get me whatever I needed whenever I wanted it, especially at night.

What do you remember about the morning of surgery?

They wheel you in on a gurney and put a paper shower cap on your head, which is not so attractive, but by that time I was woozy enough not to worry about anything. In the OR they didn't strap me in because, as promised, my doctor was there. You wake up in the recovery room. There was a girl right next to me who was very sick. I remember hearing lots of crying and whining. I remember the nurses calling my name, trying to wake me up. They just want to make sure you're alive, I guess. You go right back to sleep, and they wheel you back to your room. And you're on an IV.

Do you feel the IV?

No, you're just exhausted. I probably slept for hours. And when I woke up, my parents were there. You're not in pain, you're just pretty uncomfortable. All these bandages are on your stomach and you've got this IV. I remember it was very difficult for me to turn over. Not because of the IV—it's in your wrist and has a long leash; it's just very uncomfortable.

How much painkiller did they give you?

A lot. I just kept asking for injections. I didn't want the pain at all.

Can you describe the recovery process?

I could walk slowly by the next day, but I developed a bladder infection, and that made me very uncomfortable. Once that cleared up—it took two days at least—I felt better. I think I felt worse the second night. Some of the anesthesia was wearing off. You're more conscious of what just happened. They've asked you to move around. After the second night, it started to get progressively better. By the third or fourth day, you're walking up and down the hall, you're eating. I talked on the phone. I always talk on the phone.

Once you get home, that's when you really feel it. I couldn't bend over or lift anything. You know how you go into the kitchen and you pull something out of the refrigerator and put it in the oven? You can't even do that. The second week you can get around a little better, but you don't feel like it. So for two weeks you need someone to at least bring breakfast to you, start your day, someone to leave lunch and dinner out for you. And I needed someone there to wash my hair, because I couldn't take a shower. I had a housekeeper come in more often, a few times a week, and I arranged for someone else to come in when she couldn't make it. I know that most people cannot afford to do this, but I considered it the most important thing for me. I think indulging yourself for that two- or three-week period as much as you can makes for better health, too. I think that you recuperate better—you alleviate all of the stress.

I would say it took six months for me to heal enough so I could walk and move and exercise normally after the hysterectomy. My recovery time was abnormally long, I think, because of a subsequent discovery that I had a punctured bladder. I am not sure that the punctured bladder was due to the hysterectomy. It certainly could have been; and other people say they've heard of other organs being punctured during a hysterectomy operation. But since I only discovered the problem six months after the operation, there was no way to prove that the two were related. It's about two years since the hysterectomy, and a year since the repair operation, and it is only now that I feel I want to resume my social life. The hysterectomy, along with the leakage that was due to the puncture in my bladder, made me feel very unfeminine. They had cauterized my urethra because of the leakage, before they knew what it was. Sometimes, after a hysterectomy, you can lose control of the vaginal sphincter muscle.*

Were you on drugs for pain at home?
No, I had some pain that was centralized in my stomach area—your stomach is swollen, and you're still very full of fluid—but you don't need painkillers. There's the discomfort of the healing process—a knitting, an itching and pulling. You have to clean the incision, you know. You do that with peroxide, dabbing very lightly.

What kind of incision did you have?
Horizontal. He just went right over the myomectomy incision.

Did you start taking hormones while you were in the hospital?
No, it was a few weeks after. The doctor was saying, "Wait and see." He wanted to know how my body was reacting so he could decide how many milligrams of hormones to give me. And I remember getting hot flashes, not knowing what they were. About the third week, when I was home, it was really very debilitating. I was up at night, I was perspiring—it's everything they say it is. The flash only lasts two minutes or something, but it's the coming-up of them that's uncomfortable. You just want to take your clothes off. And for a person who had claustrophobia . . . I re-

---

* According to *Understanding Your Body*, the bladder muscles, after hysterectomy, may not be strong enough to contract. The weakness usually lasts only a few days.

member thinking, If I get one of these in an elevator, I'm a real goner.

After the first or second post-op examination, he put me on hormones. I take maybe six milligrams of estrogen once a day for three weeks, and progesterone once a day along with the estrogen, and then progesterone alone for the fourth week.

Are you aware of any changes in yourself related to the hormones?

No, though I'm not happy about being on the hormones. Sometimes I feel bloated. I've been concerned that I might gain a few pounds, but I've been able to maintain my weight; I just watch what I eat. And because I don't get my period, I don't get my premenstrual crazies.

What would you advise a woman considering this kind of surgery?

Learn medical terminology—I always found that doctors would use terms that meant nothing to me. And learn more about your body. I found that I knew very little about what was where. At the age of thirty-two—where *were* my ovaries, what *is* my uterus? And later—where *is* my bladder; why did this puncture happen—is my bladder that close to my vagina? I mean, I was so ignorant!

Another piece of advice is that you don't have to do what they say right away. You can say, "Let me think about it, and I'll call you tomorrow or I'll come back next week."

What about the emotional effects of the surgery?

Until the hysterectomy, I never had the feeling that I wanted to give birth. After, I realized I didn't have a choice anymore. I didn't really worry about that, but it was hard for me to say that I was going to have a hysterectomy: it had very negative connotations—that you're old, that you aren't going to be a woman anymore, that you aren't sensual and sexual anymore—you're dried up.

And after the surgery, I was so debilitated, between the hysterectomy and the bladder leakage, that I never came back to feeling wonderful. As far as my sexuality goes, I felt just horrible—it was because of the punctured bladder, but I didn't know that. To be honest with you, from the hysterectomy on, I just canceled my social life. I didn't feel sensual at all, or feminine. That's just coming back now.

"DOCTORS RESPOND TO PATIENTS' DEMANDS—DOCTORS
KNOW WHERE THEIR BREAD IS BUTTERED."

*Karen Blanchard, M.D., is a Los Angeles gynecologist who
had a complete hysterectomy when she was thirty-eight,
fourteen months before we interviewed her as both a patient and a physician. She started the Women's Medical
Group in 1977, now a five-doctor practice: four women who
do general OB/GYN, one "very profeminist" man who specializes in infertility and endocrinology, and one nurse-
practitioner. Dr. Blanchard, who completed her medical
training at Johns Hopkins University, is assistant clinical
professor at UCLA and on the staff of UCLA, St. John's, and
Santa Monica hospitals in California.*

*Let's begin with your own surgery. Why did you need a
hysterectomy?*
I had endometriosis and I had fibroid tumors—a little of everything. I'd had heavy bleeding and irregular bleeding and pelvic
pain for about three years.
Who is your gynecologist?
One of my partners. Well, actually, two of my partners were there
to do the surgery.
Obviously you didn't have to go for a second opinion.
No, we were fairly certain about what was happening and what
the options were to take care of it.
*Do you think that your experience as a doctor made a
difference in how you faced this surgery? Was it your
first?*
I'd had rather minor things done before. A tonsillectomy when I
was nineteen, and arthroscopic surgery on my knee. But I think
that being a surgeon myself made me more concerned about the
anesthesia than about the surgery. I was sure that the surgery
would be fine, but I was very nervous about the anesthesia. So I
chose to be awake for the surgery. I had an epidural anesthesia,
which I felt was wonderful.
Did you choose your anesthesiologist?
Yes, I chose one who wasn't a very close friend of mine but who
thought that an epidural would be okay and was very skilled at

doing it. It's a different kind of anesthetic procedure, and some very good anesthesiologists are just not skilled at doing it.

With an epidural, you're awake during the surgery. Could you see what was going on?

I couldn't really see it, no—there are drapes, and you're lying down—but I knew what was happening.

Did going through the surgery confirm anything you suspected as a surgeon?

I don't know that I learned anything about what happens to the patient in the operating room—there was nothing very unexpected about that. But I was surprised about things that happened outside the operating room. I went to give blood for myself several weeks before the surgery, in case transfusion would be necessary, and I was sort of appalled at the way patients were treated in the laboratory. It was kind of an unpleasant experience. And on the day of the surgery, they started my IV four times before they got one in me—and I have huge veins. But that, maybe, was nervousness on the nurse's part, because she did know me.

How long was the surgery?

The surgery itself was only about an hour and a half, and I was in the operating room about two hours.

And how long were you in the hospital?

Three days. I wanted to get home. I think it was okay to leave that early, but I probably did go back to work too quickly. I scheduled myself away from work for one month. But considering that I work eighty to a hundred hours a week, I don't think that four weeks was really adequate. For several months after the surgery, I was more tired than I expected. I'd say I felt absolutely back to normal three to four months after the surgery. I would probably have recovered quicker if I'd given myself a little more time to recover: two months would have been more sensible.

Were you in much pain from the surgery?

Surprisingly little. And I had an abdominal hysterectomy—it's much less painful if one has it done through the vagina.

Is that often possible?

Yes, especially if one has had children. Even quite large fibroids can be taken out through the vagina—I'd say up to a three-month gestation size.

Does that take a particularly skilled doctor?
Well, yes, the vaginal approach to surgery does require a higher
level of skill than the abdominal.
*In New York, the vaginal hysterectomy isn't offered
frequently as far as we know. Is it common on the West
Coast?*
It's actually the central United States where the vaginal hyster-
ectomy is more often performed, but I would think that at least
in any large city, there'll be skilled vaginal surgeons.
So that's another surgical option for a woman.
Right, given that we're talking about benign disease. Hysterectomies for cancer are usually not done through the vagina.
*You had your ovaries removed. Is that common practice
when a woman is in her late thirties?*
I'd say that gynecologists in general are taught to remove wom-
en's ovaries at the time of hysterectomy if the woman is past her
childbearing years. The justification is that ovarian cancer is a
devastating disease and very difficult to diagnose.

On the other hand, removing the ovaries is not without complications, too—the woman will need to take estrogen replacement therapy (ERT). These days, however, we feel that women
should take ERT when their ovaries stop working, too. So most
women who are in good health are probably going to experience
ERT at some time in their life. Experiencing it a few years
earlier because the ovaries are removed isn't that much of an
issue.

But my own personal opinion as a gynecologist is that women
need to understand those choices and that there really is no reason to remove ovaries except for diseases that involve the ovaries. Endometriosis, unfortunately, is one of the diseases that
attack the ovaries even after the uterus is removed. Even if the
ovaries look normal at the time of the procedure, the endometriosis is probably already on them. Most people would like to avoid
another surgery. I certainly did.
Are you on ERT?
Yes.
How is it administered?
I take pills. It can be taken in shots, and there's even a new type
of ERT available now using a patch—the hormone is absorbed
through the skin.

We call it estrogen replacement therapy, but it's actually estrogen and progesterone: both of the ovarian hormones need to be given to all women.

Do you feel that most gynecologists know enough about hormonal therapy, or should a woman consult an endocrinologist?

I think the awareness is certainly increasing among gynecologists. Now that we have excellent means of estrogen and progesterone replacement therapy available for postmenopausal women, and there's such a high benefit-risk ratio, gynecologists are getting more and better experience in using ERT. I'd like to see internists and family practitioners learn a lot more about it, too, because there's a tremendous amount of misconception in the medical community.

With the exception of women who have had active breast cancer in the past five years, every woman should take estrogen replacement therapy once she needs it. A lot of people disagree with me on this. Feminists say menopause is a natural process. Fine. Death is a natural process. Appendicitis is a natural process. You want to go back to the natural process? Living without ovarian hormones is appropriate in a society where women die in their mid-forties. It doesn't make any sense in a world where women are going to live forty or fifty years beyond menopause. Osteoporosis, stroke, heart attacks—these things are significantly reduced with appropriate ERT. Osteoporosis can be done away with, essentially, by ERT.

Some women who've had hysterectomies say there's now less sense of an explosion during orgasm. Did you experience that?

I can't tell the difference in sexual satisfaction since having the hysterectomy. I would say, though, that there was certainly less sexual interest on my part for maybe six months.

Do you think that had to do with the removal of the ovaries?

I'm certainly not wise enough to answer that question. Perhaps in my situation it was because I was still recovering.

In your medical practice, what is the major cause of hysterectomies?

Probably complicated fibroids that are either causing pressure or pain or bleeding problems. That's the most common cause. Weakening of the pelvic floor would come very close after that—

where the uterus is prolapsed [sinking down into the vaginal canal], and one is trying to reconstruct the pelvic floor to reestablish a good bladder base and separation of the vagina from the rectum. Removal of the uterus is part of the reconstructive surgery. This is more common in postmenopausal women—you rarely see it in a woman prior to her menopause. And I'd say endometriosis is probably third on the list. Although we have good nonsurgical treatment these days for endometriosis, we still have treatment failures and people who prefer surgical therapy to hormonal manipulation.

Are there people who really prefer surgery?

Yes, and again, that's very individual. There are people who have had hormonal therapy, who have had children, and the endometriosis comes back: it's really more appropriate to use surgery in a situation like this.

How do most doctors learn to perform this surgery? Is it during their residency?

Everyone finishing gynecological residency would be skilled enough to do a hysterectomy. So yes, they all learn to do it in residency.

Women are surprised—and disturbed—to find out that a resident has performed the surgery on them while their doctor stood by.

I would say that, in general, they're probably getting very good care that way. There are some surgeons who are very skilled at doing a hysterectomy after doing six, and others who could do six hundred and never be good.

On fibroids: There's been a lot written about the contributions of diet to both cause and cure. Do you think there's any connection?

There's a lot of that sort of thinking in California. I've seen people who have fibroids try every type of dietary intervention from a yearlong protein fast to megavitamin therapy—and I have never seen any benefit. As to preventing fibroids from starting, there may be a dietary link, but there's certainly nothing that suggests it in the medical literature. I hear acupuncturists and chiropractors say they can cure fibroids, but again, I've never seen anybody get any benefit from them. That's been my experience. So I think that fibroids are an area in tremendous need for research. I'm sure that within a few decades we'll look back on this time when we were treating them with surgery and think us very barbaric.

But we really have no other mode of treatment that looks good at present.

One woman told us she had a fibroid the size of a pear,
went on a strict macrobiotic diet, and within a year's time
the fibroid was gone.

I'd like to see the documentation—really, I'd love to. Because as I say, I've seen it tried by at least half a dozen of my patients. Mind you, I always encourage women to try it. Because diet is reversible. The surgery isn't.

Is there a fibroid size that makes surgery mandatory?

No, there's no magic size, in my opinion. Fibroids can do significant damage just by being large. They can obstruct the ureters—the tubes that go from the kidneys into the bladder—and can actually make someone uremic: shut down their kidneys totally, cause high blood pressure and some very severe problems. So size alone is an issue, but one needs to investigate whether the only problem is that they're big. The question is, is their bigness causing any problems?

Many women with large fibroids are scared into surgery by
the doctor's raising the possibility that the tumors might
really be cancer. This seems cruel. Is the fear justified?

There's always the question, How did this fibroid get to be this big? Are we missing an underlying malignancy? I mean, every obstetrician/gynecologist has a story of some woman who was watched for fibroids for several years, and when she was operated on, she had no fibroids, but she did have cancer.

So that makes one worried about a mass that grows big: is it really a fibroid, or are we missing something? I had to admit I had a moment of anxiety at the time of my surgery that maybe we'd been wrong all this time and it really was cancer, not a benign process. You know, it was just a thought, but it's human that we as patients have those feelings. Well, doctors, as doctors, have those human feelings, too. That fear—"Well, maybe I'm not doing everything that I should be doing for this woman. Maybe I'm wrong and this is not really a fibroid."

One of the most brilliant professors that I ever knew, a world-renowned gynecologist, had followed a patient for several years. He happened to be away on vacation when this woman developed a problem and was operated on by another gynecologist, who found no fibroid tumors at all but ovarian cancer that had been going for some time. And that is the best gynecologist, the very best. For those of us who are not the best in the world, and who recognize that we have human failings, this kind of thing is frightening.

Does a fibroid ever become cancerous?

Well, there is a malignant tumor that develops in the same place that fibroids do, that often mimics exactly what a fibroid feels like and in fact looks very much like a fibroid under the microscope. That kind of tumor is called a sarcoma or a leiomyosarcoma. It's actually very rare. But does a fibroid itself ever become cancerous? Probably not.

But a doctor might fear that a fibroid is actually a leiomyosarcoma?

Yes, especially if it had grown very quickly.

Does size have any bearing on the difficulty of surgery?

If you're going to do an abdominal hysterectomy, size isn't an issue, but if you're going to try to take out the fibroids and repair the uterus, and come out with a good, functioning uterus, it is a real issue. And it is if you're going to try to take the fibroids out through the vagina. Occasionally, I do a hysterectomy for size only: we have fibroids that have grown to the point where they are as big as I can get them out through the vagina. And I tell the woman, "Well, we're coming to a milestone. At their present size I have maybe a 95 percent chance of getting them out through the vagina. If they get much bigger, neither I nor anybody else is going to be able to get them out vaginally. That's not a decision that we ought to do a hysterectomy; but it's a piece of information that you ought to have in order to make the decision for yourself."

Is the decision between a horizontal or vertical incision a matter of size?

For benign disease, I'd never do a vertical incision. The horizontal—the bikini incision, as it's called—is just so much stronger and less complicated. It's actually two incisions that cross. One goes straight across, through the fascia [a thin layer of connective tissue covering the muscles]. Under the fascia, the muscles and the peritoneum [membrane lining the abdominal cavity] are opened vertically in the midline. So there are two crossing incisions. There's no way you can herniate that; it will last all your life. An up-and-down incision frequently will develop hernias.

What exactly is going on when people speak of a fibroid "rotting" or "degenerating"?

It generally means that the fibroid has grown so quickly that it's outgrown its blood supply; it's not being nourished adequately and will liquefy. Or a fibroid can twist on its pedicle [stem], cutting off its own blood supply and becoming gangrenous. If that occurs, it is very painful and needs immediate surgery.

Is a transfusion often needed during a myomectomy?
Rarely, although more commonly than during a hysterectomy.

Why is endometriosis so hard to diagnose?
It's very tiny. There are no characteristic symptoms. It's in a very hidden place, very difficult to get to. It doesn't show up on ultrasound. The only way to diagnose it, at present, is with a laparoscopy.

Is it true that having children early in your life protects you from endometriosis?
Well, having children early does protect you, but that's kind of a judgmental issue. You can wind up with endometriosis at forty, or you can wind up with children when you're twenty-two. And one wonders which way your life would have been more difficult or productive, or more in tune with your needs and your society and the time that you live in. Women need to protect their ability to get an education, to be able to have skills that are salable, because these days no one is assured of a husband who will stay with you for the rest of your life. And if you're going to have children, you're going to have to be sure that you can support them if something happens to your husband. So you're really caught in a double bind. On the one hand, you need to have twenty years of education behind you, and on the other hand you need to have your children early. Women can't win.

There's a lot written now in the popular press indicating that women who have very active sex lives with different partners are more prone to cervical cancer. Is that real information or another judgmental issue?
No, it's real information. Cervical cancer is venereally related. Having intercourse at an early age and multiple sexual partners —those are very real correlates. Prostitutes almost always get cervical cancer; nuns never do. Cervical cancer is in part a viral disease, and there are perhaps other environmental factors that come into play. That's the way it is. Sex is getting a bad name. The movement away from barrier methods of contraception is very unfortunate in terms of spreading venereal disease. The birth control pill is a wonderful thing—thank God we have it.

However, it leaves both sexual partners totally open to transmission of venereal diseases. We used to think of someone who had three sexual partners as maybe very liberated; now, someone may have three hundred.

We're just beginning to see some of the effects of what's been happening sexually. I tell my adolescent patients especially that a package of condoms is just as important as a package of birth control pills. I say, "If you're going to have sex with somebody you don't know, *assume* that they have a venereal disease."

Is it more difficult to operate on a fat person than on a skinny person?

Yes, very much more difficult. And the risks in the procedure are much higher, from complications in anesthesia as well as postoperative. There's more necrosis in the womb—more likelihood of a womb infection. There's usually poor aeration in the lungs and a greater likelihood of infections occurring in the lungs afterwards. There's more likelihood of bleeding problems. It's technically a much more difficult situation.

So if someone is fit and doesn't smoke . . .

She's going to recover faster—that's just a fact.

A few women have talked about the difference in recovery between West Coast and East Coast practices. Do you see any difference?

Yes, I think there are stylistic differences. I think we in California are, as a group, much more preventive-health oriented, maybe personally as well as professionally. And we tend to believe in the body's healing powers a little more. We push people to get out and be themselves again very quickly. We do that with our birth practices, too. And that may be helpful for some people and not helpful for others. I'm not suggesting that our way is superior but that there are different styles. I think East Coast medicine is traditionally more conservative, and I think it's a wonderful tradition. West Coast medicine has been much more affected by quackery and paramedical things.

We deal with different kinds of populations, too. People on the West Coast demand different things from doctors—and doctors respond to patients' demands. Doctors know where their bread is buttered.

What's the best way to find a good doctor or a solid second opinion?

I tend to think that patient referrals are probably the best, say

from a friend who has an established relationship with a gynecologist, including, perhaps, a surgery. Or go to the nearest university and see a professor: they're probably up on what's going
on. Call your local hospital and ask to speak to labor and delivery,
or the recovery room, and ask the nurse on duty who she would
go to if she was going to have surgery. Nurses very rarely give
people bad information; they really know what doctors are like.

What's your definition of the ideal patient?

Somebody who comes prepared to take responsibility for herself,
for all the decisions made and for the treatment format. And she
expects that the doctor expects her to make those decisions.
Never, ever let any doctor make any decisions for you. If the
doctor wants to make decisions for you, you've got the wrong
doctor. That's my opinion. As a doctor, it's my responsibility to
educate, to supply more information where it can be helpful in
the patient's decision-making process. But it is not my decision,
is it? The patient is more than part of the decision-making process; she is the process. I'm the outside element. The whole concept that doctors are supposed to take care of people is a really
bad concept: doctors are supposed to provide services and help
people to take care of themselves.

The ideal patient collects information so that what she tells you
is really the most important thing you're going to find out, a lot
more important than what you'll find on an examination. (By the
way, never go to a doctor who only examines you and doesn't talk
to you—because he'll not get enough information.) She's been
watching her body and she knows what her body is like and
what's happening. If the doctor suggests something that she
doesn't understand, she'll ask the doctor, "Do you have something that I could read about that?" If the doctor doesn't, she'll
go to the library. I honestly think that most doctors don't mean to
be mysterious. They just don't realize that the words they're
using are not appropriate to the person they're talking to. The
fact that they're not communicating doesn't get through to them.

That's the kind of patient I like—somebody who is responsible
and who demands the kind of care that she wants.

"EVERYONE ASSUMES THAT WHEN YOU SAY, 'I DON'T
WANT A HYSTERECTOMY,' IT'S BECAUSE YOU WANT A

KID. IT HAD NOTHING TO DO WITH WANTING A KID! IT
HAD TO DO WITH DEFINING MYSELF AS A SEXUAL
BEING.''

*An actress in her early forties, married, with no children.
She first underwent a myomectomy in 1983, followed by a
complete hysterectomy in 1985 that launched her into a
very difficult menopause.*

How did you discover you had a problem?
I had been going to a doctor for almost ten years. And all those
years, I'd have regular six-month checkups. In October 1982,
during my last checkup, he asked if I was pregnant. He said the
womb looked as if it were three months into pregnancy. I knew I
wasn't, but I didn't focus on what the problem might be. Yet
something in my brain said, "Change doctors. It's time to change
doctors." I started asking around, and in March 1983 I found this
great doctor with this terrific reputation. A real fancy guy, Fifth
Avenue address and all that stuff. I walked into his office only to
discover I had a fibroid tumor that was bigger than a grapefruit.
The thing was, I always had this sort of tenderness on one side,
but no one had ever noticed this growth. Being the type of woman
I am, I was in a mad fury. I went back to my old gynecologist's
office, demanding all my files. The nurse said she couldn't release
them. But I said, "Either you give them to me, or I'm going to get
a lawyer to call them in." So she handed them over.
What was your second doctor's recommendation?
He said, "Look, we'll leave it alone for now." He said that fibroids
do only one of two things. They start bleeding or start hurting.
Well, no sooner did he say that than I started bleeding. It was
just massive bleeding—I couldn't get from the bed to the bathroom. So I called him up and said, "Let's do this, and let's do it
right away." Part of what happened then, when I finally went in
for surgery, was my own fault. He wanted to give me a partial
hysterectomy, but somehow I was under the impression he was
talking about a myomectomy.
What kind of surgery did you have?
I had a myomectomy. The night before the surgery, this little
intern came in and demanded I sign a federal form permitting a
hysterectomy. I said, "I'm not having a hysterectomy." He said,
"Well, if you don't sign this, they'll cancel your surgery." I said,
"Are you threatening me?" He looked at me and said, "No, I

wouldn't call it a threat." I said, "Would you sign a piece of paper
that would allow someone to cut off your penis or your testicles?"
He said, "I don't think this is comparable." I said, "You may not,
but I do." I said, "Why don't you leave here before you upset me
further." And I wouldn't sign the paper.

By eleven o'clock that night, I was freaked! My gynecologist
showed up, and because he could tell I was upset, he said he
would do a myomectomy. If he had just taken the time to explain
a partial hysterectomy, and how I could keep my ovaries, perhaps
I would have acquiesced. Instead, he placated me by saying,
"Oh, no, no. You don't have to have a complete hysterectomy.
You don't even have to have a partial hysterectomy—we can take
just the fibroids." I think he interpreted my *not* wanting a hysterectomy as *wanting* a kid. He didn't understand that I just didn't
want to be missing any action. Everyone assumes that when you
say, "I don't want a hysterectomy," it's because you want a kid.
It had nothing to do with wanting a kid! It had to do with defining
myself as a sexual being. Anyway, everyone calmed me down—
my doctor and my best friend, Barbara, an RN who flew in from
California to take care of me. But I never signed the form. He
had no choice except to do a myomectomy. I tied his hands. I did
a foolish thing.

How did the surgery go?

The operation took an incredibly long time. I was in surgery for
eight hours. It was because I was bleeding profusely. There was
a string of fibroids. And, since I hadn't signed the form, the doctor
could not use his judgment to take my uterus and try to save my
ovaries as he originally wanted to do. I was a waif when I got out.
I was very weak. I couldn't get up for over a day. But because I
am the way I am, by the next afternoon I was figuring out a way
to get off the bed. I knew that the longer I was immobile, the
bigger trouble I was going to be in. Barbara was an enormous
help to me. And I was out of the hospital in six days. But back
home I couldn't walk. I was really clobbered.

Considering how much you were bleeding before the
surgery, you must have felt much better after.

I was coming along fine. It was summertime and I was recovering and feeling pretty good. My husband and I went on vacation,
and while we were gone, my gynecologist suddenly died. So that
was the end of my gynecologist.

I muddled around and finally went to a colleague of his. A nice guy. A young guy. And everything was fine, and I was getting checkups regularly.

One day, I'm being examined and he says to me, "There's something peculiar in here, and I want you to go have a sonogram." My heart just sank to my feet. My breath was gone. I said, "What's wrong?" He said, "Nothing. I just want to make sure." So I went to get a sonogram. And I was slowly moving into a nervous panic because these people hovered over me while I was on the table. And they kept doing the test over and over and over. And I said, "Look, guys, either tell me what's going on or get out of here!"

They said there was an "indiscrete tumor," which cracked me up. It meant that the tumor had no edges. A CAT scan then showed that my ovary was completely enmeshed in this tumor. The doctor tells me on the phone that this is a tumor that is almost never cancerous. I say, "Fine," but the only thing I'm hoping is that I won't need a hysterectomy. I'm hysterical. Because I know in my heart of hearts that that's what is going to happen, whether I want it or not.

What did the mass turn out to be?

Everyone—my internist, the head of ovarian cancer at the hospital, and my gynecologist—had a different opinion. Nobody knew what kind of tumor I had. And I sat with them in an office, crying and trying to be calm at the same time. I said, "Can't this wait for a while? Can't we just sort of fuss it out a little more?" My internist says, "Well, this could be life-endangering." I say, "But I thought this was the kind of tumor that in a woman of my age is very rarely cancerous." The cancer specialist, who is a very orderly man, said, "Yes, but you don't want to take that kind of chance." He went on to say that if they could just see the ovary or feel it, they wouldn't worry so much. He said, "Don't you understand? The tumor has engulfed the ovary. If it is cancer, you could be in big trouble."

And so I went home and I cried some more. But here's what happened. My body made a great big announcement: I was getting my period every two weeks, and I was sure there was some connection between the bleeding and what was wrong with me. There was. It turned out I had an endometrial tumor. I had endometriosis, not cancer.

Did you go in for surgery immediately?

So fast that I'm not even scheduled for this operation. I'm taken into the hospital and it's done! This time it was a hysterectomy. There was no question about it. I signed the form. I was willing to settle for a piece of an ovary. I'm going into the operating room, crying my eyes out, saying, "Please leave me something." I didn't want to get thrown into menopause.

I had endometriosis, according to my doctor, that had wrapped itself around everything. It was entwined in my intestines. It had shoved up underneath my stomach.

After the surgery, the doctor told me one of the ovaries had looked okay in the beginning and they were planning to save it. The other was completely gone. The uterus was just laden with endometrial fabric. They removed it all—that's why this surgery, too, took so long. He said, "Then, by the time we got back to the first ovary, and looked at it closely, we saw endometrial cells growing on it. Once that starts, you cannot stop it." He said, "We tried. We really honestly tried." I cried.

How long did you spend in the hospital?

I was there a week. And again, I pushed to get out, because hospitals get me very depressed.

Did you begin hormone treatments right away?

A couple of days after my internist informed me I didn't have cancer, he came in and I said to him, "Do I have to take estrogen?" He said, "Of course you do." I said, "What do you mean, of course I do?" He said, "Well, otherwise you're going to get wrinkled." His insensitivity made me furious. I wouldn't speak to him for four days, and I won't go back to him.

I was concerned about what I would have to take for maintenance. And for how much time. And what kind of cancer it could give me, potentially. That was my major concern. Then I went home for a week in Connecticut to recuperate. Of course it wasn't recuperation at all, because there were too many things going on. I went into serious cold sweats and hot flashes and the whole thing. That starts when you're in the hospital.

I called up my surgeon and he started me on estrogen and Provera. Provera is a cleansing hormone, so you don't get a buildup of estrogen. Well, unfortunately, in my body, forget it! I was an emotional rag. I was snapping at people. And I blew up— I looked like an elephant. The hormones sit in the tissues and the body retains water—at least in my tissue it does.* Some women take hormones and there's no problem.

So, again I call up the cancer doctor. We had all kinds of conversations, but he's a cancer specialist, and he's not going to worry about my levels of hormones. I went to see him once and explained I was having all the highs and lows I used to get with my period when I was in my twenties. He said, "That's what this medication we're giving you is supposed to prevent." I said, "It's not preventing anything. I've never been so overemotional."

Christmas came, and I woke up on Christmas day and thought, This is it, no more. And I warned my husband: "I have no idea how I'm going to react. I don't know if I'm going to go crazy on you. I don't know if I'm going to try to kill you in my sleep. But we are going to have to retain a sense of humor about this." I stopped the hormones, and I haven't taken anything since. I can't believe what they tell us women. If I spend the next ten years looking like a plumped-up turkey and not having any wrinkles, am I going to get breast cancer or any other form of cancer that the estrogen may bring on? They don't know! That's a simple fact. All we know for sure is that I need a lot of calcium.

Now I feel good, although I'm seriously overweight. I'm hitting 150 pounds and for me that's no joke, because I'm only five feet three inches. I don't think the weight is caused by estrogen or the lack of it. I just think it's my thing and I'm probably sort of using it as a slight excuse. I'm nearing the one-year mark without hormones. I have aches and pains, but I think they're just related to getting to my mid-forties.

Have you noticed any other changes since stopping the hormones?

Well, I am about to go to an endocrinologist. The reason is that the one thing I can assure anybody who reads this is that one's libido quietly and slowly disappears. And it's very disconcerting. I have always been a very sexual person. Sex doesn't even cross my mind now. Also, at night—but only at night—I feel very hot.

But everyone has commented on how calm I am. I've always been classified as slightly hyper. I'm not slow now, but I am calm.

---

* According to Lila Nachtigall, M.D., in her book, *Estrogen*, the weight gain may also be caused by "estrogen's tendency to encourage fat tissue, just as the male hormones encourage muscle tissue." [p. 185]

Can you describe hot flashes?

It feels like you're a torch. And sometimes you get cold sweats, too. It's a combination of events. You just get so uncomfortable. You get very warm. Then you get drained of color. There's a little bit of nausea, but you don't throw up, and you get damp. And you feel pretty terrible. Then you calm down.

If it happens at dinner, it's a bore. Sometimes I think it's correlated to drinking wine. I can drink white wine, but when I go near red wine, my body temperature seems to rise. I want to walk outside. And sometimes I do, and I'll come back and sit down and I'm just fine.

What advice would you give women considering a hysterectomy?

Don't ever, ever, let a doctor talk you into doing anything until you can gather all the facts. I believe in waiting. If it hadn't been for the bleeding, I would have put off the second surgery. Because now, just a year after the hysterectomy, they have a drug, Danazol, that puts a woman into menopause and shrinks the endometriosis. New things are always being developed.

Did your friends help you through this?

If there was anyone who was supportive, it was my husband. All he wanted was to make sure that I was alive and well.

I couldn't tell anybody else. It was embarrassing. It makes you feel terribly inadequate. Someone at a dinner party, who knew I had been in the hospital, said, "Did you have a hysterectomy?" I couldn't speak! I don't know why I feel this way. I have only just been able to talk about it the last two months.

I think it has a lot to do with lack of sexual interest. You come away from something like this thinking you're not a woman anymore, and why would anybody want to have a sexual relationship with you? Your body has been carved up to pieces. You've got scars going every which way. You've gained weight. Your whole self-image goes right out the window. You're not going to get any help by going back to the doctor. He's done what he considered his duty—he's saved your life.

But I know that there has been a cessation in my life of certain things, mentally and physically. My next-door neighbor, who is fifty-three years old, has had cancer. She had ovarian radiation: what happens is that your ovaries shrivel and become useless. She said to me, "Sex hurts because the vagina atrophies." I'm just starting to get to that part of it, because the estrogen kept the tissues pumped up.

FOLLOW-UP: About two weeks after our interview, she consulted an endocrinologist. "He gave me Premarin in a cream form that I could apply to the vaginal tissues to help correct the dryness, with no side effects. He said I also might reconsider using Premarin and Provera again sometime even though I had problems with them because I was in the risk group for osteoporosis. But for the present he recommended diet and exercise to get my weight down to between 135 and 140. He raised my calcium intake to 1500 milligrams and said three Tums was the cheapest form. For the hot flashes at night, he prescribed Periactin, which he described as an antihistamine that cuts down flushing in about half the women using it. The only side effect, he said, is sleepiness."

HYSTERECTOMY FOR CANCER

"THE ONLY CHANGE, SINCE THE SURGERY, IS THE FEELING THAT I HAVEN'T GOT FOREVER ON THIS PLANET. AND THAT'S A GIFT. BECAUSE IT'S THE TRUTH."

A forty-five-year-old psychotherapist, diagnosed as having carcinoma in situ, Class IV, had a complete hysterectomy at age forty-three; divorced mother of a fourteen-year-old daughter.

How did you discover you had a problem?
I went in for a routine six-month Pap smear, and then my doctor's office called me and said something's wrong. He wanted me to have a D&C, in the hospital, and after that, he called me to say, "We have what we call Class IV cells." I asked a doctor friend to explain what that is—he said it's like precancer—and then I had a few other consultations with other doctors.

I was pretty terrified, but my doctor said, "People come in here and it's as though there's a fire going through the room and I can't put it out. You have a fire in the corner, and I could put it out with a teakettle—it's not so bad." I really listened to him and said to myself: This is not life-threatening.

How did you decide what to do next?

There was a big debate about whether or not I should have a hysterectomy.

My gynecologist felt that since I was past childbearing age, I should have a hysterectomy. Another doctor said I would be okay with a cone biopsy, which would mean removing the top of my cervix and leaving the rest intact. And a third doctor, who was pretty upsetting, said, "I think you have Class V cells—cancer that calls for a radical hysterectomy."

Those are three totally different answers. How did you
choose between them?

I was really very confused. With the cone biopsy, there would be a 5 percent chance of the cancer recurring, and I thought that was too much. I couldn't live with that kind of worry. I wanted to get it over with.

And I thought the doctor recommending the radical hysterectomy was off the wall. I thought, This guy is a hotshot—he's got a busy practice, he's written a couple of books, and he's a little bit of a performer. I didn't take him seriously. He said, "Take out your ovaries—you don't need them." I was angry with him. These doctors are fast and loose with your organs. I said to myself, How would they feel if they came into my office and I said, "Well, we're going to have to cut one of your balls off"?

But I had a lot of confidence in my gynecologist, and I had done a lot of reading, talking about it, educating myself. I had the feeling that I wanted to turn myself into a doctor so I could do it myself—I wanted control over it. I had no control, of course, but I did everything I could to think about it well and make a decision that I felt comfortable with. I decided on a complete hysterectomy, and I never regretted it.

My doctor couldn't do the operation himself because he was too old. That upset me a lot. He had a younger man do it, and he assisted. I went to see this doctor, who's a really nice guy—funny, in his fifties—and I found myself attracted to him. I have a feeling that under other circumstances, I wouldn't have been attracted to him that much. But I think I figured that if there were some sort of sexual bond between us, I could rest assured that he'd take good care of me.

What hospital arrangements did you make?
I didn't want a private room because I have to have people around me. I did have private nurses, for two days. The doctor said that I should, and I'm glad I did. Especially the first day. You're like a lump of salmon. There you are, flat on your bed. If you have to roll over, the nurses roll you over; if you have to roll back, they roll you back. They were wonderful. For me, it's very important when I'm stressed to be with women who are warm. And I had my friends, too. There was someone to go with me to the hospital, and I knew I would be taken care of when I got home—I have a lot of friends who, I knew, would be helpful to me.

I think when somebody gets sick it gives other people the opportunity to express a lot of feelings toward them. I got a lot of help and support from my friends. I think that's why I was able to go through this as easily as I did. You almost need mothering in a high-stress situation like this where your body has been affected.

How was the admissions process?
During the physical they found something wrong with my heart. I became hysterical. They repeated the test the next day, and the problem was in the machine. But that upset me, and I was also scared about the anesthesia. I threw myself into a kind of sociability to cover up. I made great friends with the woman in the next bed.

Another problem I had was that, as a recovering alcoholic, I really have to stay away from sedatives as much as possible. The night before, they wanted to give me a sleeping pill. I said, "I'll take it, but I'll try not to take too much else." That's a problem people with an addiction face when they're going to go into surgery—how to handle the medication: Will I start to want the painkillers afterward? And with alcoholics, you have to give them more anesthesia to put them out. So you have to tell the anesthesiologist that you're an alcoholic. [See interview with anesthesiologist Marilyn Kritchman, M.D., page 249.]

The next day I had a cone biopsy—it's a very short procedure, I felt no pain—to see if there were Class V cells, which there weren't. If there were, I would have had chemotherapy.

I stayed in the hospital over the weekend to have the hysterectomy, first thing, on Monday.

Were you in pain when you woke up?

Yes . . . I don't know. Maybe for a day I had a hard time. I maybe didn't take as much medication as they were trying to give me—I was trying to limit that. I was on Demerol, and I tried to take myself off as soon as possible—maybe day three. But in the beginning, you know, you just think maybe you're never going to be all right again. I remember one day my aunt came, and she just sat there and held my hand for about two hours. That was so comforting. What helped me, too, was that I had chosen a terrific nurse. I'm very influenced by the people around me: if I have a good person, who's there for me, it makes my experience much better. This nurse would tell me all about her boyfriends, and I'd lie there giving her little whimpering pieces of advice.

And so it passed. I think it's important for people who feel the way I do to know you really need support. It's hard to impose on people, but don't try to be king of the mountain or Amazon lady.

I think you have to break down the process of recovery—whether it's physical or emotional—into little pieces so you have little successes. The third day they came to me and said, "You have to get out of bed." And they put my feet on the ground and there I was, standing up. I thought I would never stand up again. I kind of hobbled out to the hall and walked to the window, and it was very exciting to me. I made little plans for myself. The next day, I could walk down the hall and I turned the corner! There was a day room, and I used to hobble out there, and I'd sit in the sun and read, and that made me feel like a real person.

Going home . . .

I left on day six, really tired and frightened, disturbed by all the sounds of the city—it's like you can't take too much stimulation when you've had that much shock. So I stayed in my house. My roommate was very good—she got a lot of food and made a stew. A lot of people called, and I read, and I slept a lot. You're still an invalid the first week. That weekend, two guys came over to see me, and that was wonderful. The second week was the same thing—but I was getting restless and bored. The third week, after a checkup where my doctor said I was fine, I started to go out. I went out on a date—it was downtown where there are cobbled streets, and he kept losing his way and driving over the cobbles! I could feel every bump, and I kept saying, "Park the car, we'll walk!"

When did you feel you were back to normal?

In August, about three months later. I was with my daughter on the beach with a friend who was trying to stop smoking. She started to reach for my cigarettes—they were tucked in my bathing suit—and I took off down the beach, running and laughing hysterically. It was a gorgeous day, and all of a sudden—it was like a movie shot that froze into a still—I realized I'm okay.

Sex . . .

I was still nervous about sex. The doctor told me that most people are. I was developing some kind of fear about not being all right inside—it's not a rational fear, but I thought about things like what if they stitched me together, and the stitches don't hold? What if my insides are screwed up in some way—I won't be able to see it. There's an analyst who's written about female sexuality and the problems in feeling that the interior space is not knowable.

The other point is that the body is a metaphor for the soul. My analyst said that all the primitive feelings come out when you have surgery—the fear of abandonment, fear of engulfment, fear of attack. I think my fear that something was wrong inside was metaphorical as well as literal. I developed a little hypochondriasis after the surgery, jumping from something's wrong inside of me to something's wrong with my body. I saw a spot on my breast and got absolutely terrified that I was going to have skin cancer. It turned out to be nothing—I was just spooked a little bit.

One weekend, a good male friend came with me to Fire Island. I trusted him, and I went right to bed with him. Afterward, he laughed, "I think you're completely recovered!" It was the best thing I could have done under the circumstances.

About six or seven months after the operation, I had a wonderful affair with someone. I can remember worrying: What's he going to think about the scar? He didn't even know the scar was there. I have a bikini scar, and you can hardly see it.

That affair really helped me. The hysterectomy introduces you to middle age. You feel in some way you're damaged goods: you've been kind of tampered with; you're not okay. But he responded to me as if I were a normal, attractive person.

I think there's another fear—that you're not going to respond. And once I saw that that was not so, I never worried about it again.

Any emotional ramifications from the surgery?

The only emotional change is the feeling of transitoriness on this planet. The feeling that I haven't got forever. And, in a sense, that's a gift. Because I think it's the truth. And I might not have realized it if this hadn't happened. All these things that happen to you are not only tragedies—they're also opportunities.

"I THINK A LOT OF WOMEN DO NOT WANT TO DEAL WITH THE POSSIBILITY THAT THEIR FIBROIDS COULD BE MALIGNANT."

The promotion manager of a record company who has been happily married for twenty-five years and has two grown children. Five years before this interview she was scheduled for a routine hysterectomy for fibroids; the tumors turned out to be cancerous.

When did you first discover you had fibroids?
Let's see, it was in early 1980 or 1981. My doctor said, "The fibroids have gotten a little bigger." I said, "What do you mean? How long have we been watching these fibroids I don't know about?" It turned out he had first noticed them three years before and was keeping track of them. It wasn't really scary to me. My mother and her two sisters had fibroids and they all had hysterectomies because of them, so I knew about fibroids.

I have always been very good about medical care, so once I found out I had the tumors I went back for another checkup within less than a year. At that time the doctor noticed they had gotten even bigger, so we decided to do a sonogram. They had grown 18 to 20 percent in size. I would lie in bed and I could feel this lump in my uterus that felt as large as a grapefruit.

Was the fruit analogy yours or your doctor's?
It was mine, and the size really worried me. The doctor said, "You don't need to worry. The mass is big, but when you go through the change of life, the fibroids will decrease, so there's nothing to be concerned about." I was forty-three years old at the time. He kept saying that, and I went back to see him constantly. I wasn't feeling great, but I thought that it could have all been in my head. Nevertheless, it continued to bother me, so I had another sonogram a couple of months later. This time the radiologist called me into the office and closed the door. He said, "I am not supposed to tell you what I'm going to tell you. I am supposed to give

the results directly to your gynecologist. But I want to tell you that your fibroids are growing too fast, and I feel you should consider removing them."

But when I went back to see my gynecologist, he said, "There's no need to worry." I sort of put aside what the radiologist had said, but I did see other gynecologists, all of them top doctors—you know, the ones who are always written up. And they all said the same things: I didn't have a malignancy, not to worry; yes, they're big, not to worry. "Just watch and wait." Never, never, never did they say it might be malignant. I've got to tell you—I hate them all.

Did you ever go back to your original gynecologist?

Yes, somewhere toward the end of June 1983. He wasn't there, so I saw one of his assistants. And he says, "They're growing a lot, so I would suggest you have an IVP [a test to check urinary functioning] the next time you have a sonogram because the fibroids may be starting to block your kidneys and ureters." Then he asks me when I'm scheduled for my next sonogram. I said, "In September." "You can wait until September," he said. And I said, "No, listen, we'll do it now." And two days later I was having another sonogram, and my gynecologist called me to tell me that, in fact, the fibroids were beginning to block my ureters. I said, "Shall we do the hysterectomy?" He said, "Let's wait until I come back from my vacation in September." I said, "No. We'll do it the earliest date possible." That turned out to be August 25. I went on vacation because my brother, sister, and I were taking my mother to Europe for her seventieth birthday. I went into the hospital two days after I got back.

How did the surgery go?

A quick operation on a Monday. No big deal, like they said. Everything seemed fine, and I was recovering in the hospital. Then Wednesday night at six o'clock my husband walked in with my gynecologist by his side. The pathology report had come back, and, in fact, those fibroids were malignant.

How many fibroids did you have?

Half a dozen, maybe. I don't know. They were very large. It makes me *crazy* to think about this. My doctor kept trying to calm me, saying it was a very low level of malignancy, and I shouldn't worry. But meanwhile he was calling in cancer specialists. His best buddy, the head of gynecology and oncology at another major New York hospital, comes in and says, "We should move you down to my hospital and start you on chemotherapy right away." Now, I have not seen any other doctors who can confirm that, in fact, I have a low-level malignancy. I am supposed to take their word that the cancer has not spread beyond my uterus. I didn't know what to do. I hadn't read anything about it.

What did you do?

With tears running down my face and my husband supporting me, I said, "Let me get back on my feet first before I make a decision. I want to see someone at a cancer institution." Also, I have a *wonderful* internist who came to see me every night. And he arranged for me to see the head of gynecological oncology at another hospital.

Had the doctor removed your ovaries?

No. Just the uterus, because he diagnosed it as a situation calling for a routine hysterectomy. But I said to my gynecologist, "While you were in there why didn't you do a frozen section [a biopsy] on the fibroids?" He said to me, "We never do a frozen section on fibroids. It's unnecessary. They're never malignant!" After just telling me I have malignant fibroids, he's telling *me* that fibroids are never malignant! I couldn't believe it. I went to my house in the country to recover for three weeks. When I came back I went to the cancer hospital, and I think that was probably the most humiliating experience I ever had. Not that I'm an elitist, but you feel like you're just a number. It was totally impersonal. The senior in the department was interviewing me and sort of showing off for his resident. He said things like "I don't know if we should give you chemotherapy because the numbers are not really good on cancerous fibroids. In 50 percent of our patients cancer never returns, and in 50 percent there is a recurrence." But the truth of the matter is the sample is so small, there's nothing to base the 50-50 percentage on. I mean, is it 50 percent of two people? I didn't want any part of this hospital. I felt they weren't on my side. They didn't want for me what I wanted.

What did you want?

What I wanted was to be able to say, five or ten years down the road, that I had done everything that I could do. My husband wanted that for me, too. I had major thyroid surgery when I was a child, and surgery didn't frighten me. If I had to have more surgery or if I had to face chemotherapy—none of that really scared me.

Did you find a doctor you had confidence in?
Yes. And he was the total opposite of all these social doctors. He has a small office in the hospital even though he is the head of gynecological oncology of a major institution. He is an intellectual. He is very cool and very reserved. I didn't even have an appointment with him until I had another sonogram, and he didn't see me until he had another reading on my pathology report by *the* maven on sarcomas—my cancer is a form of sarcoma. He had the full picture when I saw him. And what he wanted for me was what I wanted for myself. By the way, it turned out that my original gynecologist had never filled out the proper post-op papers. He said only that the fibroids appeared to be normal, but the uterus looked "funny," whatever that means.

What did your specialist say about that?
He said, "Based on the look of the uterus and the growth pattern, I would have done a frozen section. You would have been asleep long enough for me to know how involved the other organs were. If I had had the full picture and all the organs looked clean and the frozen section showed irregularities, I probably would have monitored you before recommending chemotherapy. But since I did not have that luxury, I want to put you on chemotherapy for six or seven months." Then he said, "I want to follow that with a look-see, to see what's going on. And we will remove your ovaries —we don't want to chance ovarian cancer. I asked him, "Why don't we do it now?" He said, "No. We should get whatever if anything is there before I go in."

When did you begin your chemotherapy?
It started mid-September, about a month after my operation. I had a drug called Adriamycin. I went to the doctor's office every three weeks on a Thursday about four o'clock and took my treatment by intravenous. Then I would be off work on Friday and sick for a few days. I'd feel like a rag on Monday, but most of the time I made it back to work. All my hair fell out. Before I started chemo I had a beautiful wig made, and I did something my sister advised me to do. She suggested I have a nurse at home to give me Compazine by injection. It's really as good as you're going to get in terms of controlling the nausea and keeping you in a relaxed state. The doctors won't let you have it unless you have a nurse. I tried Compazine by pill, but it didn't work, and I also tried grass, which actually made the nausea worse. The nurse

used to go to the hospital with me while my husband waited in the car. She would usually stay two days. That was really an incredible period.

> *Weren't you recovering from the abdominal surgery while undergoing the chemo?*

Yes. But I healed very quickly. I didn't go back to work for six weeks after the hysterectomy, but I really could have gone back sooner.

> *How was the look-see surgery?*

It was terrifying. The anesthesiologist came in the night before the surgery. He said, "I want to take you through the procedure. Prior to the general anesthesia we're going to give you an epidural, and you'll feel great. We want you to wake up without pain and be comfortable." I said, "But I've read there's a possibility I could wake up with an intense headache." He said, "Yes." And I said, "Isn't it also possible that there could be partial or, if you fuck up, permanent paralysis?" He said, "Yes." I said, "I'll cope with the pain." And I made the choice not to have an epidural.

I also started seeing a special therapist who deals with very ill people who are facing chemotherapy and cancer, and I did a lot of visualization directed toward coming out of the operation clean. It was enormously helpful and a real stress reliever. I was terrified about being put to sleep again for this operation. I visualized the operation being over and everything being okay and my being awake. The doctor said he would not put me to sleep until he was in the operating room. I trusted him. He was a little late, so I was kept in the hallway. When he arrived they rolled me into the operating room. I said, "Gee, you look so slim in your scrubs. Now let's get going." He put me to sleep at around one o'clock. He removed my ovaries and kept me on the table for five hours while he did the look-see. He biopsied everything: my intestines, liver, kidneys, and whatever else is down there. And then I felt somebody holding my hand. I was still on the table, and I looked up at the clock. It was 5:15 and he said, "All the biopsies came back, and everything looks good."

Everything was clean, absolutely clean. And then I fell back asleep, and they took me to the recovery room. The doctor is a fabulous man—not fabulous-sweet, but a cool, thorough professional.

> *Why did he feel it was necessary to remove the ovaries?*

He believes that the hormones played a part in causing the cancer, but after he removed my ovaries he wanted me to go on estrogen replacement therapy. I said I was very reluctant to do that because I had heard it caused cancer. Now this is a very cautious man, and he said, "Let me tell you this. Number one, you don't have a uterus, so you can't get uterine cancer. We know ERT protects women against heart disease and it protects women against osteoporosis." And, second, he pointed out that breast cancer doesn't run in my family. Some studies are even saying that ERT protects your breasts against cancer, but he said the story on that is not really in. Finally, he thought I would be more comfortable on ERT because I'd gone into instant menopause. But I was too nervous about it to start it then. My mother fell and broke her hip because she has osteoporosis. The day she fell I started ERT—that was four years ago. And now we've changed my prescription a little because I had put on a lot of weight. He took me off the Provera, the synthetic progesterone that's supposed to protect you from uterine cancer. Another doctor in Florida at a spa I go to also said he saw no reason for me to be taking Provera. So with two doctors' opinions I've been on Premarin alone for a year and a half. I started an exercise program and lost all the weight I gained, and so far I'm feeling fine.

Among all the women we've interviewed, you're the only one whose "fibroids" were found to be malignant—the exception to the rule. Do you have any advice for women who are facing surgery for fibroids?

I think a lot of women do not want to deal with the possibility that their fibroids could be malignant, but mine were—so it can happen. I am a real advocate of getting out growths. Malignant or nonmalignant, I don't think growths should remain inside your body. But if you want children and the doctors are saying, "Watch the fibroids," then you watch them. You have sonograms and watch.

Where did you get the courage to keep questioning your doctor when he was so reluctant to perform surgery?

I'm not intimidated by doctors, but the truth is I was really motivated by an intense fear of dying. I will do anything to make my life as long as possible. I was willing to face chemotherapy if it would give me more life. I don't know if I have any more courage than other people, but I do know that if you can fight for yourself in an office to get a raise, if you can take on a boss, you can certainly face surgery. It's really no worse.

"I TELL EVERYONE GOING THROUGH THIS, 'BRING SOME-
ONE WITH YOU TO CHEMOTHERAPY.' I TELL THEM,
'DON'T TAKE ANY SHIT.' "

*A thirty-three-year-old owner of a small printing house who
was operated on for ovarian cancer when she was twenty-
eight. She started the conversation by explaining why she
agreed to be interviewed.*

I'm always willing to talk to anybody about this. There is so much
fear, and in an age where there's so much information about
everything, there's very little information about this. You never
find anyone who has the exact same experience, and the experience is never what you anticipate, medically or emotionally. And
you read in a thousand different places, "Don't be afraid to ask
your doctor as many questions . . ." but I think you *are* intimidated. Also, doctors don't tell you much. Although I really love
my surgeon, he told me nothing. Everything that I know I found
out from other people or from my own digging. He still tells me
nothing. It's outrageous!

*Let's start at the beginning. When did you first know
something was wrong?*

I've always been high-strung and always had lots of symptoms—
headaches, stomachaches. I always didn't feel well. But about a
year and a half before this happened, I started to have these . . .
all I can call them is gas attacks. The first time, I suddenly felt
terribly bloated, and my belly hurt. It lasted for two days, and it
was so bad I couldn't even ride in a car because the bumps just
killed me. But it went away, and I figured it was because I didn't
eat well. I was living on Tab and cigarettes—I was a smoker at
the time.

Then I started to have attacks more frequently. They would
come in the night and would always pass. But they started to get
so bad that I would have to leave the store, and I could barely
walk home. Finally I had a really bad attack. The pain was so
bad I went to my internist, who examined me and sent me for an
upper and lower GI series [X-rays of the gastrointestinal system].
She called me the day after and said, "I want you to go for a
sonogram." She was very cryptic and wouldn't tell me why. By
then I was scared.

I went up to this lab and had the sonogram. Everybody says the sonogram is nothing, but it was like torture to me. They fill you with water until you're ready to explode, and then they push this flat paddle on you and very slowly press it into you. It's one of these medical things that's like the marquis de Sade: they figure out what would be the most quirky thing to do and that's what they do.

Right after that, my doctor scheduled me to see a gynecologist. It's only fair to say I hadn't ever been to a gynecologist. I had internals when I went to my regular doctor, which was intermittently. Now, I would never not go on a regular basis, but then . . . For me, everything is BC and AC—before cancer and after cancer. And BC is very dim in my memory.

So my doctor sent me to this woman gynecologist in her building, who said, "Yup, that's what it is. You've got fibroid tumors the size of grapefruits and you have to have them out and there's no option and it's a snap." She was, of course, dead wrong. Thank God I didn't go with her.

Had she read the sonogram?

No. The reports were not ready yet. One thing I found out that's very interesting is that there are very few doctors who can read sonograms. What most of them read is the written report from whoever does the sonograms. One of the reasons I liked the guy I finally went with was that he could read them himself.

This woman then took out a picture book. On one page was an anatomical drawing of the internal woman, and facing it was a drawing of how you look after your organs are removed. Another page showed a really fat woman with hairs growing out of her chin. I don't remember what the operation was, but that's what stuck with me. It was unbelievable.

This was Friday. The doctor wanted to admit me on Sunday and do the operation on Monday. What I found out later was that on Tuesday she was going on vacation for two weeks. I was in such a state at that point that I said okay. Then, all weekend long, I brainstormed with my family about it. They said, "You can't rush into this. One step at a time. You've got to see somebody else."

On Monday I went back to my internist, and she said that I was lucky because if you have to have something wrong with you, fibroid tumors are the thing to have. Every surgeon in the world will fight to have you as a patient because the surgery makes them seem like gods: you've had this growth sapping your strength, and after, you feel so wonderful and give the doctor all the credit. She told me I was going to be in great shape, and what I had to do now was go shopping for a surgeon. And then she washed her hands of me completely. I think she called me once after that to see how I was.

How did you go shopping for a surgeon?

The worst thing was not knowing what I was looking for—it's more than just looking for somebody you can trust. And you have to subject yourself to the same thing over and over again. They're all doctors; they've all got that authoritarian thing. They run you around. You're sitting in offices. You're getting like a million internals. It's the pits.

Luckily, a friend of mine had a doctor she liked very much. She had an appointment with him the day I saw the internist, which I took—otherwise I never would have gotten to see this guy. He's an old man, in his seventies, a very vibrant man. And maybe because he is such an old guy and he's been around so long, he's got a very gentle way. None of these paper nightgowns. He has a woman who isn't a nurse whose job is just to be nice to you. And he's very paternal.

The interesting thing is when I started out, I wanted to know everything. By the time I had seen three doctors, and seen that book the first woman doctor showed me, all I wanted was somebody I liked to take care of it—because I realized I could not operate on myself, and I could not determine whether or not I should be operated on. I wasn't going to be able to figure it out. I was scared to death.

This man immediately treated me like I was his child, and at that point, that's all I wanted to be. I'm not really that kind of person, and I didn't really end up being that kind of patient. But there is a limit to what I want to know. I didn't realize at the time that, although he was an OB/GYN, he also had a specialty in cancer. I feel that my stars were in the right place. Anyway, I brought my sonogram with me.

Were you walking around with your sonogram?

Yes! I had to fight like hell to get it, but for some reason I knew it was important to have that in my possession. The other doctors I saw got really frustrated with me and said, "Where's the report?" which hadn't been written yet. They couldn't do anything without the report. And he didn't even ask for it—he could read the sonogram himself. One doctor had said it was a cyst, one that it was a fibroid. This doctor called it a mass. He then made me go have an IVP, where they shoot dye into your arm and take pictures. And then I had to have a barium enema, which was the thing I had feared the most. And it was nothing. Of all the tests I had, those two really didn't bother me at all. I can't say enough about the technicians—they were absolutely as pleasant and understanding and kind and efficient as they could possibly be.

Would you describe the IVP and barium enema?
It's so high-tech! The lab was all stainless steel, with incredible monitors and television graphics—it's like the twenty-first century. You're on this clean-as-a-whistle, made-out-of-kryptonite table.

Are you clothed?
You perpetually are wearing one of those robes with the back open. For the IVP, they give you a needle in a vein in your elbow —it's some kind of iodine (they want to know first if you're allergic to it), and you feel a burning sensation right under your skin. They have a big cameralike thing over the table, and they shoot pictures of you. It takes no more than fifteen or twenty minutes. And it's completely painless.

For the barium enema, you have to lie in different positions, holding the fluid in you while they take pictures. And that's that.

The conclusion was that they didn't know what the mass was, but I was booked into the hospital for surgery. And thanks to somebody intervening, I was able to get a bed only a week and a half later.

What kind of hospital arrangements did you make?
I wanted a private room, and I got one. And I ended up having a private nurse for two nights.

How did you feel, going into the hospital?
Strange as it sounds, I didn't feel nervous at all. First of all, the people were so lovely there. The nurses—as far as I'm concerned, there are no better people on earth. I've heard other stories, but without exception, the nurses were wonderful to me. Of course, I had my two partners, my sister, and my mother and father around almost all the time, so the nurses didn't have to do that much for me. Another reason they were so great to me, I think, was that I was about the same age as a lot of them. Everything conspired to get me this really wonderful, loving attention. What did freak me out was someone coming in the night before to read

me the consent form saying what they could do during surgery. But I had to sign it, so I did.

Also that night, I did a really stupid thing. The doctor had told me that I would be shaved partly. For some reason, I so much didn't want anybody else to do it that I did it. And I shaved my whole self. It was the biggest mistake! Because they just shave a little bit. And during that whole stay in the hospital, one of the most uncomfortable things was my hair growing back.

In the morning, they were so kind to me. That's what I remember more than anything. They came in and said, "They're calling for you upstairs." So gently. All these West Indian hospital workers—they're like sent from God or something, with that gentle patois they speak. On the way up, the elevator man talked to me. I was semiconscious from the tranquilizer they give you, but he kept saying, "Don't worry." Then, in the operating room, my doctor came over and held my face. . . . I had a great experience.

And after the surgery?

It was a much more complicated operation than they thought it would be. Much to everybody's shock, I had ovarian cancer, which is very unusual in someone my age. Where it's most often found, though this is changing, is in women in their fifties and sixties. It's generally got a very high mortality rate because the symptoms are so mild that it's usually not caught until it's in an advanced stage [it has spread from the site of origin to other parts of the body]. It's amazing they caught it in me in an early stage.

I had a big tumor on one ovary, and it had just begun to metastasize on the other. So they removed both ovaries, the uterus, the works.

Then they rinse you with saline solution. I don't know what that means; just the thought of it grosses me out. Apparently it's a very standard thing. And then they sew you up.

The doctor did not tell me about the cancer right away. He told my family, who then went into a huge fit that they were being asked to lie to me. But the doctor was right. When you're just coming out of something like that, you don't want to know from cancer.

Were you in much pain after the surgery?

I timed it so I wasn't in any pain. As soon as it was getting to be fifteen minutes before I was due for another painkiller, I'd start ringing, "Bring me the shot."

One thing that's inexcusable in hospitals is, whatever you're in for, they come every morning and take blood. Why? They don't know why. They don't need the blood. My arms were black and blue from their taking blood and from the IV (I had developed pneumonia from the anesthesia, and they were giving me something for it through the IV). I didn't realize until I was there about four or five days that I could refuse to have blood taken. All you have to do is say, "I don't want it," and they stop. So that was great, when I discovered that.

I also exploded when a resident couldn't get a needle in my vein. Have you ever had an IV? It doesn't hurt. It's amazing and wonderful. But after a while on IV, the vein will collapse, and the needle pops out. And this jerk couldn't get a needle in. He tried seven, eight times, and the vein would collapse, and he'd say, "Goddamnit!" He said, "What do you think this does for my ego?" At that point, I jumped out of bed and said, "You get out of my room!" and went down to the nurses' station and said, "Put it on my chart! Keep this man out of here." Three or four nurses came in and apologized; my doctor apologized.

I'm impressed that complaining had an impact.
This is one of my big points when I talk to anybody about hospitals. Unless you're in a place where the people are subhuman, you can complain. You should.

When were you told that the mass was cancer?
One morning, when I was really cognizant and getting around, the doctor came in. And in this most downplayed way, he says, "We found cancer, but we got it all. You're going to have a little bit of treatment, and you're going to be fine."

"Okay," I said. I mean—I was stunned. It was like suddenly looking down the wrong side of the telescope, as though he was in a building across the street.

Then the nurse immediately came for me and walked me back and forth in the hall.

A while later, a little resident, a young woman who was absolutely great, came in. I said, "Am I going to die?" She said, "I'll guarantee you this. If you die of anything in the next thirty years, it's not going to be of this. Don't worry."

On what basis was she reassuring you?
I don't know. She probably meant that for cancer in that stage— it was on the cusp between stage I and II—the treatment was highly successful. And that's what she kept saying. Their line was that if it had been stage I, they wouldn't even have bothered

with chemotherapy. I suspect that they would have done it anyway, since they're so aggressive about cancer. But I'm unclear about that. No matter how much you learn, it's really hard to get a very clear picture of their rules. They don't really want you to get it all.

When did you begin chemotherapy?
First, the resident brought the oncologist they were recommending for me. This guy sat there for an hour and a half describing to me what the protocol was for this thing and how Ella Grasso was a perfect example of somebody where it hadn't worked. I hated him. That's all I remember. And I remember sitting in a puddle of sweat, and it was awful. At this point no one had said to me, "You have had a radical hysterectomy. You have instant menopause. You are going to have unbelievable hot flashes." I didn't even find out until three weeks after I left the hospital that I had had a hysterectomy. I guess they figured that I had more than I could deal with, but somebody should have told me.

The hot flashes started in the hospital?
They started immediately. As soon as I was conscious, I started to feel different—violently different. A hot flash would wake me up in the middle of the night. And, horribly enough, what I've found out since is that the hot flashes almost always correspond to some disturbing thought—for me, anyway. I was at a point where I was having nothing but disturbing thoughts. It seemed like I went from one violent hot flash to the next. I was constantly changing my clothes, because I would get soaking wet. The worst thing was this awful feeling that would come up maybe three minutes before a flash. I don't know how to describe it. All I can liken it to is dread, feeling disturbed about something that is inescapable. It was a long time before I recognized that the feeling was a precursor to a hot flash. I still have that, but it isn't anywhere near as violent nor as frequent. This is something I hate my gynecologist for, because he told me that it would be over in four or five months. I asked him recently, "How long is this going to last?" "Oh, darling," he said, "it could last your whole life."

Can you take estrogen replacement therapy?
He recommended that I didn't, and I don't want to at this point. I know there are all sorts of theories about it. But I am so paranoid, I don't want to take anything. I've changed everything in my whole life. I'm not going to start taking estrogen. And I can

live with it. This is the first winter in five years I've been able to wear a turtleneck.

What did the oncologist recommend?

The standard protocol for this stage of ovarian cancer, which is called CHAD. It's Cytoxan, hexamethylmelamine, Adriamycin, and the key ingredient—cisplatin. Everybody I checked with said that's it. At this point, my family talked to the oncologist. I didn't. I wouldn't stay in the room with him. I was in a panic. The first thing I looked for was a hypnotist, because I knew I could not deal with the fear. They want you to have your first treatment before you leave the hospital, but I wouldn't do it. All the nurses begged me, and the doctor begged me, but I was too afraid. So I went home.

How did you decide what to do about chemotherapy?

I went through a long period of denial. My mother wanted to try alternatives—macrobiotics, everything. I did, too, anything to avoid the chemo. And I found myself a nutritionist, a psychiatrist, and a hypnotist to deal with the fear of chemo. But there's a woman in California who's been working on a book about women and cancer for eight years. She gave a friend of mine the name of the top man in New York for ovarian cancer. So we got an appointment, and that's when I saw the unbelievable cancer mill, the insensitive, grotesque kind of medical experience.

I had called his office and said, "Look, I'm a week and a half post-op, I can't sit in a chair." "Oh, don't worry," they said. "We'll take you right away." He had a roomful of thirty people. I waited for two hours. Then, the guy was a ghoul. He sat there, eyes drooping with fatigue, saying unconvincingly, "Well, you're going to be fine." I hated this guy so much that I thought, I'm going to have to go back to the first oncologist. Because besides hating this uptown guy more than the downtown guy, I did not want to be traveling uptown and down. And boy, that was one of the best decisions I could have made. If I'd had to have those treatments *and* travel, I would never have done it.

So, a month after I got out of the hospital, I went back in.

Do you have to stay in the hospital for the treatment?

Yes. The platinum is so deadly that you have to be in the hospital. Plus, they give it to you all night. But luckily I found a woman who had been through the same thing—except that she had had a much more advanced stage—who had made it her business to find out everything. She died. The best thing she did for me, aside from telling me about this nutritionist that I go to, and about exercise, was to say, "Don't go to the hospital alone. Have somebody stay with you, and don't let the hospital tell you the friend has to leave." So one of my partners, Jill, came with me every time and stayed all night. And without that, first of all, I wouldn't have gone, and also, I do not know how you get through that without somebody staying in the room with you.

Where did she sleep?
She didn't sleep. She sat. All night. You're sick all night. What happens is they tell you that you have to come into the hospital at noon. I kept pushing it back until I was going in at five or six at night. First, they'd take blood, to see where your platelets are —they have to know if you can take the assault. Then they start an IV with sugar water, to wash you out. They put something in it so you pee and pee and pee. It's another of these marquis de Sade things. At some point, they put up a bag of this platinum, which is like $1,000 a bag—it's kind of incredible, when you think about it. I had it once a month for six months, and each time they tried something else to relieve the nausea—Compazine, Thorazine. They tell you that some people don't get sick. I think they say that to you so that they won't plant nausea in your mind.

Then they come in in the middle of the night and do this thing called the "push." They take this gigantic needle and put it in one of the little tubes of the IV—they don't put it in your skin. And talk about burn! I don't mean heat—it's like a pain. They do this for about fifteen minutes. Then, usually, I would wake up at one or two in the morning. You feel nauseated, but not like throwing up. It's like gagging and retching, every half hour, all night long. [Judging from the experience of a woman who had chemotherapy more recently, the process is much improved. See interview, page 236.]

It's horrible. Once I threw a fit in Admissions. Every time I went in, they put me on a different floor, and this time they were about to put me on a floor where the nurses were awful; they kept making mistakes, and their mistakes can kill you. Once, I had such fear that I couldn't stop my teeth from chattering. My doctor felt so bad for me that he did the setup himself. He hooked it up all wrong, so all night long I had these people coming in and trying to get it right. Anyway, this time I said, "I will not go anywhere but the floor where I had the surgery." The Admissions woman threatened that she wouldn't admit me, or she would call the doctor—as though I would shrivel in fear if she paged the doctor. I didn't give a damn at that point, so I got my way.

Did you try marijuana to relieve the symptoms of the chemo?

Yes, I smoked a lot of pot during this whole thing, and I swear that if anything got me through, it was that. Because I had to take the edge off reality. I insisted my doctor get me THC pills, the essence of marijuana, so he did an incredible amount of legal paperwork, and I had to sign form after form and promise that if there was any left, I would bring it back. I took it with a friend, because I was afraid to take it alone. And nothing happened. It didn't relieve any nausea. Nothing did. I tried going to a hypnotist. He was a jerk, but hypnosis helped control the fear a little bit.

Tell us what you did for yourself in terms of nutrition, exercise . . .

The key to all these things, whether they work or don't work, is that they give you a feeling that you're not a victim. If you don't die in the cancer mill, you may wish you did. They make you feel like a pincushion and a hunk of flesh. Even if they're nice people. They just have so many people to deal with. You hear about the epidemic proportions of cancer, but until you wait in one of these oncologists' offices, you don't have any idea of how many people are going through this. The things I tried gave me a feeling that I was a little bit in control, that I hadn't given up all my rights, that I wasn't kneeling at the altar of the medical profession to cure me. That's one thing about the Simontons' work [see Glossary] that I absolutely agree with—they try to make you feel you're in control.

My doctor kept saying to me, "You're so difficult. You ask me all these questions"—which he really didn't answer. He said, "Most of these people come and don't ask me anything." You should see those people. They sit there like they're waiting to die.

How long did it take to recover from the chemo?

I'd go home and go to sleep, and be kind of a wreck for two days. I would have terrible muscle and bone aches; I could never get comfortable. I didn't feel nauseated; I just felt weak and achy. Everybody I know who had the kind of chemo I had has terrible aches. I arranged to have a Swedish massage once a week. I basically did everything I could to make myself feel better. Anything I wanted to do.

Then, usually the third day, my partners would drag me out and I would swim one lap in the pool; then they would drag me home. And the next day I'd be better. After about a week, I would be completely fine. I'd go in to have my blood tested, to see if the platelets were coming up. I'd wait two hours to see the doctor, who would tell me he was having a nervous breakdown, because what did I think it was like to be in this business where everybody died. Then I'd go home and start to fear the next one.

Did you lose your hair?

Oh, yeah. I couldn't imagine wearing a wig, and I did not want to see big clumps of hair all over, so I shaved it. It was really short. A lot of people thought I had gone punk. It didn't look that bad. I always had fuzz. I got a fur hat for winter. The hair part wasn't so bad. I know that's a big thing. One of the reasons I went to that big specialist uptown was because he had something like an ice hat that supposedly keeps the Adriamycin from making your hair fall out. But since the whole idea of chemo is that it's after a wild cancer cell that could be anywhere, it didn't make much sense to me to cut off my head from access. If you're going to do something as drastic as chemo, so what if you lose your hair? It just seems so minor to me.

And all this time, you were recovering from major
abdominal surgery.

Yes, that's another story. I know that after an oophorectomy, I have to worry about heart problems first and osteoporosis second. [Oophorectomy removes the ovaries, ending production of the hormone estrogen, which protects against heart attack, osteoporosis, and stroke.] Now, no medical person ever warned me of that. I've had to root that out myself. My nutritionist has told me to take calcium [thought to strengthen bones against osteoporosis] and everything else. Vitamin C, 3,000 units of E for the hot flashes. Large doses of evening primrose oil—I believed at the time it was the magic elixir; it has an intense anticancer component. I was taking chelated dolomite until I found out it has lead in it; a heavy-hitting multivitamin; and selenium. I also completely changed my diet. I cut out fats and everything fried, became a vegetarian—steamed vegetables and raw salads, all organic. You really come to love it. And I had a regular masseuse, and I exercised—I swam, I walked.

Both my doctors said that I was on the mend faster than any other patient they had ever seen, and they were willing to admit that maybe some of the things I'd done had helped. But when I asked about diet, their attitude was, "Just don't eat too many hot dogs."

What happened at the end of the six months of chemo?
Nothing much. I thought there would be something they tested, but that was it. I'm supposed to be seeing the gynecologist every six months, but I go every three or four months. That's the longest I can go without starting to think I have cancer again. And though the oncologist wanted to see me in two months, I saw no point to sitting in that office for two hours to wait and hear his problems.

After a year you're supposed to have a second-look operation. But I had been strenuously warned by this woman who was researching women and cancer that one of the drawbacks to second-look operations was—and I hope I'm getting this right—that anesthesia depresses the immune system, so maybe it wasn't a good idea for people who had cancer. I became fixated on that. Also, I think, I didn't want to know if there was anything there. Basically that's my attitude now. I went through it once, but I ain't going through it again—I did my time.

I did have a sonogram and a CAT scan. They were fine. And at some point, I'll have another CAT scan. But there doesn't seem to be a scheduled program of events to follow, at least with the medical people I have—which maybe shows that they're inferior. On the other hand, when you go through a medical emergency like this, you get so worn out and worn down that you don't want to deal with it. I have spent the last four years interviewing all these internists to find a regular doctor, and so far, I hate them all. I can't find a doctor who pays attention. And all these internists do nothing but refer you to specialists. They're great clearing houses.

After almost five years, do you feel back to normal?
For somebody like me, who had a really easy life, something like finding you have cancer becomes a turning point or a new reality. It changes your idea that things will go the way you think they should. Life packs a wallop, suddenly. I don't sit and talk about

cancer. My only big thing about it now is that I don't want it again. For a long time I lived in fear, but that has also kind of gone away—and that scares me. I don't want it to go too far away, because I'm afraid that if it does—if I forget it—I'll get a big surprise. That's one reason I will talk to anybody about this— call me up! Because I don't want to forget it. I think that would be a bad move.

What do you tell the women who do call you? Do you tell them chemo is horrible?

I don't, because the way it will be terrible for them is going to be different from the way it was terrible for me. I don't say it's a piece of cake. I tell them all it's extremely unpleasant. I tell them all, Bring someone with you. I tell them, Don't take any shit. But I understand why doctors say, "Hey, some people don't get sick." Because probably there are some who don't.

Why do you stay with your doctor despite the fact that you're "outraged" by his not giving you enough information?

In a way, as I said, there is a limit to what I want to know. I think I'm really doing well. I don't want any more things to worry about. I believe in the power of the mind, and I believe that I have a very powerful mind and that I could create problems for myself where they don't exist. And I have a feeling that this doctor of mine knows that about me. I think that's part of the reason he plays it as close to the collar as he does. If I were cooler and calmer, maybe he would throw me a couple more little bits about what's going on, although I don't think he'd ever be really all that revealing. I think they play you for who you are.

And I think he's been very responsive to me in other ways. If I call in the afternoon, freaking out for the five-hundredth time, he'll see me then. When his office gets test results back, the nurse calls me instantly because she knows I'm waiting. I haven't gotten that from anybody else, and I appreciate it. And nobody else I know has gotten that—I've heard nothing but awful stories. It's too bad that there isn't someone who watches and helps you through something like this.

An ombudsman . . .

Yes. In the hospital, when I first knew about the cancer and was so freaked out, they sent in a psychiatrist. And she was the dumbest. Asking, "Are you angry?" Things like that. And it made me so mad! Because it would be so easy to organize something that helped. With somebody who actually had an idea of what was going to happen to you. Who called you up, maybe, at home, and asked, "How are you?"

In the beginning, with my oncologist, I would call and call him, because I had feelings that I didn't know if I should have. My bones would ache until they felt like they were busting open, or I would have a metal taste in my mouth. He would call me back three or four hours later. Meanwhile, I would be ready to jump out the window—I was worried about all of it. He didn't tell me what to expect because he didn't want me to talk myself into those symptoms, and I understand that. But then there should be somebody who called me the day after chemo and said, "How are you feeling?" And if I said, "Well, I have a metal taste in my mouth," this person would say, "Oh, that's the platinum."

Is there anything else you think people ought to know?
Yes! Never go to a doctor alone if you're going to talk about something important. Take either a tape recorder or another person. Because you will find, nine out of ten times, that you walk out and either you remember very selectively or you don't remember at all.

"I HAD NEVER BEEN SO RADIANT IN MY DAY-TO-DAY LIFE AS I WAS FIGHTING THIS THING."
A playwright who was operated on for ovarian cancer a year and a half before, when she was thirty-six. She was reluctant to relive the experience by telling the story; but prompted, perhaps, by anger against the medical establishment—"I was totally disillusioned, not to say appalled, by callousness, brutality, every sort of technical mishap"—she began to speak before the first question.

The only way I got through this thing was to shift my sense of who I was going to depend on to myself. To myself and to certain other things that are basically myself—like diet, like yoga, like reading. You read everything, and you make up your own mind. You find out who is the best doctor in the field—that's the kind of research you have to do. But you don't think that a doctor is going to be your friend in any way. You get support from your friends and family; you don't go to a doctor for support.

You sound as though you prepared yourself for combat.
I was in a very critical situation. My prognosis was damn awful. I spoke to one oncologist, a top guy in the South, and after he saw my slides, we had the following dialogue on the telephone. He said, "Are you the patient?" I said yes. He said, "Well, I must say this is the most virulent cancer I've ever seen." That was shocking, shattering. I mean, there is such a thing as diplomacy—not lying, but leaving a certain amount of hope for the patient. You have to be left with something to do—like yoga, like fighting.

The surgeon I ended up with had a policy of not saying anything until he was asked. And when I asked, he gave me a statistic like 40 percent—that was my chance of surviving. It gradually became clear that I had more like a 30 to 25 percent chance and, eventually, a 12 percent chance. Now, that is really pretty slim. Given the utter horror of the chemotherapy that I had to go through, if I had been told I had a 12 percent chance, it would have made it almost impossible.

So you want to know everything there is to know, but also you have to leave yourself some room for faith. Because I did survive. Because I am a medical miracle. Because somebody *makes up* those statistics—they speak as though the numbers are written in stone.

The thing about cancer is that they really don't know that much. I got quite a range of procedural advice, from having chemotherapy in Paris two or three weeks out of every month for two to three years; to having one day a month on a smaller dosage; to having the kind of dosage that the National Institutes of Health was experimenting with, where they tolerated side effects like a 20 percent death rate, loss of tactile sensation, and kidney failure. They don't like to tell you this. They say, "Well, we've got this experimental program that has very good results."

How did this all begin?
I had symptoms of what I thought was appendicitis or colitis—cramps—and sometimes in the middle of the night, I'd wake up with very sharp pains. I went to see a doctor. I was living alone, very romantically, at the beach, in the late autumn of 1984, trying to get my head together and my work together.

A doctor checked me out, but he didn't check me out gynecologically because he was a regular GP. He said, "Well, it's not appendicitis. If it doesn't go away in a couple of weeks, we'll run a G.I.

series." In the meantime, I changed my diet totally—to a vegetarian diet—and the symptoms disappeared, which is weird.

I was feeling fine, and I was active. The only thing I did notice
was that in certain exercise positions, like lying on my stomach,
it occasionally felt like there was a rock in my side. But I always
suspected myself of hypochondria, and besides, I'd been to this
doctor.

About a month later, I got the most ferocious attack of diarrhea, just when I had to drive six hours back to New York. I'd
been up all night, doubled over. One of the doctors I later saw, an
expert in this kind of cancer, found many women who had gastrointestinal symptoms months before they were diagnosed,
symptoms of indigestion like gassiness, a feeling of fullness after
eating small amounts of food.

When I got home I made an appointment to see a doctor I'd
used before. So two days later, December 23, right before Christmas, after four months of living alone at the beach, really happy
to be back in the world of human beings and my friends—no more
sea gulls—I go to see this doctor. "What's this?" she said. I said,
"What's what?" She sent me immediately to the sonogram lady,
who was very sweet.

You're building up a sense that this could be serious, but you
have to cool out to get across time. You have to say, "One step at
a time." In fact, that was the phrase that got me through the
whole thing: "I don't have to die today, so I'm not going to worry
about dying right now. I'm just going to do this one day at a
time." And look, folks, here I am—touch wood.

I'm not really into terror at this point, but the sonogram lady
says a slightly ominous thing when she finishes. She says, "Good
luck."

It's four-thirty in the afternoon, and the GP said that she had
to read the sonograms to me herself, and she was leaving for the
Virgin Islands in two hours, and I had to cross town in half an
hour, and the snow and the rain were coming down, and I
couldn't get a taxi, and I suddenly got hysterical. I banged on an
off-duty cab's window and showed him the envelope that said,
"Radiology: X-rays." I said, "Do you see this? I could have cancer. You've got to get me to the doctor." And he rolls up his window and pushes on.

Downtown, the lady with the Virgin Islands holiday delivers

the most extraordinary speech to me. It's like in a movie. She says, "Well, I'm sorry to tell you this, but I'm afraid it's serious." It sounds like a joke, right? You sit there and she says, "You've got a massive ovarian tumor, and although we can't be sure, and it might be all right, it looks malignant, and I'm booking you with the surgeon who saved my sister-in-law."

She said, "I want to tell you that ovarian cancer is one of the few cancers that is curable." I for some reason misunderstood and said, "You mean, I can't die?" She said, "Oh, no, you can very well die." She said, "Look, I've got to take this plane. I'm really sorry to leave you like this. Are you going to be alone tonight? I don't want you to be alone." She said, "Well, I've got to go." It was like that.

She is the one person I was angry with, unreasonably angry, and I've never gone back to her to tell her that I'm still alive.

How did you go about shopping for a doctor?

I saw five surgeons in one week. It was absolutely haphazard. First I saw the guy who saved the Virgin Islands lady's sister-in-law, and he's very jolly and says, "Well, it's pretty bad and we're going to cut you open and you'll probably be in chemotherapy for a year, and you may live, you may not." Nobody said, "Darling girl! You poor thing! How could this happen to you!" Naturally not.

Another doctor said, "Come see me, I'll be in my office on Christmas morning." So I ended up wandering around the halls of his hospital Christmas morning. He wasn't there. I arrived the day after, and he said, "Of course I wasn't here. I was on my yacht." I went to another doctor, who was the top surgeon in the field. He said, "Look, I think it's probably Stage II, it's contained, you've got a good chance." And I went with him because his prognosis was better than any of those other jerks'.

But, in fact, it turned out to be Stage III, and I had a massive tumor on one ovary and a small tumor on another, and an exploding appendix. They took lots of stuff out of me—both ovaries, the uterus, fallopian tubes, and the appendix. Then, this doctor wouldn't speak to me! He told me what the situation was and that it wasn't good. He seemed to be furious with me for coming to die on his doorstep. They were cold as can be, he and the other doctors, and the nurses were hell. I had been opened up at least twelve inches and couldn't move, and the nurses would sort of just jerk me around when they gave me morphine so that I was literally screaming.

Did you have private nurses, a private room?

No, I shared a room with this rather marvelous girl who was scared as can be. Her family would sing hymns over her, and her sister stayed with her. I found that I was able to comfort the sister. I said, "Don't be afraid. What's the worst thing that could happen to your sister? She could die, right? But you believe in reincarnation, don't you? You know she's going to come back, her spirit will live." And she said, "Yes, I surely do." I don't know where this stuff came from in me, but it's there fast. What you need is there in you, and it stayed with me.

How did you manage with money?

I went into debt. I had various people helping me, others offering to help. My friends were amazing. There's a tendency to withdraw from someone who might disappear, to save yourself pain. But the day-to-day evidence was of me in the fight, so they were in that fight with me. I had one friend who would come and sleep on the sofa every weekend after chemotherapy and take care of me. I had a friend who is an actress who spent money she didn't have buying me a wig. A friend who is a literary agent—whom I had left; we'd had a fight—got me a grant and sold some writing for me and refused to take a cut. Just people taking me to the doctor. . . . I've never felt so terribly loved.

Did your doctors discuss estrogen replacement therapy with you?

I take pills now, Premarin.

What chemotherapy did you have?

It's a combination of three things. Cisplatin, which was discovered eight years ago—it makes you sick as a dog, but before it was discovered, there was no chance with ovarian cancer, and now there's normally a 30 percent chance. Another one is Cytoxan . . . even to name them, I feel sick . . . and the other one is called Adriamycin. I had to shop around again for a chemotherapist, going around with my slides, asking, "What would you do?"

I took it once a month for seven months. Then they opened me up and I was clear. You get a final hit of chemotherapy after the operation. So twice now, with stitches still in me, I had the che-

motherapy. You have to have a corset, because you're convulsing
with the chemo, you're throwing up every twenty minutes for
nine hours overnight, you're pulling all the stitches. It's the most
torturous thing. [For an account of a more recent and less
wrenching experience of chemotherapy, see the interview on
page 236.] Typical of the nursing care: the chemo was mixed
with a diuretic, which makes you have to pee all the time, and
instead of giving you a bedpan, the nurses make you get up eight
times in the first hour of the chemo, drag your IV, maneuver to
the bathroom, pee, and try to get back into bed. On one of these
trips I blacked out. My head hit the floor. I nearly gave myself a
concussion. From then on, I hired my own nurse, who dealt with
the bedpans.

It's unbelievably grotesque. The only thing that got me through
it was that I had been told I was going to be okay. That, and the
extraordinary experience of discovering other people's and one's
own strength, my own strength. That has changed my sense of
myself.

How did you change?

I've never been particularly courageous. I've never been in a hospital, I didn't even have my tonsils out. I'm basically a chicken-
shit—I get anxiety attacks all the time over nothing. But very
early on with this, in the first week or two, I remember thinking,
I can't believe how I'm behaving. I don't recognize myself. I
couldn't believe I was helping other people deal with it. I was
making jokes. I was on the phone in the hospital the day after
they gave me the diagnosis, saying, "These guys are really
creeps. Come and visit me, I'm bored." That kind of thing. It was
totally instinctive. And that put other people at their ease and
they were able to give to me, enormous amounts.

I had a sense that whatever happened, I could somehow do it.
And it was exhilarating. I had never been so radiant in my day-
to-day life as I was fighting this thing.

And later, when I lost my hair, which was terribly frightening
to me—it was such an image of disintegration—I made elaborate
turbans. I had been wearing a lot of black, and then I remember
dressing against the situation, wearing color as much as I could.
Going out as much as I could. Intense involvement in life to counteract this huge threat of death. Deep, deep love for people. Love
for people I thought I would never talk to again—enormous sense

of reconciliation. And a sense of detachment from the normal kind of pettiness: all that matters is human life. That kind of freedom was extraordinary. And it existed only in the spaces of this prison-and-torture world that I was in. I mean, to go into chemotherapy was like going down death row. And then you have to crawl back up.

So—trust yourself, trust your friends, fuck the doctors. I remember deciding on this attitude in the first month: "Fuck those bastards. I'm not going to let them get me. I'm going to fight this. They're not going to win."

Where do you think this fighting spirit came from?
Grace. Whatever that is. It may be God, it may be the will to live, I don't know. I remember asking Susan Sontag how she got through the terror. Just the terrors at night. I mean, I was living alone, I was doing this alone. And I thought, Susan Sontag's going to have an incredible reading list or something. I asked, "What did you do about the fear of death, Susan?" And in all seriousness, she said, "I slept with the lights on."

How would you answer your own question now?
I discovered this very simple thing. I would say, "Well, today— this particular day—you're still okay. You don't even have to do chemotherapy today. So this day belongs to you. Enjoy it." I remember telling my friend with AIDS, "The thing about dying is that you don't have to go when they tell you to go. You can go when you want to." These ways of coping bubble up from somewhere when you're in a gravely serious situation. No one is helpless, is what I mean.

This sounds very arrogant, but I feel that I took care of myself last year. I organized the defensive parts of me—yoga, people, macrobiotics. However fatuous it was, I organized it. And therefore I felt competent. I could look after myself. And now I feel that I'll be okay. I actually also feel something will look after me, even if it's only me.

I still feel that I am not living productively, I'm not doing the right things, I'm impatient with myself—the neuroses survived this. But the basic trust of self has been changed forever, I think.

Have you kept up your diet and the yoga?
Yoga, no. I stayed on macrobiotics for three months, but it's so antisocial—I needed people more than the diet.

"I TAUGHT MYSELF THAT I CAN'T THINK AHEAD. I CAN
ONLY DO WHAT COMES NEXT."

*A sixty-six-year-old speech coach, married and the mother
of two, who is currently undergoing chemotherapy for ovarian cancer. We interviewed her a few hours before she was
due at the hospital for her fifth treatment. An attractive
woman with short gray hair (a new wig, she said), she
began by talking about chemo—about overcoming her fear
of it.*

After my first treatment, another woman told me that it gets
worse each time. Worse *how*? I wanted to know. I was relieved
as all hell that it didn't get worse physically, because I sure didn't
like what I'd been through. This woman said no, it gets worse
psychologically. Now, I'm beginning to see what she meant. It's
like Pavlov's dogs, as my daughter explained. You've been con-
ditioned: you know what you're going to go through. Last time,
there was a crucial moment in which I felt for the first time a
kind of panic. I thought, I'm going to tear this IV out of my arm
and just run away. And then I thought, Oh, maybe that's what
that woman was talking about. She'd said, "Your thoughts aren't
your own—you think in a way that's not you. It must be the chemicals."

I figured, if I can control the psychological thing, I don't have
to go through that! So, I got myself to the American Cancer Society. Their support group has its pros and cons. The first time I
went, a woman walked in, pulled off her scarf, and she was bald
except for dark little patches. I thought, Wow, that's gutsy. But
then she started talking and couldn't stop for a half hour. She
had a horrible story to tell. Somebody else, a small girl in the
corner, had a worse story. I thought, Jesus, I'm not too bad. The
fact is that one of the advantages of this group—and I am
ashamed to say it—is you tell yourself, "Listen, kid. You're not
the worst situation by a very long shot!"

How did this begin for you?
It began with stupidity. I went through menopause fairly early,
and I was relieved as hell to be through with it. My gynecologist
retired, and approximately five years went by—I hate to say this
—without a pelvic exam. I finally decided I'd better go—the day

after my birthday this year—and they found a three-inch cyst on my right ovary. This gynecologist said, "We'd better have a sonogram very soon." There was a certain urgency in his voice, so I said, "Let's do it right now." And I went right over and had a sonogram.

You're paranoid in that situation—which makes you a good observer. So I'm watching the nurse do the sonogram, then go out and bring in the doctor, and out of the corner of my eye I see some big thing in the sonogram . . . and the nurses and attendants all begin to talk to me a little differently. I thought, I think I'm in for something here.

I get back to my doctor's office and he says, "You have a large cyst, and it has to come out. And with a woman of your age, postmenopause, we always take out everything—we do a hysterectomy." So I said, "Okay."

Your surgery was probably overshadowed by the chemo,
but did you have good hospital care, good nursing care?
I had private nurses all the time. My nephew, who's a doctor and teaches at the University of California, said that everybody working in these big city hospitals is absolutely overburdened. And I read somewhere that if you go to the hospital, either take a loved one with you or a private nurse or both. My husband and I can afford this. It's the best use of our money.

The surgery went well, and when I woke up from it, they said, in their nice polite way, "Well, we found something we weren't expecting. There was a tumor on your left ovary, and we got it all out." And *luckily,* they said, a doctor from the GYN-oncology group was next door and came in on the surgery. That word *luckily* froze me! You want to say, "You dumb bastards—don't you know this is the sort of thing that might happen? What if he hadn't been there?"

The oncologist who luckily turned out to be next door came in after the surgery and told me that the cancer had spread a little, and there was some on the bowel and he had removed that tissue. I later got a bill from him for $1,500 (and the gynecologist cost $4,000). The oncologist was a darling young man who had the grace to sit down in my room. All of these guys come in and they want to leave. When he actually sat down, I thought, You're my man. And I said, "May I ask you some questions?" He said, "As many as you like." I asked him the fearful ones. I asked him about the chemo: "Is this something I can bear?" There's this terrible fear that you'll become a screaming animal. You'll come unhinged. He said, "Yes, you can."

I found out that the normal course of chemo is eight, but they said I was going to have ten, because this little thing had begun to colonize. They did not use the word *metastasize*. After the chemo, they would do what they call a "look-see," which is the laughingest description of a major operation known to man. They take about fifty samples of tissue for biopsies, to be sure that there's no more in there. If there is, you get to have some more chemo.

What did you decide to do about the chemo?
They want to give you the first treatment right then, while you're still in the hospital. I was too terrified. I said I'd come back in a week. The only thing I knew about chemotherapy was that it's a living hell. I had a friend who chose not to do it. She said, "If I've only a year to live, I'm going to really live it." She went to see her grandchildren out west, she went to see the Grand Canyon, and she spent her money on herself nicely. I called our mutual friend and asked how she died. She said, "Oh, you don't want to do that. And she was so stupid. She had lung cancer and she kept smoking."

I thought, Jesus, she isn't a role model for me. I did think seriously about suicide for the first month. I read a book called *Let Me Die Before I Wake,* by Derek Humphrey [published by the Hemlock Society, it argues for the right of the incurably ill to kill themselves and explains how to do it]. I realized it's very hard to commit suicide successfully.

I also realized I couldn't go through chemo alone. The American Cancer Society group seemed to be run by amateurs, so I got the name of a therapist who was a chemo nurse for seventeen years, a social worker-therapist. She has been wonderful.

And I taught myself that I can't think ahead. I can only do what comes next. What happens is, a few days before you're due in, you start to be fearful and weepy. That's the conditioning getting to you, but it's also reasonable. One time in chemo they poked me five times before they found a vein. Oh, I was furious as hell! And hurt and crying.

The next nurse said, "Oh, dear, that's not necessary, there's nothing wrong with your veins," and found it the first time. But then you hear from everybody that it's luck—sometimes the vein just won't hold. You learn that chemo destroys your veins and, as time goes by, it's sometimes harder to find a vein.

So this is not going to get any better. And everybody has different theories about what you should do. Put ice packs on the spot and then a heating pad. Or soak your arm in hot water, and squeeze sponges with your hands to flush the blood through your veins. The last nurse told me, "You should put vitamin E on it, to prevent scarring."

Today, when I go in, I have to steel myself for the fact that we're not going to get it the first time. If we do, that will just be sensational.

How do you rate the medical care you're receiving?

Let me go back to what happened after the operation that I'm so angry about: the fact that everything is so departmentalized that you never hear again from the doctor who did the surgery; the gynecologist hands you over to the chemotherapist and washes his hands of you. The fourth day after the operation, I'm feeling marvelous, and I'm running up and down the halls. I don't care about the incision, I'm going to go home! On the fifth day, I start to have gas pains. I ask for something, and they bring me Simethacone [nonprescription antigas drug]—you take a couple of drops every four hours. They give me Mylanta [an antacid], too. In the middle of the night I wake up with these awful pains—you don't know what to do with yourself, you can't move. But they can't find the Simethacone! And the pharmacy can't make up more without a doctor's approval! And who's your doctor? The resident on the floor, and he's out doing a thousand things. It's this kind of idiocy that drives me mad—it's what I call falling between two chairs.

I finally got the Simethacone, and I took it home with me. When I go back in for my operation [the look-see], I'll have that little bottle in my hand.

Another example: On my fourth chemo, I began to have a feeling of panic. I asked for some Valium. My doctor was in OR, and I couldn't find anybody to okay a Valium. Here I am in tears, and I'm sitting there saying, "This is *stupid!*"

The young oncologist I liked so much left the hospital to go back to Boston. The doctor he recommended came in one day, said hello, and that was that. I'm now going in for my fifth treatment, and I have never seen him again!

At the American Cancer Society, several people said that what was most important in chemotherapy was a supportive doctor. Well, I don't *have* a fucking doctor! The time they stabbed me five times and nobody could find a vein, my husband went to the main office and raised his voice and said, "Something has to be done here!" Later, the head of the oncology group—who's highly respected, famous world over, and a prima donna—appeared in my doorway in his OR clothes and introduced himself. I knew he was angry. He said, "Chemotherapy is difficult. You just have to put down your head and go for it. And there will be many difficulties—not just physical ones, but administrative and bureaucratic ones." And I thought, You son of a bitch. Those are *your* problems. How dare you bring them up here! I was so mad I could have killed him.

The doctor who's supposed to be looking after me has his own problems—his son is sick. I called him—he was kind enough to leave me his home phone number—and said, "It is important for me to feel that I have a relationship with you. I do hope that I will see you this time when I come in for my treatment." And he said yes, he'd be there today. But he's said yes before. I said, "I have a list of questions for you." He said, "Write them down, I'll answer them all." So I'm going in today with a list of questions.

What kind of chemotherapy are you getting?

I go in on Monday, get the chemo on Tuesday. Tuesday evening I recover, and Wednesday I go home. You have the saline first, three bags of it in my case, all the first night. Then at about eleven in the morning, they start an antiemetic that has some sedative in it. Then you go to sleep and they throw in the real tough stuff, the platinum, which gives you what I call the dead battery acid taste. And I'm sick for about an hour and a half. Then I get more of the antiemetic to stop the vomiting. Then more saline.

It sounds as though this particular chemo has improved since the other women we've interviewed went through it. They describe being up all night.

When I told the nurse at the American Cancer Society that I'd heard chemo was a living hell, she said, "Who told you, and when did they have it?" I said, "Well, quite a few years ago. Has it changed?" She said, "Oh, yes, we have much better controls now."

What have you learned about getting through this
psychologically?

I have never had an endgame, and this requires one. You know what having an endgame means in chess? It means that you're still operative, smart, strategic when the game is coming to a close. The other person may be winning, but if you have an endgame, you can save yourself.

I never had an endgame. I am marvelous at the beginning. I am creative, intelligent, talented, physically skilled. I am the first kid out of the box. And I am lousy at the long haul, when it gets to be a matter of maintenance. If I played a game, and if the odds looked like they were beginning to fall on the other side, I'd give up and say, Well, I don't care.

Now I'm faced with the ultimate endgame: Are you going to play this game out, or are you going to give up?

When I went to the American Cancer Society group, I said I had hoped to get out of this life without having to develop an endgame, because I knew that was my weakest point. I'd gone through psychoanalysis, I said, and I didn't solve it there. Now, here I am at sixty-six, and I've got to solve it.

And the little girl in the far corner, who was shaking and had liver cancer, looked at me as if to say "The problem is, *I'm* not a fighter." And I thought, Jesus, I *am* a fighter, I really am one.

And here I am, and I've got to do what I've got to do, as my best friend said. She's always had an endgame. I'm the hare and she is the tortoise, and she is doing beautifully with her older age. I'm having a rougher time with my older age. When I was deeply depressed, I said to her, "Betty, if I didn't have my husband, I couldn't and wouldn't go through this." She said, "Oh, yes, you would. You just do what you gotta do."

It is such a dumb little chestnut, but it hit me. That's what she's always done that I have envied. And now it's become my mantra: "You just do what you gotta do."

People sent me off to some yoga institute, to find "peace in my healing body," as they say. I tried it. It's not me. You've got to find what works for you. What I am is a competitor. I'm not this serene, let's-meditate-with-the-yellow-disk person. When I work with women who seem absolutely without any kind of passion, I say, "What makes you angry? What makes you cry?" Whatever it is, I've got to help them find it. For me, anger is the best stuff!

THREE

Consultations with Specialists

DIAGNOSTIC TESTS

ANESTHESIOLOGY

SURGERY AND ANESTHESIA CONSENT FORM

ESTROGEN REPLACEMENT THERAPY

ON LASER, MYOMECTOMY, ENDOMETRIOSIS,
FERTILITY, AND THE RISK OF CANCER

HYSTEROSCOPY: OPTIONS IN FIBROID SURGERY

CHEMOTHERAPY

CHEMOTHERAPY CONSENT FORMS

ONCOLOGY NURSING

SCRIPTS: QUESTIONS TO ASK YOUR DOCTORS

DIAGNOSTIC TESTS

JEROLD D. KURZBAN, M.D.

"I CAN'T EXPECT EVEN THE BEST GYNECOLOGIST TO BE ABLE TO READ AS ACCURATELY AS WE CAN. ONE SPECIALTY HAS TO DEPEND ON ANOTHER."

SONOGRAM

BARIUM ENEMA

IVP (INTRAVENOUS PYELOGRAM)

HYSTEROGRAM

HYSTEROSALPINGOGRAM

All of these tests are simply ways of seeing into the body. The organs in the pelvic cavity are "soft"—boneless—and so won't show up on X-ray film unless they're outlined by a radio-opaque dye. Sonogram uses sound waves instead of dye to "sketch" the various masses in the belly.

A medical doctor with a specialty in radiology performs the tests and interprets the results for the gynecologist. Says Jerold D. Kurzban, M.D., a New York City radiologist: "It's nice when you come into your doctor's office, and he holds up the film and says, 'Well, here's your tumor'—the Marcus Welby kind of thing. But medicine has become too complex: I can't expect even the best gynecologist to be able to read as accurately as we can, the same way a gynecologist can't expect me to be a good surgeon. One specialty has to depend on another."

Within twelve to fourteen hours after the test, the gynecologist has the report and the "film," meaning X-ray or sonogram images. "Some gynecologists don't want to see the film itself—they want just our report," Kurzban says. But whatever the findings, it is not the radiologist's job to reveal them to the patient. "Ninety-nine percent of our doctors don't want us to tell the patients anything," Kurzban says, "and I agree with that. We've only just met the patient. You can't just walk her back to the room and say, 'Well, you have an ovarian cancer, and it has to be addressed.' "

According to law, the woman is not entitled to her films—"which is odd," he says—but she is entitled to her report. "If she wanted a second opinion, she would ask her doctor for the film. I don't think any doctor would withhold it."

SONOGRAM

Pelvic sonogram is a painless test that allows visualization of the ovaries, fallopian tubes, and uterus, as well as the kidneys, ureters, and bladder. Sonogram is considered totally safe, with none of the risks of radiation. The only discomfort is that caused by a full bladder: you have to drink four or five glasses of liquid to inflate the bladder.

"It could be mineral water, tap water, soda, coffee, anything," Kurzban says. "Why do we need the patient's bladder filled? For several reasons. One, ultrasound works on the same principle as sonar detection of submarines. We're looking through a fluid-filled structure. Water is a great transmitter of sound, and a full bladder is a great ecogenic window to look through, to see the pelvic wall.

"The second reason we need to fill the bladder is because the full bladder elevates the bowel out of the pelvic cavity. The bowel interferes with the transmission of sound because it contains gas and food.

"The third reason is that fluid in the bladder makes for a cystic structure. If the patient has a cyst in the pelvic cavity, we can compare densities. A cyst in the ovaries should have the same sonar characteristics as the bladder."

During the pelvic sonogram, the patient lies on her back while her abdomen is coated with mineral oil, which helps conduct sound. A paddle (called a transducer) is then rubbed across the belly, emitting high-frequency (inaudible) sound waves that bounce back: the speed and strength of the returning waves indicate what's there, how dense it is, what size, what kind of tissue it is—all of which is transformed instantaneously into a TV-screen image, read by the radiologist.

BARIUM ENEMA

Barium is a chalky-white liquid used to coat the lining of the colon (the large intestine) and make it possible to see any tumors or polyps. Twenty-four hours before the test, the patient goes on a liquid diet—clear soup, soda, juice, no milk. The night before, she takes a series of laxatives and an enema. "You need an absolutely clean colon," Kurzban says, "because food could simulate a polyp or a growth."

The test itself consists of X-rays taken in three stages: before the enema; while the barium is in the colon; and after the barium is expelled. The whole process takes about an hour.

"It's not a pleasant procedure," Kurzban admits, "but the rewards far outweigh any discomfort that you may have." The discomfort arises from dilating the bowel with the liquid and lasts about ten minutes.

IVP (INTRAVENOUS PYELOGRAM)

This test allows visualization of the urinary system. A contrast dye is injected into a vein (in the crook of the elbow), and then X-rays are taken at short intervals over the next fifteen minutes. The dye makes it possible to see tumors, kidney stones, or signs of kidney disease. Some people feel a slight wave of nausea or a sensation of warmth as the dye is introduced—because the dye is dilating the vessels in the stomach, Kurzban says. These are normal reactions, especially for women, because of the huge vascular supply to their pelvic organs. You may also have a metallic taste in your mouth. The dye may contain iodine and could cause an allergic reaction. (Some new dyes are free of iodine.)

HYSTEROGRAM

"This is mainly done to detect fibroids in the uterus, and to see how they're growing," Kurzban says, "to learn if they're projecting into the uterus or if they are embedded in the uterine wall. You can find other things, too, such as polyps and small cysts in the uterus."

The patient is in standard gynecological position—feet in stirrups. The gynecologist inserts first a speculum to expose the cervix; second, a clamp to grip the cervix; and then dye is introduced into the uterus through a tube. X-rays are then taken.

HYSTEROSALPINGOGRAM

This is used for women who have difficulties in conceiving. The purpose is to evaluate the patency of the fallopian tubes—to find out if they are blocked in any way. With the woman in the usual gynecological position, the speculum is inserted, the cervix is dilated, and the womb is cleaned with methylate to prevent any infection. The uterus is then dilated and sounded so you know how far to put in the injecting instrument. "Dilating the cervix may cause slight pain," Kurzban says, "which can be made worse if you tense up and clamp down." Then dye is introduced into the uterine cavity. "You may need as little as 2 ccs. or as much as 10 ccs. The whole procedure takes about four minutes. Most women come in here with abnormal fears, but 99 percent of them leave here with no pain. They may have some bleeding —because you've interrupted the lining of the uterus, just as when you're shedding the lining during a normal period—and the bleeding may last as long as a normal period."

The newest technique is endovaginal sonography, using a probe that comes into almost direct contact with the pelvic organs (the uterus and ovaries). "We still do transabdominal sonography," Kurzban says, "but the probe allows us to see the finer details of early gestation, do more accurate dating, and more easily detect any early fetal abnormalities. It also enables us to better visualize any ovarian and uterine abnormalities, and help us distinguish between benign and malignant conditions. The probe is sterilized each time and used with a condom. It's an expensive instrument—$20,000—but the benefits far outweigh the cost."

ANESTHESIOLOGY

MARILYN KRITCHMAN, M.D.

"DURING SURGERY WE'RE METERING IN THE ANES-
THESIA TO THE PROPER DEPTH OF RELAXATION. IT'S
CONSTANT ATTENDANCE, MONITORING, AND SUPPORT OF
VITAL FUNCTIONS."

*Dr. Kritchman is director of the residency training program
in the Department of Anesthesiology and associate professor of clinical anesthesiology at New York University Medical Center.*

*Anesthesia is a mystery to most people. Many don't know,
for instance, that anesthesiologists are doctors. Would you
tell us about the training of an anesthesiologist?*
After medical school, we encourage our residents to take a full
year of internal medicine because we function as the internist for
the patient in the operating room. Then, as residents, there is a
three-year postgraduate program in anesthesiology, which is the
same length as the programs for ophthalmologists, obstetricians,
gynecologists, urologists—many of the subspecialties.
Who chooses the anesthesiologist in any particular case?
In most instances, anesthesiologists practice in groups, with a
rotating schedule. But it is possible, always, for a patient to make
a request.
*A gynecologist who underwent a complete hysterectomy
wanted to have an epidural rather than general
anesthesia. She found that many anesthesiologists were
"uncomfortable" with the prospect of doing an epidural.
Why isn't that method used more frequently?*
It varies with the region of the country and the sophistication of
the anesthesiology department. Here at New York University
Medical Center, many patients get an epidural for a number of
different procedures, among them a hysterectomy.

249

Do the patients request it, or is the epidural standard?

Nothing is standard. There are as many people who are afraid of being awake during surgery as there are people who are afraid of going to sleep. Assuming a patient doesn't have any contraindications to a particular type of anesthesia, the choice is hers. An anesthesiologist interviews each patient beforehand and explains the options. One of our physicians was scheduled for a hysterectomy recently, and she called me because she wanted to be awake. There was no problem—she had the surgery under epidural.

Though epidural is not new, it is newer than the spinal in terms of the training process. A doctor who has been out of medical school perhaps twenty-five to thirty years may not be as comfortable with it.

Does it take more skill to do an epidural or a spinal than a general?

Not more skill. It's just a different skill and must be learned.

What's the difference between a spinal and an epidural?

The approach through the skin is the same; the end point differs. A spinal just perforates the envelope around the spine, where there's fluid; when you reach that point, you get fluid back, so you know where you are. The reason that epidural is a little more difficult is that the epidural space is a *potential* space between the bone and some ligaments and the spinal canal; you perform the injection by feel more than by having a real end point.

Each technique has its own possible complications, none of which makes it less safe than general anesthesia.

One of the reasons that people choose epidural over spinal is to avoid the so-called spinal headache, [pain caused by the loss of spinal fluid, which supports the brain] which is not inevitable— occurring in less than 5 percent of patients—but it is a possible complication. On the other hand, there are complications that can occur with epidural. The anesthetic drug is given in larger concentration in the epidural space, so there is a greater potential for toxicity.

Are patients who choose epidural often unnerved by being awake? Are they given tranquilizers as well?

You can have as much or as little sedation as you want. Some people don't want any sedation—they want to be totally awake, and they are more relaxed that way. Many people are afraid that if they go to sleep, they won't wake up. More people are afraid of that possibility than voice it.

Could you wear a Walkman and listen to music during surgery?

Yes, of course.

The most common complaint about general anesthesia is that it causes a loss of concentration. Is this a known side effect?

It has been shown that after general anesthesia, judgment is impaired for a few hours, and it is suggested that, besides not driving home from the procedure, you don't make any significant decisions about your stocks and bonds and that sort of thing.

But remember that the kinds of surgery you're dealing with are very emotional experiences, and when you're emotionally involved, I think, your concentration diminishes anyhow. Let's say that if you had a prolonged anesthesia—three to four hours—your concentration, or your ability to judge, would be affected until the next day. But after shorter surgical procedures, I think the larger cause for the loss of concentration is emotional.

Now, nobody suggests that anesthesia will *add* to your health. Our only idea is to try, as the expression goes, "to do no harm" in terms of the anesthesia.

Could you take us through the surgical process, focusing on the anesthesia? Say I'm a woman who's checked into the hospital, scheduled for a hysterectomy the next day.

Anesthesiologists will come to see you after reviewing your chart. If there's anything on the chart that concerns them, they will speak either to your gynecologist or to a medical person who has been taking care of you, as well as interview you intensively.

What are they looking for?

They're looking for significant disease, especially circulatory and respiratory—heart disease, respiratory problems, smoking. People who smoke have irritated airways and reduced power to pick up oxygen because they have a lot of carbon monoxide in their blood. It is also important to determine what specific medications patients are taking since many interact with anesthetic agents and drugs.

Is there a good reason to stop smoking before surgery?

It helps to stop two weeks or more before surgery. Some people say the anxiety associated with trying to give it up at that point is not worth it, but I would rather see them stop smoking and take Valium. It's my experience that general anesthesia is easier to induce and maintain if the patient reduces or desists completely for that period of time.

The night before surgery, what do you need to tell your anesthesiologist?

Ideally, anesthesiologists should ask you everything so you shouldn't need to add anything. They should know of any drugs that you've been taking, because there are interactions between drugs—even aspirin, because it may have an effect on your blood's ability to clot. They should know about any untoward reaction you've had to a drug, any specific allergies, although allergies to drugs are a little less common than people think they are. Very important is a previous history of difficulty during anesthesia.

A woman who is in Alcoholics Anonymous suggested that anyone who is an alcoholic tell her anesthesiologist because she'll need more anesthesia. Is that accurate?

Alcoholics may need more if they're drinking up to the time of the surgery. Patients who come in drunk, however, need less because alcohol is a depressant. Patients who maintain a steady, continuous intake of alcohol often require larger doses of drugs to reach the same end point. In that respect one can consider them "more tolerant" to anesthetic medication.

Is there anything else the anesthesiologist and the patient should discuss the night before?

In the best of all practices the anesthesiologist will describe the kinds of anesthesia that are possible. That is how I practice. It's an opportunity for the patient, if she has a special request, to bring it up. Patients should ask for this discussion of their choices if the anesthesiologist doesn't initiate it. If the procedure is a hysterectomy, vaginal plastic [for prolapsed uterus], or face lift, a choice does exist for the healthy patient.

What would your choice be?

In the best of all worlds, I would have a regional—an epidural or a spinal—for a hysterectomy. But if my anesthesiologist or surgeon was not comfortable with it, it wouldn't bother me to go to sleep. It *does* make a very big difference to me who my anesthesiologist is.

How can the ordinary patient judge the competence of her anesthesiologist?

I admit that's a very difficult problem. You have to depend on your surgeon, I guess. But on the other hand, how does the woman know that her surgeon is the best?

You get to know your surgeon.

Yes, in terms of personality. But you have no way of knowing about his surgical skills any more than you do about the anesthesiologist's.

What is the purpose of the tube inserted after you're under general anesthesia?

You're thinking about endotracheal intubation, which means that a tube is placed in the trachea, the major air passage. We use that to ventilate the patient and also to keep fluids from the gastrointestinal tract from getting into the lungs. General anesthetics eliminate the gag reflex, so you have no protection against aspirating gastric juices into the respiratory tract. Intubation is customary practice for, say, a hysterectomy, as opposed to a D&C, because of the longer time, the greater depth of anesthesia and of muscular relaxation, and the position of the patient, all of which facilitate access of fluid from the stomach into the trachea.

What are anesthesiologists doing during surgery?

They are monitoring your vital signs at all times, making sure they're physiologically normal. If the patient is under general anesthesia, anesthesiologists are maintaining a proper depth of anesthesia and relaxation by metering in, if you will, the anesthetics. They're administering fluids and blood, if necessary, to keep your circulation adequate. With the muscle relaxation, your breathing ceases, so they utilize a ventilator and assure its proper functioning, or they hand-ventilate the patient.

If the surgery is being performed under an epidural, they will also be giving you sedatives or oxygen, or supporting the circulation if your blood pressure goes down.

It's constant attendance, monitoring, and support of vital functions. And at the end, they want to wake you up, want you to breathe properly, so that they can take out the tube.

When does the anesthesiologist's job end?

When you are transferred from the recovery room to another area of the hospital. They do, however, make postoperative rounds. And, should you have a spinal headache or other complications, they will attend to ameliorate your discomfort. But their major work is over after the recovery room. In every hospital today, the anesthesiologists are in charge of the recovery room care.

Why are patients in the recovery room allowed only crushed ice or lemon soaked in water to appease their thirst?

After general anesthesia, your peristalsis tends to stop. Normal elimination is slowed, so volume tends to increase in the stomach. We could give you a teaspoon of liquid—the idea is just to keep a minimum volume of fluid in your stomach.

What are the risks of anesthesia? Why are people so scared of it?

Statistically, we are safer than we've ever been. I always say it's more dangerous to go on the Long Island Expressway or the Los Angeles Freeway than it is to have an anesthetic. The risk of a problem occurring is something like one in two thousand, and most of those problems are minor. Paralysis from a well-conducted spinal or epidural is really unheard-of today. Sometimes, after a spinal or epidural, there is a persistent nerve tingling for some months afterward—that can happen.

The accidents that may occur under general anesthesia in a healthy patient are usually misadventures—a problem with the machine and oxygen deprivation. Vigilance overcomes these.

I think that the fear you're hearing is less related to the science of anesthesia than, say, to the women's fears of these particular surgeries, hysterectomy or mastectomy, where there are issues related to body image and disfigurement. Many people are afraid of going to sleep and having no control or never waking up. There's no question that once you get the hospital gown on, you feel that you've lost your self, your image, your control. But as far as the anesthesia goes—maybe because I'm involved in the specialty—I've never been concerned about going to sleep or of receiving a spinal or epidural. I've always picked my anesthesiologist, and when he said, "What do you want?" I've always said, "Whatever you want to give me." I have personally experienced both types of anesthesia without concern and, happily, without complications. As long as it's done well, what difference does it make?

SURGERY AND ANESTHESIA CONSENT FORM

PERMISSION FOR OPERATION AND/OR PROCEDURE AND ANESTHESIA

1. I hereby authorize Dr. _____ (NAME) _____
   or associates or assistants of his/her choice at _____
   Hospital to perform upon me or the above-named patient the
   following operations and/or procedures (*please type or print*):

   _____

   _____

2. Dr. _____ (NAME) _____ has fully ex-
   plained to me the nature and purposes of the operation/proce-
   dure and has also informed me of expected benefits and complications (from known and unknown causes), attendant
   discomforts and risks that may arise, as well as possible alternatives to the proposed treatment. I have been given an opportunity to ask questions, and all my questions have been
   answered fully and satisfactorily.

3. I understand that during the course of the operation or procedure unforeseen conditions may arise which necessitate procedures different from those contemplated. I therefore consent to
   the performance of additional operations and procedures which
   the above-named physician or his/her associates or assistants
   may consider necessary.

4. I further consent to the administration of such anesthetics as
   may be considered necessary. I recognize that there are always
   risks to life and health associated with anesthesia and such
   risks have been fully explained to me.

5. For the purpose of advancing medical knowledge and education,
   I consent to the photographing, videotaping or televising of the

(continued)

255

operation or procedure to be performed, provided my/the patient's identity is not disclosed. I also consent to the admission of observers to the operating or treatment room.

6. Any organs or tissues surgically removed may be examined and retained by the Hospital for medical, scientific or educational purposes and such tissues or organs may be disposed of in accordance with accustomed practice.

7. I acknowledge that no guarantees or assurances have been made to me concerning the results intended from the operation or procedure.

8. I confirm that I have read and fully understand the above and that all the blank spaces have been completed prior to my signing. I have crossed out any paragraphs above which do not pertain to me.

Witness   Patient/Relative

(Optional): _____   or Guardian*: _____

        (SIGNATURE)   (SIGNATURE)

_____   _____

    (PRINT NAME)   (PRINT NAME)

Date: _____   _____

                        (RELATIONSHIP, IF SIGNED BY

                        PERSON OTHER THAN PATIENT)

    I hereby certify that I have explained the nature, purpose, benefits, risks of, and alternatives to, the proposed procedure/operation, have offered to answer any questions and have fully answered all such questions. I believe that the patient/relative/guardian fully understands what I have explained and answered.

Date: _____   Physician: _____

                                     (SIGNATURE)

The signature of the patient must be obtained unless the patient is under the age of 18 or incompetent.

NOTE: THIS DOCUMENT MUST BE MADE PART OF THE PATIENT'S MEDICAL RECORD.

ESTROGEN REPLACEMENT THERAPY

LILA NACHTIGALL, M.D.

"GOING WITHOUT ERT IS REALLY TORTURING WOMEN FOR NO GOOD REASON."

Dr. Nachtigall is considered one of the country's leading specialists in female hormones. She is associate professor of obstetrics and gynecology at New York University Medical Center, director of gynecological endocrinology at Goldwater Memorial Hospital and of Bellevue Hospital Outpatient Services. She is the author of two books for the general audience; the more recent is Estrogen: The Facts Can Change Your Life *(Harper & Row, 1986).*

A convincing advocate of estrogen replacement therapy (ERT), she is eager to dispel fears that such treatment causes cancer. On the contrary, she reports, ERT protects against uterine cancer, osteoporosis, heart attack, and stroke and can relieve women of the discomfort caused either by the natural aging process or by surgery. ERT cannot be used by women with "estrogen-dependent" breast cancer or endometrial cancer: the risks of both increase in the presence of estrogen.

What is the difference between surgical menopause and natural menopause?

Surgical menopause is the removal of the ovaries, the source of estrogen, causing the most dramatic kind of menopause known, especially if you had a good level of estrogen before. If your ovaries are removed *after* menopause, you won't know the difference.

Estrogen falls off by degrees. The younger you are, the more estrogen you make. The body seems to get used to the changes with time. That's why surgical menopause is the worst. Everything's been normal. One day you're making 75 micrograms of estrogen, and the next day you're making zero. That throws the vasomotor [blood circulatory] system into disarray. To try to compensate for the sudden drop of estrogen, the body produces huge amounts of FSH [follicle stimulating hormone—its job is to trigger the release of estrogen], and many control mechanisms go awry. Women can be very miserable. It's very sad, particularly if it happens because of an estrogen-dependent cancer [a cancer that flourishes under the influence of estrogen]. I see this all the time. Following endometrial cancer, for example, when estrogen is contraindicated and progesterone is not, the progesterone at least stops some of the flushing.

What causes the flush?

No one completely understands it. At one time it was thought to be set off by a high amount of the stimulating hormone for FSH, called luteinizing hormone release hormone—LHRH. The latest theory is that estrogen receptors in the hypothalmus need to be satisfied. When they are not satisfied, they release a chemical-like substance that causes vasoconstriction, giving the intense feelings of warmth. It's interesting that the flush is almost exclusively over the face and neck, sometimes the chest—just the upper part of your body. No one has been able to explain why.

It ends in a sweat, with the dilation of all the same vessels. The flush rarely lasts longer than a few minutes. When measured scientifically, the longest one ever reported was three minutes from start to end. No patient of mine believes that. They all say, "Can't be true. Mine lasts twenty-five minutes." When you actually sit there and time it, they say, "No kidding! Boy, that was the longest three minutes I ever had." It must really be uncomfortable.

Some women say that the worst part is right before the
flash itself. A young woman who had ovarian cancer
described a terribly unsettling, depressive few minutes.

But ovarian cancer—I see no reason why she couldn't be given estrogen. It's not an estrogen-dependent cancer. With breast cancer and with endometrial cancer, one can't take estrogen, but I give it to women after ovarian cancer if there's been no spread, no endometrial involvement. Going without is really torturing women for no good reason. It's just because we're frightened of the word *cancer*.

After a total hysterectomy, you recommend taking both
estrogen and progesterone—both Premarin and Provera,

*for instance. A lot of the women we speak to are just taking
Premarin.*

We use Provera because we think it offers some protection from
breast cancer. When there's no uterus, of course, there's no need
for the Provera, but several studies seem to indicate that there's
a less than normal incidence of breast cancer if you take both
hormones. So I *add* the progesterone—the estrogen continues all
the time—although less progesterone than needed to prevent
buildup of the uterine lining.

*Women tell us that after going through a total
hysterectomy their doctor instructed them to go home and
await symptoms before beginning hormone therapy. So the
women went home and had hot flashes for three weeks. Is
there enough variation in body response and dosage to
justify the few weeks of discomfort?*

Every woman is different, there's no doubt about it. Nothing I
see in all of medicine takes more individualization than using
estrogen. If the patient is twenty-eight years old and she's losing
her ovaries, I could think of very few reasons why she wouldn't
desperately need estrogen. If she's fifty-two and losing her ovaries, and is a tall, dark-skinned woman who's at low risk for osteoporosis, and doesn't get symptoms—and there are many who
don't—then you might say to her, "Go home, and if you have
symptoms, call me." She may never need estrogen replacement.
And if she does, I don't think she has to wait for three weeks. If
she starts getting terrible flashes in three days, she should be
treated.

*Do gynecologists generally know enough about hormone
therapy to prescribe it—or should a woman consult a
specialist?*

I would say that for the average woman, a board-certified gynecologist knows enough—unless the doctor is very, very old and
doesn't understand some of the new ways of giving estrogen. I
think you only need a reproductive endocrinologist if you're having trouble with the therapy or symptoms are not completely
abolished.

*Some women who've had a partial [simple] hysterectomy
for fibroids say that not only has their premenstrual
tension continued, but so have menstrual cramps.*

Premenstrual tension would be expected because they still have
their ovaries. If they have cramps, it would have to be from the

bowel. The bowel is right there, and it's very hard to tell one kind of cramp from the other. I've had patients who say they have exactly the same findings that they had with their period or when they were pregnant. They're just relating it to what they know. Women tend to revolve symptoms around the period—I guess they've been taught to do this—and say, "Oh, I get a headache every time before my period." But if you have them charted, "before their period" can mean three weeks before their period.

One woman was operated on for ovarian cysts, and because she was only thirty-eight and wanted to have a child, the surgeon left half an ovary. After a few months, her period stopped and she went into a clinical depression. Why does menopause cause depression? And how likely was it that one-half an ovary might have functioned?

No one knows the reason for the depression, but we do know that sudden drops in estrogen do lead to depression. Some people think—this is a very new theory—that estrogen itself is a MAO inhibitor,* which is similar to some mood-elevating drugs. And it really might be.

Isn't that what happens with premenstrual syndrome—the sudden drop in estrogen?

Nobody is sure that that's really the cause. We believe PMS is real, but we don't know if it's from the estrogen decrease, or if, when the estrogen drops, the endorphins decrease, or if a serotonin † release comes at the same time. There are so many hormonal changes that we don't understand. But depression postpartum is so common that everybody expects it, and that's thought to be from the estrogen drop. So it's not surprising that in menopause depression occurs, and that in sudden menopause, it would be worse—because the drop is much more precipitous.

Are you surprised that half an ovary wouldn't function at all?

During surgery, when you leave something behind, you have to clamp and tie to control bleeding. It's not unusual that, with all the clamping and tying off, an ovary you hoped would function

---

* MAO inhibitor: Monoamine oxidase inhibitors are antidepressants. According to *The Women's Drugstore* (Dell, 1985), by Harold M. Silverman, Pharm.D., monoamine oxidase is an enzyme that "is responsible for breaking down the natural stimulants." Drugs that inhibit the action of MAO allow the stimulants to work at full force.
† Serotonin is one of the natural stimulants.

would lose its circulation and not function. I have seen it work a couple of times. I was at the operation of a friend's daughter who had a huge dermoid cyst—a very common kind of ovarian cyst. She was in her early twenties, and everyone was hysterical. I had promised to keep my eye on her and just be there for support. The surgeon had to remove the ovary that was affected as well as a section of the other ovary where there was another cyst, which is not unusual. They actually removed one and a half ovaries. She's been pregnant four times since then and has three healthy children.

From what we hear, doctors seem to be cavalier about taking out a woman's ovaries. One gynecologist in his late thirties said, "If a patient is really old, it's an absolute rule that you take out the ovaries if you're going in for surgery." We asked, "What's really old?" He said forty.

Well, I think that has been a problem. For the doctor, obviously, if you're not thinking about the whole patient, if you're thinking about not getting sued, or not feeling guilty, you figure, "We're in there anyway, let's take out the ovaries." One very good cancer surgeon and I have had this discussion innumerable times. He always says, "I take them out because there is nothing worse than having a patient come back with ovarian cancer, and you know you were in that abdomen and could have taken them out." Most women, if they're still menstruating—whether they're forty-five or fifty-five—would rather take a chance. Some patients think that a partial hysterectomy increases your chance of getting ovarian cancer—and, of course, it does not. It doesn't lower the chance, but it doesn't increase it. This doctor's point is that the patients can go on estrogen. My point is that they're probably going to go on estrogen eventually; leaving the ovaries gives a couple of years without medication while estrogen is still produced. And there's nothing like the natural estrogen.

I always advise that the doctor leave in the ovaries. But you don't want to tie the doctor's hands. You make a deal in advance. The deal is that if everything looks fine, he'll leave the ovaries; if there's any question, he'll take them out. Of course, you have to trust your surgeon—otherwise you shouldn't be using him.

It's definitely harder to examine a woman's ovaries when she no longer has her uterus. What we use to hold down the ovaries is the uterus. In an examination, you feel the uterus, then you slide off the uterus, and there are the ovaries. When the uterus is gone, the ovaries are floating somewhere and you can't always feel them. Now we have ultrasound, and if a woman has had a partial hysterectomy and you can't really feel her ovaries, it's appropriate to get an ultrasound once a year as a checkup, a cancer detection.

A young woman who just called is an example of that. She had huge fibroids. . . .

How old is "young"?

Young to me is forty-five. I think this woman was forty-two. In surgery, her ovaries were fine, and her doctor left them in. She still is cycling. She won't have periods, of course, but she has had no flashing, no menopausal symptoms, and it's almost a year. Even if she got one year out of it, I think it was worth the risk.

The risk of ovarian cancer is quite small, isn't it?

Small but scary, because, of all the GYN diseases, ovarian cancer is still the most common cause of death. The statistics are one percent. The survival rate is getting better because of cisplatin, the wonder treatment we have been using in the last four or five years. I think survival is up to 30 percent. But the risk of one percent is still a risk. You go down to zero percent if the ovaries are taken out. The decision depends on a lot of things. If the ovaries are fine and you're still menstruating, I usually recommend leaving them in and watching them with ultrasound as well as physical examination.

There's no risk in ultrasound?

None that we know of. We use it in pregnancy.

You say there is nobody for whom ERT is not safe except for those with uterine cancer or estrogen-dependent breast cancer. In the minds of many people outside the medical profession, hormones are linked to an increased risk of cancer, a fear that started when the Pill was first introduced. Obviously, something has changed in hormone therapy since then.

You know how people, including medical writers, can get on a bandwagon. About two years ago, you would have thought that one of the worst things that could happen to anybody on this earth was herpes. Now, herpes hasn't changed in the last two years—the incidence is still high. But AIDS came in, and AIDS was much more scary.

The same thing happened with estrogen. People were frightened in the early seventies when estrogen was being given without progesterone and it came out there was about a six times increase in endometrial cancer with unopposed estrogen. All the newspapers wrote that up, and people don't forget. And I must say that for twenty-two years I've only given estrogen with progesterone. It makes good physiological sense; it's the way you function normally.

But it became clear that if you watched the dose, and used estrogen with progesterone, it doesn't cause cancer. It was never shown to increase the risk of cancer of the breast: if there is already a cancer in the breast, it does accelerate its growth. Now that we're doing mammographies routinely—on every woman over fifty and some over forty-five—I think you're less likely to miss those preexisting cancers.

Poor birth control pills! They've never been shown to cause cancer of anything, anywhere, any time. Because they have progesterone in them. They're perfectly safe. They have other problems, but they don't cause cancer. In fact, if you're on the Pill for a long period of time, it decreases the incidence of ovarian cancer to practically zero.

How long would a woman who's thrown into surgical menopause stay on ERT?

That's something that you have to individualize. If you're putting her on it to prevent flashes, usually two years is adequate, and then you gradually withdraw it. If you're putting her on it because she's at high risk for osteoporosis, she's going to be on it for ten, maybe fifteen years. We have studies to show that she'll be perfectly safe.

There can be other little problems with hormones—liver, gall bladder, blood clotting, enzyme problems. The new transdermal patch [worn like a Band-Aid] avoids some of those, and you're left, really, with only a couple of minor contraindications. Of course, every woman has to be individually evaluated, but it's certainly a lot safer than the overall impression people gave us in the seventies.

In your book, you urge people to make sure they're taking the lowest possible dose of hormones. How is a patient to know?

The patient can't know it. The doctor has to know. We start with about 0.65 mg. of Premarin or the equivalent because 0.3 is too low to prevent osteoporosis. If you're not having flashes, if the vaginal mucus is more than adequate or adequate, there's no dryness, and you feel well—then that is all the dose you need. If you're still having flashes, if you're not making good mucus—you may need more. The point is that we've learned to lower the dose. At one time we thought replacement levels comparable to what you had when you were menstruating were needed. They're not.

Are you comfortable with the way gynecological surgeons
talk about their patients, their work?

It depends on where they trained and who they trained with. We still see this male chauvinistic attitude of superiority to women. I'm not an archfeminist, but I've certainly been through good times and bad. Some doctors are very cavalier—I agree with you. I've had patients tell me that they were shocked after surgery when they didn't get their period anymore. They weren't told that would happen. And women who are fifty-five years old now really didn't learn about physiology. I think the younger women are better informed.

Most of the men that I work with, that I refer to, are very sensitive. Most. They will talk to a patient before surgery and tell her what's going to happen. But I think a lot of them still say things like "You might as well take out your ovaries." And women say, "If you were having a testicular biopsy, would you feel you might as well have your testes out?" Nothing makes a doctor angrier. He'll say, "It has nothing to do with it!" Well, it does have to do with it. There is an incidence of testicular cancer as well. We don't talk about "prophylactically removing the testes."

Is there a clue that tells you you've got a decent doctor?
The clue is if he or she will spend time with you. And don't think the women doctors are exempt from these criticisms. I know just as many women who are as cavalier as the men or worse. It varies. People are short-tempered and overworked and tired, and they get sued for nothing. It gets to you; you bring all that to your work. But the clue is the time. A doctor should spend more than five minutes with you, telling you why you need surgery and explaining it; or he should say, "I very much feel you need this surgery. If you want a second opinion, you should have it. Then come back and I'll tell you all the implications of how I do it, what it means, what the changes will be," and so on.

One woman advised anyone searching for a surgeon to go
for skill—she said you don't have to like the doctor.
There's one cancer surgeon whom I refer patients to, who will remain nameless, who is always a little flip and uses expressions

that make me sick—like "You'll be screwin' your pants off within two weeks"—to somebody who would never think of screwing her pants off. And yet he is one of the most skilled surgeons I know, and I would let him operate on me. When I refer to him, I always tell the patient, "You're not going there for TLC, and if you have questions, call me."

So there are skilled surgeons who have no bedside manner. That's probably why they went into surgery. You have to deal with that. But I think you can get both skill and sensitivity. I know surgeons who have both. And I do think the patient should expect to be told whether she's going to have a period again, whether she's going to have hot flashes, what can be done about them, and is there a chance that she can have hormone therapy.

ON LASER, MYOMECTOMY, ENDOMETRIOSIS, FERTILITY, AND THE RISK OF CANCER

J. VICTOR REYNIAK, M.D.

"LASER IS A TWENTY-FIRST-CENTURY TOOL, ELEGANT AND EXTREMELY PRECISE. IT CAUSES LESS TISSUE IN-JURY, SO THE HEALING PROCESS IS BETTER."

Dr. Reyniak specializes in infertility and reproductive endocrinology. He is an expert on laser surgery, which has created alternative ways to treat fibroids, cure infertility, deal with excessive bleeding and ectopic pregnancies, manage endometriosis, and remove certain kinds of malignancies. He is clinical professor of obstetrics and gynecology, and director, Division of Reproductive Endocrinology, at Mount Sinai Medical Center in New York City and is coauthor of Principles of Microsurgical Techniques in Infertility *(Plenum Publishing Co., New York, 1982). He ended the interview with encouragement to call if we had any questions left unasked: "Remember, there are no stupid questions."*

Would you begin by explaining what laser is?
Laser is basically a surgical tool, an elegant, extremely precise surgical tool. It can be used as a cutting tool, a coagulating tool, or a combination of both.

Some specialties could not live without laser—ophthalmology, for instance. Gynecology could probably do very well without laser, relying on a knife or cautery. Laser is just a little more advanced, a twenty-first-century tool, that, when applied properly, offers advantages. Surgeons can use mechanical energy: a hand pushing a knife, leaving a raw surface with bleeding, which you have to control. You can also use electrical energy,

266

such as electrocautery. This obliterates small vessels by heat as
it cuts; however, in the body, electric current travels in a conical
shape—spreading out to other tissues—so it splatters, causing
thermal injury to other tissues, which then can undergo necrosis
and adhesions. Or you can use laser.

Laser is simply a collimated parallel beam of light—intensified
light that has been concentrated in a very small spot. The light
has been centered on spots the size of 0.2 millimeters. And this
spot, when in focus, can actually work as a surgical blade. As
that light strikes the tissue, it heats the cell water to flash boil,
vaporizing the cells. It cuts the tissue, assuring coagulation of
small blood vessels as it cuts and causing no thermal damage to
the lateral tissues. The laser impact is a clean, thin line. The
depth of the necrosis—the wounding of tissue that is inevitable
in surgery—is absolutely minute, in a range of 100 microns.

What are some of the uses of laser?
It's ideal for, let's say, endometriosis. Endometriosis right now
has reached almost epidemic proportions, and one of the ways of
managing it—not curing it, because there is no cure for it—is
eradication of the abnormal endometrial tissue outside the
uterus. When you take the laser out of focus, instead of cutting
you can vaporize cell layer by cell layer without causing thermal
damage to underlying organs such as the ureter or bowel. The
patient goes home the same day with minimal postoperative discomfort. The results are promising. And I'll tell you this secret:
Laser destroys the DNA of the cell, the genetic material that
guides the cell's reproduction, so the disease is less likely to recur
in the same spot. And since any procedure can be contaminated
by bacteria, infections are less likely to occur after laser because
you burn up the bacteria and viruses; you send them up in smoke.

In myomectomies, laser is an option. Myomectomy is such a
gross procedure, and so bloody, usually, because of the large area
that you have to incise. With the use of laser, we don't eliminate
the bleeding, but we minimize it. And laser probably causes less
tissue injury, so the healing process is better.

Some women who have tremendous bleeding problems connected to their menstrual cycle are no longer interested in childbearing but have some sort of contraindication to major
procedures such as hysterectomy. We can obliterate the cavity by
burning out the endometrial tissue with laser through the hysteroscope. You won't run into a great number of patients of that

sort, but in indicated cases, this solution is marvelous. Also, laser can burn off small polyps or fibroids in the cavity as a minor procedure.

The primary application of laser in gynecology is for vaginal, vulvar, and cervical malignancy. It's marvelous, again, because you vaporize the disease, destroying the DNA of the malignant cells. You can do a cervical conization with laser, almost totally bloodless, as long as the malignancy is confined to the surface—an early, intraepithelial neoplasia. That's how laser works. Look, I'll show you, and you don't have to be a physician to understand.

[He pulls out color photographs taken during a myomectomy. "This woman had a fibroid inside her uterus. Here is the villain," Reyniak says, pointing to a fibroid being lifted out of the uterus—it looks like a knot or a twisted skein of yarn. The carbon-dioxide laser beam itself is invisible; an aiming dart of helium shows the path of the beam. "I want you to look for blood," Reyniak prompts. There is none. As the laser cuts, it "seals" the blood vessels. The visibility is remarkable. "Laser seems to incise without bleeding, so it minimizes adhesions," he says. "It simply causes less tissue insult and trauma." He identifies another photograph: "Final excision. As a backstop, I am using a quartz rod, which absorbs laser and so prevents the beam from going beyond what I want it to hit. . . . And here she's all stitched up, back together again, to live happily ever after." You can see large cross-stitches running vertically up the uterus. "I love this because it's neat, it's bloodless, it's clean. Well, not bloodless—say less, much less bleeding."]

Would you use laser for a hysterectomy?
No. Any destructive procedure, you use the knife. It would be silly and time-consuming and unnecessary to use laser. You use the simplest tool that you can to do the procedure, to get it over with and finished.

On the other hand, when we're trying to reconstruct or preserve organs, we should apply the principles of microsurgery. The principles of microsurgery call for ultimate gentleness with tissues; judicious use of a variety of optic magnification, very delicate instruments like laser or electrocautery, and fine suture material; constant irrigation to prevent tissue dessication so it's less likely to cause adhesions; and most important, not pushing, pulling, tugging. And this is all to preserve the tissue, to respect it as much as we can, and to assure a good healing. Because the enemy of reconstructive procedures is scar tissue, adhesion formation.

Are the risks different with laser?

Laser is as safe as any surgical tool, providing the physician understands the principles of physics behind laser, knows how to use it, and uses simple precautions such as protection for the eyes of assistants and so on.

Is laser considered at all experimental?

No, it's totally accepted. Laser has been accepted for a long time in ophthalmology, of course, and in other specialties. In gynecology it is finally catching on and approved for use in endometriosis through the laparoscope, and for hysteroscopy, and with the open abdomen as well.

How do the costs compare between laser and scalpel procedures?

Many surgeons will charge more for laser, but I don't believe that is justified. It is a very expensive tool, of course, to the hospital— the initial investment can run from $25,000 to $100,000—but it's not a patient's responsibility: it makes my life easier, and I am more successful in managing the case with the appropriate tool.

We know you're working on a study of laser myomectomy and fertility. How is it going?

So far I have 240 myomectomy patients. Two hundred thirty-nine out of 240 went home on the fourth day after surgery, as opposed to seven to ten days for a scalpel myomectomy. A few had transfusions—autologous transfusions, of their own blood that they stored for themselves before. And unfortunately, I cannot tell you about fertility rates, because many of those women didn't want to conceive immediately or didn't have anybody to conceive the baby with. They wanted simply to preserve the uterus for possible future use. Of those who desired pregnancy, about 70 percent have become pregnant so far. It's a small number of cases—I don't know how statistically significant it is—but the pregnancy rate for standard myomectomy is 47 percent. So it seems to be a little better.

We were surprised to hear that you're willing to perform myomectomies on older women who have no intention of getting pregnant.

The indications for myomectomy have changed, not only because of several social factors, but also because of women's attitudes. The social factors are that women delay childbearing to a later age. The later the age, the greater the likelihood of benign pathology such as fibroids. Fibroids eventually affect about one-third of white women and two-thirds of black women. And they usually don't disturb you too much, but they may interfere with fertility potential.

In the past, the treatment for fibroids was hysterectomy. Right now, both women and doctors think twice before they consider a hysterectomy. Myomectomy is a less traumatic technique. One indication for it is to preserve fertility potential.

Another interesting indication is women who do not want to have hysterectomies. And if a woman who is forty-three comes in and says, "Look, I know I have fibroids. I probably won't even consider childbearing, but I don't want to close a gate for myself. I like my uterus"—I think this should be a reasonable indication to preserve a uterus, as a reflection of her wishes.

What do you think of this new impulse in the older woman to try to keep her uterus, her ovaries?

Well, I think the Greeks created the word *hysteria* from "hystet," the uterus. They thought the uterus was the center of the soul. And hysterectomy does cause some psychological depression, no doubt, because you are parting with a very essential organ of your body. But I think in a postmenopausal situation, when reproduction is no longer an issue—or even premenopausal, when the reproduction is finished—I would be much more inclined to suggest hysterectomy. What is the use of saving it? It is ridden with a disease of sorts—fibroids; let's take it out.

Some women who are now forty-five tell me, "Look, reproductive technology has progressed so far, what if I want to have a donor egg? If I have a womb, I may be able to carry the baby biologically even when I am sixty years old." Of course it's possible. On the other hand, you can ask: Psychologically, what would be the fate of a newborn of a sixty-year-old woman? When the baby is ready for college, where is the woman going to be? That is a very realistic consideration, in my opinion.

So if reproduction is no longer an objective, I would be much more inclined to recommend removal of the uterus. I am, however, becoming more and more conservative with removal of the ovaries. The rule of thumb in gynecology has been: Below forty, preserve the ovaries; over forty, take them out. But nobody says to the forty-year-old male who has had a prostatectomy [removal of all or part of the prostate gland], "Oh, while we are there, why don't we take out your testicles?" Ovaries should be respected, and if the woman can get mileage out of her own ovaries, I think it's worth a trade-off with the minimum risk of cancer—unless the woman is of such advanced age that I know her days before menopause are numbered and it's really silly to preserve them.

What's advanced age?

About forty-five. Then it's a controversial issue whether the organs should be preserved. Over forty-five, I probably would do as well removing the ovaries and putting the woman on estrogen replacement therapy and calcium.

We're interested in the fact that about a fourth of the women we've interviewed who have had hysterectomies for fibroids went into surgery with the fear of cancer planted by their doctors. How realistic is that?

The malignant transformation of the fibroid is very uncommon. *Very* uncommon. But a rapid increase in size could be the warning, you see, and then one should be prepared. I just today have a woman whose fibroid grew to a very large size within four months. I warned her, "Look, it could be malignant." We did a myomectomy, and I sent a frozen section for biopsy, and it was reported as suspicious but not conclusive. And when she woke up, I said, "Look, we've preserved your uterus right now, but there is a likelihood we'll have to go back and remove it." And that's exactly how it turned out—the tumor was malignant. That's the first time in about twelve years for me. It's a very rare situation—it's one in a million. I am extremely upset today because of this. I just don't know how to face this poor woman, and I've got the report and I know I have to go to the hospital and tell her about it. I'm extremely upset not only because she went through hell to get pregnant, and now, not only is the fertility potential over, but there is a grave threat to her life.

How old is she?

Thirty-two.

And you have been following her fibroids?

No, she was referred to me for surgery. The fibroids were discovered eight months ago. She had an ectopic pregnancy a few months ago, and they noted an increase of fibroid size, which they attributed to pregnancy. Subsequently, the fibroids grew even further, very rapidly. So we removed them, and based on examination, it was one of those unique cases where a malignant transformation has occurred. But it's very, very rare.

Do you think doctors should alarm a woman with the possibility of cancer when the chances are so remote?

Yes. If the tumor is growing very fast, it is the doctor's responsibility to inform her, and the woman should be pressured into decision making. If the fibroids are small or slow-growing or not growing at all, then leave them alone—unless they interfere with function, or reproductive potential, or cause pressure, pain, or bleeding.

HYSTEROSCOPY: OPTIONS IN FIBROID SURGERY

ROBERT NEUWIRTH, M.D.

"THE MOST POWERFUL THING ABOUT THE TECHNIQUE IS THAT YOU OBTAIN A PRECISE KNOWLEDGE OF WHAT'S GOING ON. AND WHATEVER IT IS, YOU CAN TELL THE PATIENT RIGHT THEN, AND GO ON FROM THERE."

Dr. Neuwirth is director of obstetrics and gynecology at St. Luke's-Roosevelt Hospital Center in New York City. He developed the fiberoptic technique for diagnosis and surgery in gynecology. He combines research on the hysteroscope with a private practice.

Could you give us some background on the hysteroscope?
The idea is to look into the uterus, just as you might look into any other body cavity. There are problems to be defined, and you want to use all the senses you can—including vision—to make a diagnosis. Until ten years ago, the gynecologist had only two diagnostic techniques available: first, the curettage, a tactile technique that can be used to feel the uterine walls, and second, the hysterogram, a visualization technique in which a dye is injected into the uterine cavity to outline it and X-rays are taken.

Hysteroscopy was made possible by several technical advances between 1900 and 1960 in endoscopy: the development of new instruments with fiberoptic lighting, and better lens systems and a better knowledge of how to distend the uterus properly—so you can see into it—with liquid or gas.

The hysteroscope was developed initially to get at the fallopian tubes to perform sterilizations without going through the abdom-

273

inal cavity. Diagnostic hysteroscopy, however, became important very quickly. The most powerful thing about the technique is that you obtain a precise knowledge of what's going on. The uterus may be normal, it may have a polyp, or an IUD: whatever it is, you can tell the patient right then, and go on from there. And, also, a fair amount of hysteroscopy can be done right in the office, saving time and money.

Is the major use of the hysteroscope diagnostic?

Sure, but we have gone on to more and more surgical applications. Here you marry the diagnostic technique to a variety of other tools: scissors, laser, cauterizing instruments, Silastic plugs that you can inject into the fallopian tubes for sterilization —it's a marriage of technologies to accomplish specific objectives. People call up now and say, "I want my uterus to be lasered." That's the buzzword for high-tech surgery—a laser: it's essentially a scalpel using light waves. Fiberoptics is a way to get the light into the body.

Will you describe the hysteroscopic exam?

For a diagnostic hysteroscopy, a woman is placed on an examining table just as if she's about to be examined at a routine office visit. In our place, we usually give the patient 5 milligrams of Valium a half hour before so she's relaxed. A speculum is put in, the cervix is exposed. We put a little local anesthesia in the cervix to numb it so you won't feel the passage of the hysteroscope into the uterus. (The cervix isn't sensitive to needles.) After we inject the local, the telescope is passed into the uterine cavity. We distend the uterus by passing Hyskon, a very viscous fluid, or carbon dioxide through the scope into the cavity. It takes two minutes, and you see what's inside. And that's that.

Is the cost of the hysteroscopy in addition to the cost of the visit?

Yes, because you need special equipment and you need a nurse trained to assist. It's a special procedure. We schedule it.

Is diagnostic hysteroscopy considered experimental?

No.

How widespread is the use of the hysteroscope across the country?

I would say maybe 10 percent of gynecologists are using it, now. It's been around only ten years, and it's a technique you have to learn. You've got to remember that the private practice of medicine is very influenced by economic drive. You're not going to change your practice unless it is necessary. What drove laparoscopy into prominence was tubal sterilization, not diagnosis. When women went down the street to have another doctor do a laparoscopic sterilization, their doctor was pushed to learn how to do it.

How do you use hysteroscopy to manage bleeding?

Say a woman is forty-eight years old and having abnormal bleeding. If cancer or precancer has been ruled out with curettage or endometrial biopsy, and the uterus is not so enlarged due to very large fibroids, we will give it a try. The woman must be prepared to sign a release permitting a hysterectomy if we get into trouble during a myomectomy. If there's not a submucous fibroid, we create a third-degree burn of the entire uterine cavity with a laser or cautery: we're able to visualize directly, burn out the lining, and let it scar the endometrial cavity. Most of those patients do very well. Afterward, they either have no periods or light periods. The bulk of patients will have that as the single treatment of their problem. Clearly, this burn technique is not useful in women who want to retain their fertility.

Abnormal bleeding seems to be one of the most common gynecological problems women face. Can you talk about the causes and treatment?

There really are two generic causes. The first is precancerous and cancerous problems, which, fortunately, is the less common category. The second category is hormonal or local physical problems. First you have to rule out the malignant and premalignant causes. That's critical. It's done by biopsies, curettages, and Pap smears. Once we've eliminated precancerous and cancerous states, we can deal with the broad category of benign causes of abnormal bleeding, and we've learned we can do something about it.

If a woman has a normal uterus and is young, usually the cause of her abnormal bleeding is hormonal (once pregnancy is ruled out), and usually you use some hormonal replacement treatment. You're limited by certain risks. For example, estrogen in an older woman: it's not a good idea to put a woman of forty-five on birth control pills for a long time. But it is not unreasonable to try it for a few months, and if there are no specific contraindications, I do it frequently. The woman may start cycling normally again and avoid surgery. The contraindications to estrogen with the older age group includes fibroids, hypertension, diabetes, endometrial hyperplasia.

Then there are the benign physical causes, like fibroids. There are two things we can do. One, if the woman wants to maintain her fertility option and she has submucous fibroids, we now know we can go in and shave off the part of the fibroid that is protruding into the uterine cavity. Or two, if the fibroid is pedunculated [growing on a stem like a mushroom] and it's soft, we can shave it down and pull it out. And we will often get significant improvement of the bleeding problem. If the problem cannot be handled by hysteroscopy, the patient will need an abdominal myomectomy.

The advantage of the hysteroscope is that you can make the diagnosis in the office. Not only can we tell exactly what it is, but we know if we can attack it hysteroscopically. Furthermore, if we can treat it hysteroscopically—that is, vaginally—the woman will be in the hospital for only a couple of nights and be back to work in a week. The abdominal approach requires a longer recovery.

If a woman has fibroids and wants to get pregnant, what are her chances after a hysteroscopic myomectomy?

In the beginning, we didn't know whether the area would resurface with normal endometrium, so we limited the procedure to older women. But after eight or nine years, we called up all the women and found that several in our over thirty-five group had gotten pregnant. So we began to open up the procedure to younger groups. And we found they can reproduce. At least some of them. The series is not enormous, but we have enough to know that there's a reasonable chance a woman can reproduce following this approach.

What are the risks associated with the operative hysteroscopy?

We use a laparoscope when we do a major hysteroscopic surgery. With the laparoscope, you have a gas bubble inflating the abdominal cavity. So if the hysteroscopic instruments penetrate the uterine wall, you probably won't hit a vital organ such as the intestines. You may have to stop the operation at that point, but you haven't created a serious injury. And so far, we've not injured anybody's bladder or bowel. We have put a couple of holes in the uterus. In one woman who was forty-nine, we had half the tumor out and I couldn't finish the operation due to perforation. She and I had an understanding that if that should happen, we would do a hysterectomy, which is what was done.

That brings me to the other point. Women over forty-five, nearing menopause, don't have that much to lose unless a serious injury occurs. The patient I mentioned had about one chance in a hundred of losing her uterus. She took the risk and she lost, but she was happy with the outcome. She's the only one who had to have a hysterectomy during the hysteroscopic surgery. The others have avoided major abdominal surgery and recovered from the hysteroscopic surgery quickly. Younger women, below forty, have a greater chance of requiring repeat hysteroscopic surgery or hysterectomy because they have a longer interval until menopause. About a quarter of women below forty will require additional treatment, mainly because of enlarging fibroids or recurrent bleeding.

CHEMOTHERAPY

WILLIAM GRACE, M.D.

"AMONG PATIENTS OF WORLD-CLASS ONCOLOGISTS,
NAUSEA AND VOMITING FROM CHEMOTHERAPY HAVE AL-
MOST TOTALLY DISAPPEARED."

*Dr. Grace is chief of medical oncology at St. Vincent's Hos-
pital in New York City. He is assistant professor of medicine
at New York Medical College and on the board of directors
of the American Cancer Society.*

How did chemotherapy evolve as a treatment for cancer?
It began back in the 1930s with the discovery of penicillin. Researchers found that penicillin stopped the uncontrolled growth
of bacteria by inhibiting the construction of the cell wall. It didn't
take a mental giant to hypothesize that if antibiotics worked to
stop bacteria growth, antibiotics might be effective in inhibiting
the growth of cancer cells—and that turned out to be a successful
exploration. In the early days, researchers called the use of antibiotics chemotherapy. And even today, in Europe, chemotherapy
means drug treatment for infection whereas in the United States
chemotherapy means the use of anticancer drugs.

The first step in the research process was an exploration of
what nutrients cancer cells needed to grow. Folic acid was one of
those nutrients, and they learned that it worked to inhibit the
growth of rapidly dividing cells. This discovery led to research
into the metabolic requirements of cancer cells. At the same time
researchers began experimenting with drugs that could cut off
the supply of what the cells needed. And as the research evolved,
the use of antibiotics against cancer cells increased outside the
realm of controlled studies. When I graduated from a cancer program in 1976, there were very few medical oncologists in the
country. There were physicians taking care of cancer patients
who knew very little about how to treat the disease, and there

were very few tools that could treat cancer successfully. Immunotherapy of cancer in the *classic* sense as physicians practiced
it in the 1960s and 1970s didn't pan out.* Today, we're just beginning to have some success with immunologic therapies for cancer. Interleukin II and interferon have produced some anticancer
activity by manipulating cancer cells in the patient's body, but
they are still very expensive.

How does chemotherapy work?

Chemotherapy attacks cancer cells. When you treat breast cancer with chemotherapy, seven out of ten women respond. The 30
percent who do not respond to treatment are getting poisoned
without benefit. It is important to understand that the drugs we
use are systemic metabolic poisons which optimally eliminate
the cancer without damaging the patient too severely. We have
at least five different kinds of drug combinations for women with
breast cancer. A woman could fail drug combination number one
but respond to drug combination number three or number five.
Certain cancers demand that we come up with new combinations
of drugs, and I think in this area a medical oncologist's creative
skills are tested.

*Are the side effects of chemotherapy like nausea and
vomiting dependent on the individual woman?*

No. Among patients of world-class oncologists, nausea and vomiting from chemotherapy have almost totally disappeared.

*Why is it, then, that so many of the women we interviewed
reported nausea and vomiting? Did they get the wrong
treatment?*

I don't play hockey as well as Wayne Gretzky, okay? There are
differences among oncologists as there are among hockey players. I always use three classes of antinausea medicine on every
patient. If you go to a large hospital specializing in cancer where
sixteen people are in a room getting chemotherapy, it can be a
horror show. One person vomits, and the smells get everyone

---

* According to Fredrica Preston, clinical nurse specialist, University of Pennsylvania Cancer Center, it is felt that cancer patients have a decreased immune
system. "The idea behind immunotherapy is finding a way to make the immune
system more active so it can go after cancer cells." In the 1960s and 1970s immunotherapy of cancer was far more random in its methodology. "Researchers
explored applying drugs directly on a section of malignant melanoma to see if the
immune system could be increased. Today the methodology is more specific. A
culture of a certain type of tumor is taken and grown in the lab, and its response
to different drugs is noted."

going. When a new patient walks into a room like that, she thinks everyone who has chemotherapy is supposed to puke. It's not true. Here at St. Vincent's we always use individual treatment rooms. When the one patient in twenty in our hospital gets sick, nobody else knows about it, nobody else smells it, nobody else sees it. Many of our patients are given a Walkman and/or a TV to distract them. Our nurses are compassionate and hold patients' hands. You have to treat people with dignity.

What is the most common way of giving chemotherapy?
There is no one set pattern. Cancer is six hundred different diseases. There are many good chemotherapeutic regimens: some in which the medicines are taken orally, some where they're given intravenously. Cytoxan and Methotrexate can be given by mouth or taken through the vein. If a woman doesn't like swallowing pills, I think it's better to give it by vein. It's an area of controversy as to whether one is more effective than the other.

As a chemotherapist do you consult with surgeons and
radiation oncologists?
I hate the term *chemotherapist.* I am a medical oncologist. My role is to integrate all the disciplines. To do that requires a complete understanding of cancer therapy whether it involves chemotherapy, hormones, radiation, or surgery. The oncologist is not there to push poisons—that is the definition of a chemotherapist. In the fifties, physicians were taught how to push poisons, but they didn't understand *why* they were pushing them. Oncologists are trained to provide total treatment. Before seeing a patient I see the records from every doctor she has consulted so I have as much information about the patient as possible. It's the only way to recommend the most appropriate options in therapy. I have to know the pathology. I have to know what the surgery entailed. I have to know how likely the failures are going to be. Will the failures be systemic with the possibility that the disease will return? Or is there a high probability of a local failure, in which case more local therapy is appropriate? Or maybe I might want to use some combination of different therapies.

You also have to know other things about a patient. Many of the drugs we use might be toxic to the heart, so it's important to know if a patient has good heart function. And then you have to assess psychological factors. A patient who is a famous movie star—very beautiful, very wealthy—was referred to me as a candidate for chemotherapy. She is basically a very unhappy person and has tried to commit suicide several times. Chemotherapy was out of the question for her because it was clear that anything that made her life one little bit more difficult would make her life not worth living. Basically, she said she didn't want curative management—very aggressive chemotherapy and radiotherapy—for her disease even though I can't imagine someone for whom it would have been more appropriate.

How do you find a good oncologist?
It is very difficult because a woman feels very vulnerable at the moment she's looking. Not knowing anything about therapy, she generally has to trust her surgeon. And he may not know about every option in terms of therapy, nor all the different doctors who deliver it.

I think women may want to interview more than one specialist, so I suggest they ask their surgeon for a number of names. Also the recommendations of friends are very, very important.

Do you treat younger cases more aggressively?
We know that cancer in women under the age of thirty-five responds to aggressive hormonal treatment and aggressive chemotherapy. And that the more intensely we poison our young women, the greater will be the percentage of those women who are going to have long-term freedom from their cancer and the possibility of a cure. However, every new group of cancer trial reports confirms that no matter what the patient's age, the more a number of effective drugs are used together, and the earlier and more aggressively they're used, the greater the benefits. And that trend continues. A woman's age ultimately may be less a factor than the stage of her cancer in determining treatment.

What do you see as the future of chemotherapy?
Every year we're getting better at giving chemotherapy. We are learning how to give it with less duration, more intensity, and fewer side effects. Optimally, in a few years, we'll get the toxicities down to even more manageable levels and get the postoperative efficacy up to more acceptable levels. We are making progress, and we continue to make progress. I don't think women should be afraid of it. Chemotherapy is a growing and evolving science. The new therapies will involve more drugs than we currently use—combinations of seven and eight instead of two or three. In the future, chemotherapy will probably last only three months instead of the six months or twelve months it does today.

CHEMOTHERAPY CONSENT FORMS

THE STANDARD FORM

When a patient agrees to be treated by chemotherapy, she must sign a consent form. The following is an example of a standard form.

CONSENT FOR DRUG THERAPY

1. My doctor has informed me that I have a tumor or malignant disease which requires drug treatment. I, (NAME OF PATIENT) , willingly agree to participate in the described treatment explained to me by ___(NAME OF DOCTOR)___ .

2. I understand that my participation is voluntary, and this treatment directed toward cure or improvement may result in neither.

3. I have been informed that my doctor plans to treat me with one or more of the following drugs. He has explained fully how these drugs will be given and the known side effects as set forth below. Also, I have been informed that there may be potential side effects which are not yet known. I have been assured that every attempt will be made to minimize the possible risks or side effects through careful monitoring of blood counts and body chemistries.

(continued)

DRUG	METHOD OF ADMINISTRATION	POSSIBLE SIDE EFFECTS
_____	_____	_____
_____	_____	_____
_____	_____	_____

4. I understand that I am free to withdraw my consent to participate in this treatment program without prejudice to my subsequent care and to seek care from any physician of my choice at any time.

5. I understand that a record of my progress while on this treatment will be kept in a confidential form in this office.

6. I have read all of the above, asked questions, received answers concerning areas I did not understand and willingly give my consent in this program.

_____   _____
(PATIENT SIGNATURE)   (DATE)

_____   _____
(WITNESS SIGNATURE)   (DATE)

_____   _____
(PHYSICIAN SIGNATURE)   (DATE)

CHEMOTHERAPY: RESEARCH PROGRAM CONSENT FORM

Any patient who participates in an investigational study must sign a consent form similar to the one below. All such studies must be approved by the Food and Drug Administration and the institutional review board of the hospital.

PHASE II–III STUDY OF CHEMOTHERAPY OF
(Name of Disease)

RESEARCH STUDY

I, __(NAME OF PATIENT)__ , willingly agree to participate in this treatment which has been explained to me by __(NAME OF DOCTOR)__ . This research study is being conducted by __(NAME OF ONCOLOGY GROUP)__ and by __(NAME OF HOSPITAL)__ .

PURPOSE OF THE STUDY

It has been explained to me that I have __(NAME OF DISEASE)__ . I have been invited to participate in this study. This study involves treatment with antitumor drugs and in some cases X-ray therapy to the brain. The purpose of this study is to develop new treatments which will hopefully result in the relief of symptoms and prolongation of life. To do this, the standard drug regimen of __(NAME OF REGIMEN)__ will be compared to several new experimental agents. The effectiveness of the investigational drug I may receive is unknown.

DESCRIPTION OF PROCEDURES

This study involves initially the administration of __(NUMBER OF DRUGS)__ different chemotherapeutic treatments: __(NAMES OF DRUGS)__ .

Since it is not clear which of the drug combinations is better, the drug treatment plan which is to be offered to me will be determined by chance using a method of random selection called randomization. Randomization means that my physician will call a statistical

(continued)

office which will assign one of the drug therapies to me and that the chances of my receiving one of the offered treatments are approximately equal.

(The method of administration of each of the drugs to be tested, the amount of time it takes to administer each drug, the length of time it takes to complete the course of treatment is outlined. In addition to this, the form states what course of action is to be taken if there is a complete remission of the disease, if there is partial remission, or if the treatment is not effective.)

RISKS AND DISCOMFORTS

Drugs for chemotherapy often have side effects. The drugs used in this program may cause all, some, or none of the side effects listed. In addition, there is always the risk of very uncommon or previously unknown side effects occurring.

VP-16 may cause breathing difficulties, nausea, vomiting, a lowering of the blood cell and platelet counts (leading to an increased risk of infection, easy bruising and bleeding, and anemia), temporary hair loss, loss of appetite, headache, and mild low blood pressure.

CYTOXAN may cause temporary hair loss, bladder irritation with bloody urine, nausea, a lowering of the blood cell and platelet counts (leading to an increased risk of infection, and easy bruising and bleeding).

ADRIAMYCIN may cause a lowering of the blood cell and platelet counts (leading to an increased risk of infection, easy bruising, and bleeding), ulcerations of the mouth, temporary hair loss, and severe skin ulceration if the drug is leaked when it is being given. Adriamycin can also cause heart damage.

VINCRISTINE may cause damage to the nerves of the legs and arms, constipation, muscle weakness, and jaw pain.

CISPLATIN may cause nausea, vomiting, hair loss, lowering of the blood counts (which may lead to an increased risk of infection,

(continued)

bleeding or anemia), decreased hearing, numbness or decreased sensation in hands or feet, kidney abnormalities, and, rarely, decreased vision.

TENIPOSIDE frequently causes decreases in the white blood cell and platelet counts (which increase the risk of infection, bleeding, and bruising), nausea and vomiting, and temporary loss of hair. Less frequent side effects include low blood pressure, allergic reactions that can cause breathing difficulty, and skin rashes, damage to the liver, muscle soreness, and numbness and tingling in the hands and feet.

IFOSFAMIDE commonly causes lowering of the white blood count (which increases the risk of infection), loss of hair (which is not permanent), and nausea and vomiting. Less common side effects are damage to the liver, kidneys, or bladder. Central nervous system side effects such as confusion, weakness, drowsiness, and possible coma may occur.

MESNA usually causes no side effects, but nausea, vomiting, and diarrhea could occur.

WHOLE BRAIN RADIATION THERAPY may cause temporary hair loss, scalp irritation, and alteration in taste.

My doctors and nurses will be checking me often to see if any side effects or complications are occurring. Routine blood and urine tests will be performed to monitor side effects and results of therapy. Side effects usually disappear after the drug is stopped. However, my doctors may prescribe medications to keep those side effects under control. I understand that treatment to help control side effects could result in added costs. This institution is not financially responsible for treatments of side effects caused by the study drugs.

This protocol may or may not have harmful effects on pregnancy, but, as yet, the existence of any such harmful effects are not reasonably known. I am not pregnant at this time.

If I am not pregnant but decide in the future to attempt to become pregnant, or if there is even a slight possibility that I may be-

(continued)

come pregnant, intentionally or unintentionally, I agree to notify Dr. _____(NAME)_____ immediately so that the advisability of my continued participation in this study may be discussed.

CONTACT PERSONS

The physicians involved in my care have made themselves available to answer any questions I have concerning this program. In addition, I understand that I am free to ask my physician any questions concerning this program that I wish in the future. I have been assured that any procedures related solely to research which would not otherwise be necessary will be explained to me. Some of these research procedures may result in added costs which may not be covered by insurance. My doctor has discussed these with me. If physical injury is suffered in the course of this research or for more information, I can notify _____(NAME OF DOCTOR)_____ , the investigator in charge, at _____(PHONE NUMBER)_____ .

BENEFITS

It is not possible to predict whether or not any personal benefit will result from the use of the treatment program. Possible benefits are remission of tumor and prolonged survival. It is possible that the investigational drug may prove to be less effective than the standard regimen. I understand that if I receive treatment with the experimental drug and do not show any benefit from the treatment, I will receive treatment that has previously been shown to be effective. I have been told that if my disease becomes worse, if side effects become very severe, if my doctor feels that continued treatment is not in my best interest, or if new scientific developments occur that indicate the treatment is not in my best interest, I will be so informed and the treatment program will be stopped. Further treatment will be discussed.

ALTERNATIVES

Alternatives which could be advantageous in my case include treatment with different drugs, or radiotherapy. However, there is no clear evidence that other treatments would provide an increased chance of controlling my disease, and the side effects from other

(continued)

drugs may be similar to those from the drugs proposed in this study. I understand that my doctor can provide detailed information about my disease and the benefits of the various treatments available. Another alternative is no further therapy, which would probably result in continued growth of my disease. I have been told that I should feel free to discuss my disease and my prognosis with my doctor.

VOLUNTARY PARTICIPATION

Participation in this study is voluntary. No compensation for participation will be given. I understand that I am free to withdraw my consent to participate in this treatment program at any time without prejudice to my subsequent care. Refusing to participate will involve no penalty or loss of benefits. I am free to seek care from a physician of my choice at any time. If I do not take part in or withdraw from the study, I will continue to receive care. In the event that I withdraw from the study, I will continue to be followed and clinical data will continue to be collected from my medical records.

CONFIDENTIALITY

I understand that a record of my progress while on the study will be kept in a confidential form at ___(NAME OF INSTITUTION)___ and also in the computer file at the statistical headquarters of __(NAME OF ONCOLOGY GROUP)__ . The confidentiality of the central computer record is carefully guarded, and no information by which I can be identified will be released or published. However, medical records which contain my identity may be examined by members of the Food and Drug Administration (FDA) and by the National Cancer Institute (NCI) during their required reviews. Histopathologic material, including slides, will be sent to a central office for review.

___(NAME OF HOSPITAL)___will provide immediate essential care for any physical injury resulting from my participation in this research protocol. However, neither long-term hospital treatment nor financial compensation will be available from the hospital.

(continued)

I have read all of the above, asked questions, received answers concerning areas I did not understand, and willingly give my consent to participate in this program.

_____   _____
     (PATIENT SIGNATURE)   (DATE)

_____   _____
     (WITNESS SIGNATURE)   (DATE)

_____   _____
    (PHYSICIAN SIGNATURE)   (DATE)

ONCOLOGY NURSING

FREDRICA PRESTON, R.N., M.A., O.C.N.

"I WOULD STRONGLY ENCOURAGE A WOMAN CONSIDER-
ING ADJUVANT THERAPY TO USE THE ONCOLOGY NURSE
AS A RESOURCE PERSON, PARTICULARLY IF SHE IS CON-
FUSED BY THE INFORMATION SHE IS GETTING FROM
OTHER SOURCES."

*Ms. Preston is an oncological clinical nurse specialist and
assistant director of the Hospice/Home Care Department of
the University of Pennsylvania Cancer Center. She received the 1989 American Cancer Society's Lane Adams
Award for excellence in cancer nursing.*

What do oncology nurses do?
We work closely with medical and surgical oncologists providing
physical care—chemotherapy administration, wound management. We are very good at symptom management and at coun-
seling and teaching patients with cancer. Oncology nurses
practice in a variety of settings, including hospitals, private offices, clinics, and in patients' homes. We want to help. We're well
educated—master's degrees are very common, and many nurses
are taking Ph.D.'s now—and we know the current cancer research.

I think oncology nurses are the true patient advocates, with the
knowledge, skill, and authority to meet the needs of our patients.
We try to make the treatment fit the patient's life-style. For instance, if we know a patient works during the day or is in school,
we will try to schedule her treatment at night or on the weekend.
I would strongly encourage a woman considering adjuvant therapy to use the oncology nurse as a resource person, particularly
if she is confused by the information she is getting from other
sources. We have our own channels of information, and if one
nurse doesn't have an answer, a friend or colleague across town

can help. I think we are an untapped resource for cancer patients.

Is oncology a new specialization in nursing?

I started in 1975, and very few nurses specialized in oncology then. I became involved right from the start. It's a wonderful field for nursing—you work with patients long-term and get to know them very well. You work with their families. You're involved with research. It's a field oncology nurses have carved out for themselves. They have seen the needs and actively gone out to meet those needs. Also, the overwhelming majority of oncologists are more than receptive to our work—they're really enthusiastic about our contribution. Oncology is a field where nurses and physicians each acknowledge the contribution the other makes. The science of oncology is not as exact as some others, so the two disciplines work hand in hand to provide quality patient care.

As a medical professional, how do you feel about alternative therapies for cancer, such as a macrobiotic diet?

If we have nothing else to offer cancer patients and if the alternative therapy isn't harmful to them, then I think it's fine. If people feel their general sense of well-being is better on a macrobiotic diet, I say good for them. Do it. But I would strongly suggest they consult someone who really knows macrobiotic nutritional principles because the body is already compromised due to the cancer and the treatments. There are also treatments like biofeedback that emphasize relaxation, and I consider them very positive. The only problem I have with many of the alternative therapies is the subtle message they communicate to a cancer patient that she is in control of her disease and has the power to change the course of her illness. That's fine as long as she remains healthy, but if she has a relapse or something goes wrong, she blames herself: "If only I had tried harder." And that's not a positive state of mind! There are charlatans out there. Everyone is looking for a miracle—that's the problem. However, having said that, most alternative treatments are *not* toxic, and they can assist patients in developing a sense of inner peace. At the center we offer people relaxation tapes, and I think massage is wonderful relaxation.

I have patients who have read Bernie Siegel's *Love, Medicine & Miracles* and were helped by it. I really think that's great. But I feel a patient has to consider the stage of her disease before turning to alternative treatment. If she is offered a multiple drug regimen when her cancer has metastasized to different parts of the body and the risks of treatment outweigh the potential benefits, and then she says, "No, I don't want this. I think I'm going to go to the mountains in Tibet," I'd say, "Go." But if she is in an early stage of cancer and she says, "No, I don't want surgery or chemotherapy, I'm leaving for Tibet," I'd say, "You're a fool." I would try to make sure she understands the ramifications of her decision to reject treatment of a potentially curable disease. But in my experience if a person gets strong emotional support and good medical care in managing her side effects from the professionals caring for her, she won't get to the point where she walks away from treatment that can cure her.

SCRIPTS

Questions to Ask Your Doctors

"I WISH I'D HAD A SCRIPT WHEN I WENT IN TO THE DOCTOR: ASK THIS AND THIS," SAID A WOMAN FRUSTRATED BY A LOST OPPORTUNITY TO QUIZ HER SURGEON. WE THOUGHT THAT WAS A GREAT IDEA AND ROUGHED OUT SCRIPTS FOR EACH SURGERY.

GENERAL QUESTIONS FOR ANY GYNECOLOGICAL SURGERY

1. Is this surgery necessary or elective?

2. Is there any alternative to the surgery?

3. What does the surgery entail? [If an organ is to be removed and you are not sure where it is in your body, ask to see a model or a drawing of the abdomen and have the doctor show you exactly what he plans to do.]

4. What are the risks of this surgery?

5. Do you allow residents to participate in your operation, or do you do the surgery completely?

6. What kind of anesthesia will be used, and how will it be administered?

7. What medication will I be on, if any, after surgery? [If you are allergic to any medication, make sure your doctor knows as well as the anesthesiologist in the hospital.]

8. Do you think I should have blood drawn before surgery in case I need a transfusion? [Even if the doctor feels it is unnecessary, if you are concerned about possibly needing blood, ask him/her to arrange it.]

9. Can I be shaved under anesthesia rather than the night before surgery?

10. How long will I be in the hospital?

11. When can I expect to see you in the hospital?

12. When can I shower or bathe?

13. Should I stay in bed when I get home, and for how long?

14. When can I have intercourse?

15. When can I return to work?

16. What is your fee for the surgery?

D&C AND D&E

1. Do I have an option to have the surgery as an office procedure with local anesthesia?

2. Do you recommend that?

3. What are the risks of the procedure?

4. With local anesthesia, can I go back to work sooner, or is recovery the same?

5. How much does it cost to have the procedure in the office? How much does it cost in the hospital?

LAPAROSCOPY

1. Where will the incision be?

2. How long will it be?

3. Will it be stitched or clamped?

4. When will the stitches or clamps be removed?

5. [If the procedure is related to a cyst] What do you think about my taking the Pill for a couple of months instead of having the surgery right away? [If the ovaries have a chance to rest, the cyst could shrink.]

CONE BIOPSY

1. Does the Pap smear indicate I need a cone biopsy? [Read interviews on cone biopsy and see Glossary on staging.]

2. Is cryosurgery [an office procedure] an alternative for me?

3. Will there be a risk of my not being able to carry a pregnancy to term?

CESAREAN

1. Under what conditions would you do a C-section?

2. What do you think are the chances of my needing a cesarean?

3. If I have a cesarean, what kind of anesthesia do you plan?

MYOMECTOMY

1. Can I postpone my surgery if
   a. I'm within a few years of menopause?
   b. size is the only significant reason you feel I need surgery?

2. Can my fibroids be removed vaginally?

3. Can my fibroids be removed with laser?

4. Can I have a bikini incision?

HYSTERECTOMY

1. Can I postpone my surgery if
   a. I'm within a few years of menopause?
   b. size is the only significant reason you feel I need surgery?

2. I know I need this surgery, but can I keep my ovaries unless they are diseased?

3. Will you at least try to save a part of an ovary if there is a problem? [Even half an ovary can provide enough hormones to delay the onset of menopause.]

4. Can I have a vaginal hysterectomy?

5. Can I have a bikini incision?

6. My skin has a tendency to form keloids. Do you know any way to counteract it with different methods of suturing or clamping or injecting cortisone under the skin? [There seem to be no guarantees, but it's good to focus the doctor on your concern.]

7. Since I am having a complete hysterectomy, will you tell me the advantages and disadvantages of ERT? [See interview with Lila Nachtigall, page 257.]

ANESTHESIA

1. Will I be given any medication before going into surgery? What kind?

2. Will you be the one who administers the anesthesia?

3. What will you be giving me?

4. How will it be administered?

5. Are there alternatives, and what makes this one the best for me?

6. Are there any side effects?

7. Are there any risks?

8. After surgery, how long will it take to regain consciousness?

9. What is your fee?

FOUR

The Hospital: Routines, Procedures, and Services

THE ADMITTING PROCESS

INSURANCE PLANS

PATIENTS' RIGHTS

A PATIENT'S BILL OF RIGHTS

THE ADMITTING PROCESS

Setting the date for hospital admission and making a reservation for a room—private or semiprivate—as well as arranging a time for preadmittance lab work is usually done through the surgeon's office. The lab work must be done no longer than fourteen days before surgery so the results will be current. Many large metropolitan hospitals make every effort to settle the details concerning admission before check-in day. The procedure varies from hospital to hospital, but, generally, when the hospital takes the reservation, the preadmitting office sends the patient a questionnaire requesting personal data, such as age, sex, marital status, and so forth, and insurance information that is to be returned to the hospital within forty-eight hours. If the surgery is scheduled immediately, this information will be taken over the phone.

The preadmitting office also arranges for private nursing care, a phone, a TV, and any special diet a patient may need—vegetarian, low fat-low salt, kosher, and the like. You can make these arrangements by phone or in person. Make sure to get the name of the person you speak with so if you want to make any changes, you have a contact. Most hospitals hand out a booklet about the hospital's policies regarding fees, visiting hours, use of the telephone, social services, complaints, and so on. If the hospital has a patient representative, that person is your official ombudsman. The phone number for the department is usually prominently displayed in the admissions booklet and in each room. Use it. The patient representative's only job is to make sure your stay in the hospital is as trouble-free as possible. (See the interview with Ruth Ravich, patient representative, page 308.)

A patient has recognized rights when she is treated in a member hospital of the American Hospital Association. These rights are clearly set forth in "A Patient's Bill of Rights" (see page 315). A few women we interviewed complained about people coming in to examine them several times while they were in the hospital. Another woman talked about not understanding the reason blood

samples were taken frequently. All of them had the right to refuse examination or treatment, according to "A Patient's Bill of
Rights": "Those not directly involved in her care must have the
permission of the patient to be present."

PREADMISSION LAB TESTS

These tests are part of the check-in routine for patients undergoing general anesthesia. If a patient is scheduled for local surgery,
the tests are generally unnecessary unless the patient is old, has
severe hypertension, or has a history of heart problems. In such
cases, the patient may be given one or more of the tests to make
sure she is able to tolerate the local.

Chest X-ray. Checks that the lungs are healthy and can take the
anesthesia. Generally, if a patient has had an X-ray within two
or three months, the test need not be repeated.

Electrocardiogram (EKG). Conducted to make sure the patient's
heart is healthy enough to withstand surgery. Electrodes are
placed directly on the skin of the upper body in a painless procedure to record the heart muscle's activity. An irregular reading
may indicate heart problems that need to be reviewed by a cardiologist.

Complete blood count (CBC). A number of different tests are
performed on the blood taken from a patient to make sure she
can go through the surgery with minimum risk. The most common blood test checks the level of hemoglobin, a protein in the
red cells responsible for carrying oxygen to the body's tissues. If
a patient is found to be anemic—her hemoglobin level is low—
surgery might be delayed until her blood has built up to normal
levels, or she might be given a transfusion. A platelet count is
also done to check that the blood will clot normally. A hematocrit
reading is taken to measure the volumes of blood cells and fluid
in the body: a particularly low hematocrit reading may be an
indication that a transfusion is necessary.

Urinalysis. Tests for specific gravity (SG) compares the weight
of urine to that of plain water. If the count is low, it indicates
urinary obstruction; if high, dehydration. Also checks levels of

sugar, acidity, and protein. Abnormal readings may require further evaluation by a doctor before surgery.

These tests *can* be performed on the day a patient is admitted to the hospital, but if any problems require cancellation of surgery, the sudden change can be very stressful for everyone concerned. For this reason hospitals and physicians recommend scheduling necessary tests before admitting day.

WHAT TO TAKE TO THE HOSPITAL

Preadmittance literature at most hospitals includes tips on what to pack and what not to pack. The lists generally recommend taking a lightweight robe, nightgown or pajamas (the hospital provides a gown, but many patients prefer to wear their own), slippers, toilet articles, stationery, and an inexpensive watch or clock. You are asked to bring no more than a few dollars and no jewelry or other valuables.

Many of the women we interviewed admitted they took more than they needed to the hospital. But this is no time to deprive yourself of anything that will make you feel more comfortable about being in the hospital. If you want to take something seemingly unnecessary with you, take it. The women we interviewed had some suggestions, many that might not be on any official hospital list: a Filofax, envelopes of checks for the private nurses, insurance forms already filled out, a Walkman and favorite cassettes, books, their own pillow and fresh pillowcases, vitamins, body cream, makeup, magazines, and tapes designed to calm you before surgery and to help heal you after surgery from the Planetree Health Resource Center in San Francisco. For those having abdominal surgery: cotton underpants that come up to the waist (bikinis hit you right at the incision) and slip-on slippers because you can't bend down easily after the surgery. If you're in a room equipped with a refrigerator, the women suggest stocking up on fruit, juices, and wine to offer guests, plus extra glasses and paper napkins.

CONSENT FORM

The night before surgery you will be asked to sign the consent form reprinted below, agreeing to have a specific procedure performed on you. The form may need revisions or additions to bring it into line with the verbal agreement you have made with your doctor to have a bikini incision, for instance, or *not* to remove your ovaries unless there's an indication of cancer.

INSURANCE PLANS

PAT MCGUIER

"KNOW WHAT YOUR POLICY COVERS BEFORE YOU HAVE
TO TAKE ADVANTAGE OF IT."

*Pat McGuier, an insurance benefits manager working with
a small brokerage company in Seattle, Washington, talked
with us about health and medical plans. In 1990 a five-day
stay at a large metropolitan hospital for a hysterectomy
could cost $5,000 to $6,000 for a semiprivate room, $7,000
to $8,000 for a private room. Those figures would cover sur-
gical facilities, room, nursing care, tests, drugs, and so
forth. The surgeon's fee could be an additional $3,000–
$5,000, and the anesthesiologist could raise the total by an-
other $750. With a good insurance plan, the hospital cost
can virtually be taken care of, and with major medical
riders, a portion of the doctor's fee can be reimbursed.*

*How can a consumer get the cheapest but best possible
medical coverage?*

By working for a company or belonging to an organization that
has group insurance covering all hospital costs as well as doctors'
or surgeons' fees.

So group insurance is your recommendation?

Yes. Group insurance may be funded two different ways. The first
is noncontributory, where the company pays 100 percent of the
cost. The advantage of this type of insurance is that the individual does not bear *any* of the cost. Up until two years ago there
was an even greater advantage—a person could get coverage
under this policy without any health statement, so no prior or
current illness could affect your eligibility for coverage. But that
is no longer true because costs have risen so dramatically. To get
this type of insurance today you have to submit evidence of your
insurability. What this means is that at the time of application

303

there can be no presence of a preexisting condition such as cancer, heart disease, high blood pressure, AIDS, kidney problems, pregnancy, and so on.

The second type of funding is called contributory. The employer agrees to pay a percentage of the costs, and the employee picks up the rest. Under contributory insurance, if the employee agrees to take the coverage when it is first offered to her, no health history is required—that is, if the company she works for employs twenty or more employees. This figure depends on the area of the country and the particular policies of the insurer. However, if she works for a company that employs less than twenty people, or for any reason she declines to accept the initial offer and then *later* wants coverage, the application form requires a full health statement. Any prior illness or physical problem listed in that statement could be used as a reason for denying a person coverage if she or he is hospitalized for that illness or problem. So if a woman has a condition such as fibroids or endometriosis that might warrant future surgery, ideally she should be employed by a large company that requires no health statement.

Two common options in group insurance exist. The first offers a basic plan where certain items are paid for at the rate of 100 percent of usual and customary charges—for example, the cost of a semiprivate room—while other things such as the doctor's fee is covered at a percentage of perhaps 80 percent, 85 percent, or even 90 percent. The second common option is comprehensive major medical, where you pay a standard deductible and then everything above that is covered at an agreed-upon percentage.

What happens with individual insurance?
Today, individual insurance rates are more or less even with group insurance—that is, if you are under age forty-five. If you are forty-five or older, the cost of coverage may be greater than group insurance. Anyone applying for individual insurance is required to give the insurer health information. They ask you to tell them the last time you went to a doctor and the names of the doctors you have consulted within the past few years. When you sign your name at the bottom of the statement, you give them the right to go to those doctors to find out the nature of your visit. When the doctor responds, the information received is placed in the computer for future reference. Coverage can be denied if there is proof of illness prior to application. Also, if you have a condition that requires hospitalization or extensive outpatient

care, the insurance companies can attach riders to your policy stating they will not pay for treatment for that particular problem again. The obvious conclusion is that if you are over forty-five, with any preexisting medical condition, you could be denied individual insurance and should make every effort to get coverage through a group plan in a company that has more than twenty employees. At any age noncontributory is best because the employee does not pay. Second best is contributory when it is first offered to you.

How are rates for hospital insurance claims determined?
The rates are based on usual and customary charges for a particular area or city. Every three to six months the rates for various procedures are charted. A simple average is calculated. The rates are different across the country. For example, what a doctor or a hospital charges in Los Angeles is much higher than what they might charge in Seattle, whereas in Podunk, Iowa, the rates may be even lower.

Would it be accurate to say that a consumer is dependent on her employer's choice of carrier and plan for adequate medical coverage?
Yes. The portion of our company that works on health benefits helps design plans for individual companies. We advise them of the benefits available and advise them of what's new on the market, what might be better for their employees. The options increase depending on the size of the group. And the company usually makes the decision about what kind of plan or plans they will offer their employees based on the company's financial picture. I'm sure when people are considering the advantages of one job over another, excellent medical coverage is one of the real inducements.

Are there tremendous profits in hospital plans?
Actually the profit margins are small, but the dollars coming in are very large. The insurance companies take that money and invest it. In lots of cases the loss ratio is over 100 percent, which means they have put out far more money than has been paid in, but most insurance companies make their money from investments.

Although Blue Cross/Blue Shield is the most widely publicized of the insurance plans, there are many others.
Is there any advantage to having Blue Cross/Blue Shield?
Not particularly, even though you might think so because Blue

Cross/Blue Shield is a nonprofit carrier. All premium rates and benefits for Blue Cross/Blue Shield as well as the for-profit companies like Mutual of Omaha, Traveler's, or Metropolitan Life are based on the usual and customary charges existing in the area on the age/sex ratio of the particular firm they are insuring. And they're based on the benefits within the plan they are selling. However, for-profit carriers may provide better contracts, and they are worth investigating if you have a choice.

At this time [December 1989], there is a trend with all of the insurance carriers to go to what is called "preferred provider option" for groups. Different companies have different titles for this option, but it means that a particular carrier goes out to the various hospitals, the various doctors in all fields of medicine in a geographic area, and gets those doctors to agree to charge a certain fee for a procedure. The carrier then agrees to pay 100 percent of the bill.

The number of different doctors and hospitals you have to choose from depends on the carrier. Blue Cross/Blue Shield, because of their size and visibility, often represent a great many doctors and hospitals. The preferred option plan gives the consumer the greatest number of options. Not only can those doctors who have signed up work in whatever hospital they have agreed to work in, but they can work in other hospitals that have a similar agreement with the carriers.

So if you have a preferred option plan, you can be assured your rate with an affiliated doctor would be, say, $2,000 for a hysterectomy. But what happens if you go to the same doctor covered by another medical insurance plan?

It's possible that your cost could be higher if you are insured by a different type of plan. For example, indemnity plans which are offered by for-profit organizations might charge you more. These plans make payments to the consumer on usual and customary charges which are determined by their own figures. If your doctor charges more than their assessment of the costs, you could be responsible for the difference—even if your policy with them states they will pay 100 percent.

One forty-five-year-old woman we talked with chose a myomectomy over a hysterectomy because she wanted to keep her uterus. The insurance company wanted to cancel her insurance because she hadn't chosen a more

*conservative method. Do insurance companies have that
kind of power?*

I don't know about canceling a policy, but they could offer less
payment on a claim if you chose to go a certain way. In most
cases they can require you to get a second opinion on a particular
surgical procedure, which they will pay for. If you don't get the
second opinion, they can lower the rate at which they will pay for
a procedure. This particularly applies to certain elective procedures such as D&C's and hysterectomies.

What if you have uterine cancer?

If the recommendation is hysterectomy, insurance companies
want the second opinion to confirm the diagnosis as a measure to
reduce the number of nonessential surgeries. Many hysterectomies are statistically unnecessary, and many more of them are
performed in some states than in others. Second opinions are a
new data source for the insurance companies. They hope to pin-
point problem areas. If a physician recommends ten hysterectomies and the second opinion in eight of the cases recommends
against it, the insurance companies and eventually the hospitals
will be able to look into the physician's practice.

*What would be your advice to consumers of medical
insurance?*

To know what your policy covers before you have to take advantage of it. Does it pay for all or a percentage of the hospital costs?
Does it pay the doctor's fee? Does it cover private rooms, private
nurses? How about lab tests, drugs, and prescriptions? Does your
medical plan allow you to choose your own doctors, or is your
choice of doctors limited by the plan? What surgical procedures
does your plan cover? Are maternity benefits included? Does your
plan include physical examinations or any preventive medical
procedures? What is the policy regarding preexisting conditions?
Also, if you are changing jobs, make sure your current plan continues to give you medical coverage through the transitional period.

PATIENTS' RIGHTS

"WE HUMANIZE THE HOSPITAL EXPERIENCE FOR THE
PATIENT. WE HAVE TO SOLVE THE PROBLEMS THAT
MIGHT BE IMPEDING A PATIENT'S RECOVERY, AND WE
HELP A FAMILY COPE WITH THE HOSPITAL SYSTEM."

*Ms. Ravich has been the director of the Patient Represen-
tative Department at New York City's Mount Sinai Medical
Center since she developed the program in 1966. She was
the first president of the National Society of Patient Representatives of the American Hospital Association and a
founder and co-director of the master's program in health
advocacy at Sarah Lawrence College from 1980 to 1985. She
is currently a special consultant to that program.*

*We understand that Mount Sinai Hospital was the first in
the country to institute an advocacy program for patients.
How did that come about?*

In 1966 Medicare and Medicaid programs were altering health
care delivery systems, and Mount Sinai was developing a medical school. The director of social services felt that it was important for the hospital to have a department dedicated to
individualizing and humanizing the hospital experience for patients and to create an official channel of communication between the patients and administration. Our function was to be
patient advocates: to handle complaints, solve problems, answer
questions, and act as liaison between patients and staff. We
would also hasten solutions by negotiating the complex hospital
bureaucracy on behalf of the patient or family. Another important aspect of our job would be to assess where the bottlenecks in
the system prevented optimal care and to offer solutions and recommendations for changes from a patient perspective. We would
report our findings to hospital administrators to help them pin-

point problems in their operations and deliver more effective services.

What kind of authority do you have in the hospital?
The department has the support and cooperation of the hospital's senior management team. We have access to staff in all departments and at every level as well as access to medical records. We have an overview of the entire patient care system and the authority to cross departmental lines to advocate for the patient when necessary. Our role in patient care is to help the hospital improve its response to patient needs by pointing out the patient's view to the hospital administration. We try to do this without assigning blame or complicating issues with emotionalism. It has been my experience that this way encourages staff to listen and to help find solutions to the problems.

What aspects of this role do you feel are most important?
First, evaluating the patient's needs and wishes, then presenting the facts to the appropriate staff member. Another important facet is learning which staff members are responsive and responsible in implementing plans that have been developed for the individual patient. A patient's problem frequently involves many staff members, including doctors, nurses, and aides—often from several departments. In some cases we arrange a conference in the patient's room that can include the patient's family, the nurse, the doctor, the social worker—if there is one on the case—and a member of our staff. We discuss the patient's perception of the problem and the needs of the patient. This opens channels of communication and improves interaction between the patient, the family, and the staff.

Sometimes the staff labels a patient or family as "troublesome" or "demanding," and this is reflected in their behavior toward the patient. When a patient is very sick, or develops an infection or a reaction to medication after surgery, or falls out of bed, the staff may feel they have contributed to the problem. Instead of becoming more solicitous of the patient's needs, they can develop negative feelings, making it difficult to talk to the patient. In such cases—when communication breaks down—the patient representative can get it started again. If an impasse is reached, we might recommend that the patient be transferred to a different floor where the relationship between patient and staff is more compatible.

Patient representation is such a logical solution to better

*patient care. How many hospitals across the country have
such an organization?*
Over one-half of all hospitals in the United States have a patient
representative program now. Hospital administrators have multiple problems to deal with—budget, space allocation, research,
and meeting the needs of staff as well as patients. A patient
representative department focuses on the patient. It is a struc-
tured way to deal with patient problems, and more and more
hospitals are adopting the concept.

How large a department do you have?
Besides myself we have two coordinators—one for our In-Patient
Division, the other for the Ambulatory Care and Emergency
Room Division. We also have eight patient representatives, a
Spanish interpreter, and an administrative secretary. We are assisted by five volunteers, all of whom have been with us for at
least five years; each devotes at least two full days a week to the
department. We handle approximately forty thousand cases a
year.

How do patients find out your organization exists?
First of all, elective patients receive a packet of information before they are admitted, and the patient representative telephone
number is included. Then, when patients are admitted they are
given a welcome card that states: "If you have any questions or
concerns about hospital services that staff is unable to resolve,
please call the Patient Representative, dial 66." Also, the welcome booklet at bedside contains information about the services
the hospital provides, including the patient "hot line" number
that connects directly to our office. That number is also posted on
all patient telephones. Patients are also given the Patient's Bill
of Rights—in compliance with the New York State Health Code
—which again mentions the availability of our services and the
number to call. Spanish-speaking patients are given all information in their own language.

*Let's say a woman in a hospital lacking a patient
representative has what she considers a major problem
and can't get anyone to help. What should she do?*
Hospitals are complex organizations, and if contact can be made
with the appropriate department, the solutions may come faster.
If the problem is nursing, the woman or some member of her
family can contact the director of nursing. If the problem is with

social services, the head of that department should be contacted. Other hospital problems should be taken to the administrator or the director of the hospital. Patients must make their problems and complaints known. That's the only way a hospital can help and serve them better.

But you have to admit that all hospital staff members are not Florence Nightingales.

Absolutely. And very few people are always patient and kind. Nurses and aides and hospital staff sometimes wake up on the wrong side of the bed like everyone else. And at times that's reflected in their attitude. Nursing in particular is a very difficult job. You have to know a tremendous amount these days because the technology is always changing. The nationwide shortage of registered professional nurses is complicating the quality of health care and putting added burdens on those in the field. But I think people who work in a hospital are there to serve patients, not just to get a salary. There are other jobs where people can make the same or even more money without the particularly difficult responsibilities hospital workers assume in treating and caring for people who are ill and upset. Improving the interaction between patients and staff is often only a matter of pointing out the patient's perception.

With fewer nurses, what will happen to patient care?

I think people will become adjusted to accepting alternatives to the traditional modes of care. The number of patient representatives will increase as well as staff members with technical training. These professionals will share some of the nursing responsibilities, relieving the nurse of many of the tasks she now performs. Patients will have to recognize that some parts of today's comprehensive nursing role will be taken over by other players.

How often do nurses get in touch with your department for help with a patient?

About 30 percent of our referrals are from nurses, doctors, ancillary staff, and administration. We are often called on to handle "difficult" patients—people who are excessively anxious and require a great deal of attention and time beyond their medical needs. I had an interesting case last week, which is an example of the kind of work we do as patient representatives. A nurse called to say that a patient had to be moved to another room and that she refused. She had been assigned to a room with one nurse for two patients when she had been very ill. Now she was medically ready to be moved back to the room she had occupied before. When I approached her bed she said, "You want me to move." I explained that because she was much better now we were asking her to give up the room and the private nurse for a much sicker patient. I asked her why she didn't want to move. She said, "Well, the room I had before didn't have a telephone and my television didn't work for a day and I didn't like my bed." Everyone had assumed that she didn't want to move because she wanted the extra care and attention of the private nurse. No one had listened to her reasons for not wanting to move. I assured her that before she was moved, the television and the phone would be working. I offered to move her in the bed she was occupying and gave her credit for the days her phone hadn't worked. Responding to the concern that was shown, she willingly agreed to be moved. The arrangements were made, and the nurse was asked not to make the move until everything that had been promised was in place.

In our interviews we talked with women who want to make sure that surgery is not performed by a resident. Can that be prevented, or is it established procedure in some hospitals?

If you are a private patient, the surgery should be performed by your private physician. However, in a teaching hospital, your surgeon may be working with a resident as part of the training program. When it is determined that the resident has the necessary skills, the resident may be allowed to perform part of an operation such as opening or closing a wound. As the resident becomes proficient, increasingly complicated procedures will be performed. It is important to know that in a reputable hospital, if a resident performs any part of a procedure, an experienced surgeon will oversee the operation.

What happens when a patient doesn't like the resident assigned?

At times we are involved in cases where a patient doesn't get along with a particular resident. A patient representative can arrange for another resident to take over the case. Patients should be aware, however, that having residents on call twenty-four hours a day improves the quality of patient care. Attending physicians are not always available, and it is important that a physician who is knowledgeable about a case *is* available at all times.

Is it difficult remaining a true patient advocate when you are being paid by the hospital?

Here at Mount Sinai I know we've been able to maintain our position of patient advocate and assure that patients we see receive the best care and services that the hospital can offer. One way we can maintain our objectivity is to keep a little distance between ourselves and other departments. I think the hospital responds to our recommendations because we manage to maintain our objectivity about the patients, staff, and system. When people work closely together on the same floor or same nursing unit or department, they function as a team that can deliver efficient medical care. The team may make decisions concerning a patient without involving her or her family, and they expect the patient to understand that the best decision regarding her care has been made. When the patient or family expresses concern about that care, the patient representative can mediate and help the team find an alternative way to deal with the situation.

Are there independent patient advocates who don't work for the hospital?

This field is just opening up. There are advocates who see people in nursing homes. Usually they have hospital, nursing, social services, or patient representative experience. Some are paid by families who do not live nearby. In New York State, ombudsmen associated with the Department of Health have access to nursing homes and review the quality of care delivered. A new federal law will mandate this access to all nursing homes in the country. However, I think it's particularly difficult to advocate from outside the institution. Not knowing the staff and not having access to records can be a real stumbling block. Patient representatives working in the institution know the staff and know how the charts are organized. They know where to find laboratory and X-ray reports and whom to contact when a test must be rescheduled or when a patient is dissatisfied with some aspect of her care.

What should you look for in a patient representative?

They should be assertive without being bossy. They must be able to communicate well and have exceptional negotiation skills. They need analytic and organizational skills and problem-solving abilities as well. They must be tactful and patient, and a good sense of humor is an asset. It's very important that they be non-judgmental and accepting of the values and priorities of both patients and staff members.

Is patient advocacy a real career?

Absolutely. In 1980 I started a graduate program in health advocacy at Sarah Lawrence College in Bronxville, New York. I have two people working in my department now who are graduates of that program. They did their fieldwork here as part of their studies and became members of the staff when the department expanded. In New York City there is a patient representative department in every hospital, and almost all have expanded their programs during the year. The National Society of Patient Representatives of the American Hospital Association has over one thousand members.

What is their training?

Students analyze actual cases and discuss various ways of handling situations that may occur. There are practicums where the students work in a hospital or in an outside advocacy organization. The course in physiology helps students understand the processes and functioning of the body. "The Language of Patient Care" is a course covering surgical and X-ray procedures: what they are and how patients must prepare for them, how it feels to undergo them, and how long they take. Courses in hospital law, health care regulations, medical ethics, psychology, and medical economics are also part of the curriculum.

Sometimes people think patient representation is a hostess job designed to comfort patients or take complaints about food service. We do a lot of that, but as professionals we also have to solve the problems that might be impeding a patient's recovery, and we help a family cope with the hospital system not only while the patient is in the hospital, but in some cases after she is discharged, where continuing care might be necessary. The patient should not be released before she is medically ready to be sent home, but a problem could arise when a patient *is* medically ready for discharge according to her physician, but she doesn't feel well enough to go home. She may find it difficult to stand, to walk, to do housework, or to take care of the children. Social services and home care departments of the hospital are usually responsible for coordinating services at discharge and after the patient is at home. The patient representative is available if there is a systems breakdown or if an appeal to Medicare or other insurance company is necessary.

If a woman is preparing for an operation at Mount Sinai,
can she call you before she comes into the hospital?

Certainly. We would be happy to answer any question about the hospital, but we would encourage her to talk with her doctor about her medical concerns.

And if she isn't sure of the right way to frame a question to
her doctor, could you help her with that?

Yes, we can assist by helping her formulate the questions she would want to ask the doctor about treatment and alternatives, prognosis, length of stay, and so forth. The following American Hospital Association Patient's Bill of Rights can be used as a guide for this.

A PATIENT'S BILL OF RIGHTS

During the 1970s the board of trustees and house of delegates of the American Hospital Association developed the following statement on patients' rights. It defines the responsibilities of the physicians and medical staff. Implicitly, it expects the patient to share in her own health care by first knowing her rights, then exercising them.

The American Hospital Association presents "A Patient's Bill of Rights" with the expectation that observance of these rights will contribute to more effective patient care and greater satisfaction for the patient, her physician, and the hospital organization. Further, the association presents these rights in the expectation that they will be supported by the hospital on behalf of its patients as an integral part of the healing process. It is recognized that a personal relationship between the physician and the patient is essential for the provision of proper medical care.

The traditional physician-patient relationship takes on a new dimension when care is rendered within an organizational structure. Legal precedent has established that the institution itself also has a responsibility to the patient. It is in recognition of these factors that these rights are affirmed.

  1. The patient has the right to considerate and respectful care.

(continued)

---

2. The patient has the right to obtain from her physician complete current information concerning her diagnosis, treatment, and prognosis in terms the patient can be reasonably expected to understand. When it is not medically advisable to give such information to the patient, the information should be made available to an appropriate person in her behalf. She has the right to know, by name, the physician responsible for coordinating her care.

3. The patient has the right to receive from her physician information necessary to give informed consent prior to the start of any procedure and/or treatment. Except in emergencies, such information for informed consent should include, but not necessarily be limited to, the specific procedure and treatment, the medically significant risks involved, and the probable duration of incapacitation. Where medically significant alternatives for care or treatment exist, or when the patient requests information concerning medical alternatives, the patient has the right to such information. The patient also has the right to know the name of the person responsible for the procedures and/or treatment.

4. The patient has the right to refuse treatment to the extent permitted by law and to be informed of the medical consequences of her action.

5. The patient has the right to every consideration of her privacy concerning her own medical care program. Case discussion, consultation, examination, and treatment are confidential and should be conducted discreetly. Those not directly involved in her care must have the permission of the patient to be present.

6. The patient has the right to expect that all communications and records pertaining to her care should be treated as confidential.

7. The patient has the right to expect that within its capacity a hospital must make reasonable response to the request of a patient for services. The hospital must provide evaluation, service, and/or referral as indicated by the urgency of the case. When medically permissible, a patient may be transferred to another facility only after she has received complete information and explanation concerning the needs for and alternatives to such a transfer. The institution to which the patient is to be transferred must first have accepted the patient for transfer.

(continued)

8. The patient has the right to obtain information as to any relationship of her hospital to other health care and educational institutions insofar as her care is concerned. The patient has the right to obtain information as to the existence of any professional relationships among individuals, by name, who are treating her.

9. The patient has the right to be advised if the hospital proposes to engage in or perform human experimentation affecting her care or treatment. The patient has the right to refuse to participate in such research projects.

10. The patient has the right to expect reasonable continuity of care. She has the right to know in advance what appointment times and physicians are available and where. The patient has the right to expect that the hospital will provide a mechanism whereby she is informed by her physician of the patient's continuing health care requirements following discharge.

11. The patient has the right to examine and receive an explanation of her bill, regardless of source of payment.

12. The patient has the right to know what hospital rules and regulations apply to her conduct as a patient.

GLOSSARY
Breaking the Code—
Translating Medicalese into English

ACUPUNCTURE: A branch of traditional Chinese medicine, used to rebalance the body's energy, to cure and prevent illnesses and to anesthetize. Very fine needles are inserted into the skin at specific points along the body's meridians (fourteen invisible lines running the length of the body). The meridians are thought to form the circulatory system for the *chi,* the life force.

ADHESIONS: Internal scar tissue that forms in areas that have been traumatized by infection or surgery. Pelvic adhesions, which can range from thin strands to dense bands, may bind or block reproductive organs, causing pain and/or infertility.

ADRENALINE: A hormone produced by the adrenal glands in response to low blood sugar and at other times of physical and psychological stress. Because it constricts blood vessels, a synthetic form of adrenaline may be added to local anesthetics in spinal or epidural anesthesia to prolong numbness by confining the drug to the surgical area and to reduce toxicity by slowing its passage into the bloodstream.

AIDS (ACQUIRED IMMUNE DEFICIENCY SYNDROME): a virus-caused illness that destroys the body's immune system. It's transmitted by contaminated blood products, sexual intercourse, and intravenous needles previously used by infected people. Because AIDS is an epidemic, it is strongly suggested that anyone facing surgery in which transfusion is a possibility store her own blood for that use. (See AUTOLOGOUS TRANSFUSION.)

318

ARTHROSCOPIC SURGERY: A procedure often done on an outpatient basis that allows a surgeon to see inside the knee, shoulder, elbow, ankle, hip, or wrist. After the patient has been given a local or general anesthetic, a fiberoptic magnifying instrument called an arthroscope is inserted through a buttonhole-size incision, allowing the surgeon to diagnose joint damage due to injuries or arthritis. If treatment is necessary, the surgeon may insert another instrument through the arthroscope or through a separate incision.

ATROPINE: A drug that may be used during surgery to block glandular secretions in the gastrointestinal and urinary tracts and to control heart rate. An injection of Atropine before surgery was routine in the days when the major anesthetic used was ether, which increased salivation. Because modern anesthetics don't have this effect, Atropine is only used to prevent slowing of the heart rate, which can occur during pelvic surgery as a "reflex response" to manipulation of the uterus, according to Harry H. Bird, president of the American Society of Anesthesiologists and clinical professor of anesthesiology at Dartmouth College.

AUTOLOGOUS TRANSFUSION: The replacement of blood lost in surgery by one's own blood, which is drawn and stored in the weeks before surgery. Since the AIDS crisis, this is becoming a common procedure: it protects against the risk of unwittingly receiving contaminated blood products.

BARIUM ENEMA: A test in which X-rays are taken while the colon is coated with a chalky liquid called barium, which makes it stand out from the abdominal cavity. Barium is infused into the colon through a tube inserted in the rectum while the patient is lying on her side. In gynecology the test may be done to check for displacement of the colon by a pelvic mass or the spread of cancer to the colon.

BIKINI CUT: The incision of choice for gynecological surgery. It follows the top of the pubic hair horizontally across the bottom of the belly. (The alternative incision, called a vertical incision, extends from the navel to the top of the pubic hair.) The bikini cut is not only more attractive cosmetically, but also heals faster, and the scar is stronger because it is not subject to tension caused by normal expansion and contraction of the upper abdomen. The vertical incision, on the other hand, allows the surgeon greater visibility and freedom of motion and it is used in more radical procedures—for instance, when a hysterectomy is prompted by a malignancy or when fibroid tumors are too large to remove through the bikini cut.

BIOPSY: A procedure in which a small sample of a lump or other abnormal tissue is removed and examined by a pathologist to detect cancer and other conditions. This procedure can usually be done in a doctor's office; patients may receive a local anesthetic.

BLADDER: A muscular, expandable sac that holds urine and contracts to expel it from the body through the urethra. (See URETHRA.)

BREECH BIRTH: Delivery in which the baby's feet or buttocks precede the head through the birth canal. According to *Obstetrics and Gynecology* (J. B. Lippincott Co., 1986), babies born in this position face about 5.5 times the mortality risk of other babies. For example, the cord can be compressed, cutting off oxygen to the baby, or the cervix may not dilate enough for the head, which is the largest part of the body. In the past, cesarean section was always performed in breech births to avoid these risks, but studies have shown that, depending on fetal weight, size of the mother's pelvis, and other factors, vaginal delivery may be safe.

CALCIFICATION: Hardening of tissue by a deposit of calcium salts, which can occur in ovarian and breast tumors and other tissues. The distribution, density, and shape of calcium deposits as revealed on X-ray may help radiologists to differentiate between malignant and nonmalignant tumors.

CATHETER: Any hollow, narrow tube. During gynecological surgeries, a catheter may be inserted to drain the bladder, so it can be moved away from other pelvic organs, and/or monitor kidney function. Bladder catheters also may be inserted after surgery if a patient is temporarily unable to urinate due to pain or trauma to the bladder during surgery.

CAT SCAN (COMPUTERIZED AXIAL TOMOGRAPHY): An X-ray procedure that takes thousands of cross-sectional views of the body, which are then merged into a single image by computer. During the test, which takes less than an hour, the patient lies completely still inside a circular X-ray machine. Specific gynecological uses include determining the extent of a pelvic mass and, in cases of cancer, determining its stage by examining for evidence of spread to lymph nodes and other organs.

CAUTERIZATION: An instrument called a cautery probe delivers an electric current to tissue. One of the three methods used to treat cervical, vulvar, and vaginal abnormalities, in which diseased tissues are destroyed to promote the growth of healthy tissue. The patient is positioned with feet in stirrups, and a speculum is inserted to open the vagina as in a pelvic exam. The growth or abnormality is then destroyed with a special instrument that burns (cauterization), freezes (see CRYOSURGERY), or vaporizes (see LASER) tissue. Patients may be given local or general anesthesia.

CERVICAL BIOPSY: A procedure performed after an abnormal Pap smear that allows the pathologist to examine the full thickness of the cervical epithelium rather than just the surface layer of cells obtained from a Pap smear. The biopsy can usually be performed with no anesthesia on an outpatient basis. The physician removes one or more tiny tissue fragments using an alligator-jaws-type instrument inserted through the vagina. He or she also may use a curette to scrape some tissue from the cervical canal. In some precancerous cervical abnormalities, a cervical biopsy stimulates healing so no other treatment is necessary.

CERVICAL CAP: A small cuplike birth control device that is similar to a diaphragm except that it is smaller and forms an airtight seal over the cervical opening. They are in use in some European countries and are undergoing clinical trials in the United States.

CERVICAL STENOSIS: A narrowing of the cervical canal due to a buildup of scar tissue following infection or certain treatments (conization, cauterization, and the like) of the cervix or hormonal changes that occur with age. Although this condition usually causes no symptoms, it may cause infertility, abnormal bleeding, or excessive menstrual pain.

CERVICITIS: Inflammation of the cervix, usually caused by infection with *Chlamydia trachomatis, Neisseria gonorrhoeae,* or herpes virus. Although cervicitis frequently causes a thick discharge, pain, or bleeding, many patients have no symptoms. Sometimes women have chronic mild cervicitis, most commonly caused by trauma and tiny cuts that occur during childbirth. Because studies have linked cervicitis to cervical cancer, treatment of infections and attention to cervical injuries are essential; if cervicitis persists, treatment to eradicate the abnormal tissue (see CAUTERIZATION) may be necessary.

CERVIX: A doughnut-shaped muscular structure at the lower end of the uterus, often referred to as the "neck" or "mouth" of the uterus. The opening leads into the canal that connects the vagina to the uterine cavity.

CHAD: The acronym for one of several ovarian cancer treatments in which cisplatin (see below) is given in combination with other drugs. Patients receive intravenous doses of Adriamycin, cis-diamminedichloroplatinum (cisplatin), cyclophosphamide (Cytoxan), and an oral dose of hexamethylmelamine six times at three- to four-week intervals. Many physicians now feel that they can produce as good or better results with fewer side effects without hexamethylmelamine.

CHEMOTHERAPY: Treatment of disease with chemicals (drugs); the term is often used to refer to the use of powerful medications to treat cancer. Because cancer is characterized by cells that undergo uncontrolled division, anticancer drugs are designed to stop this process by interfering with cell growth and reproduction. This is why chemotherapy drugs are often toxic to other rapidly dividing cells, accounting for such side effects as hair loss and sores in the mouth.

CISPLATIN: Generic name for Platinol, a heavy metal complex considered to be the most effective drug in the treatment of ovarian cancer. It is given intravenously in combination with other drugs (see CHAD).

COITUS INTERRUPTUS: A birth control method that involves withdrawing the penis from the vagina just before ejaculation. It is considered very risky because it not only requires great control, but also ignores the fact that a drop of semen may well be at the tip of the penis before ejaculation.

COLOSTOMY: Creation of a (sometimes temporary) opening of the colon in the abdomen for the elimination of body wastes. The procedure may be performed if part of the colon has been removed due to cancer or disease.

COMPAZINE: Brand name of the drug prochlorperazine. It may be used for severe anxiety or relief of severe nausea and vomiting caused by chemotherapy.

CONE BIOPSY: A procedure in which a surgical knife or a laser is used to remove a cone-shaped wedge of the cervix comprising the epithelium surrounding its opening and a portion of the cervical canal. Traditionally this procedure was done following an abnormal Pap smear, but today treatment is more conservative, and a cone biopsy is only done when the disease extends into the cervical canal or to treat cancer in situ (see DYSPLASIA).

CONSENT FORM: A document stating that patients agree to surgery or certain diagnostic procedures, such as D&C. Signing the document indicates that the patient not only agrees to the procedure, but also understands her medical condition, the nature of the test or surgery, its risks and benefits, and its alternatives—a principle known as informed consent.

CONTRACEPTIVE SPONGE: Made of polyurethane, it's molded to cover the cervix and designed to release a chemical that kills sperm.

CORTISONE: A steroid hormone produced in the adrenal gland. Synthetic forms are used to treat various inflammatory or allergic reactions or abnormal tissue growths.

CRYOSURGERY: Also called cryotherapy, this is one of the treatments used for abnormal cervical and vaginal tissue. The tissue is frozen one or more times with a long metal probe cooled with nitrous oxide, carbon dioxide, or liquid Freon (see CAUTERIZATION for treatment method). Cryosurgery is less painful and poses less risk of infection, bleeding, and scarring than cauterization, according to the American College of Obstetricians and Gynecologists.

CURETTE: A long, curved, spoon-shaped instrument designed to reach through the cervix into the cervical canal or uterus. It is used to scrape off a sample of the lining for biopsy or to clean it out completely after an incomplete abortion.

CYST: See OVARIAN CYST.

CYSTOCELE: If childbirth has stretched and weakened the muscle layer separating the bladder from the vagina, the bladder may fall down into the vagina. Surgery (called an anterior colporrhaphy), tightens and repositions the muscles to better support the bladder. A similar procedure corrects a bulge in the posterior vaginal wall, called a rectocele.

DALKON SHIELD: An intrauterine device manufactured by A. H. Robins Company that was taken off the market in the United States in 1974, just three years after it was introduced, because it was implicated in miscarriages, pelvic inflammatory disease, and even death. Although it is not known exactly how many women were harmed by the Dalkon shield, 332,000 women have filed claims agains Robins; 197,000 of these suits are still pending. According to Sybil Shainwald, an attorney on the board of the National Women's Health Network who represents many of the women injured by the Dalkon shield, at least twenty deaths have been caused by complications related to the device. She said that thousands of women worldwide are still wearing the shield.

DANAZOL: Generic name of a synthetic male hormone that has become the preferred endometriosis treatment. The drug seems to work by inhibiting estrogens and progesterone as well as pituitary hormones, inducing "pseudomenopause" and causing endometrial tissue (both inside and outside the uterus) to shrink. Depending on the seriousness of the condition, danazol may be given for three to four or more than eight months. Studies have shown that this drug relieves symptoms in 70 to 100 percent of cases, and 50 percent of patients are successful in attempts to conceive following treatment. About 80 percent of women who take danazol experience some side effects, including acne, facial hair, and oily skin (due to the increased levels of male hormone) and hot flashes, vaginal dryness, and mood swings due to decreased estrogen). Nafarelin, a new drug that is given in a nasal spray, is now being tested for possible use as an alternative to danazol. Nafarelin has been shown to be as effective as danazol without causing masculinizing side effects; however, because the drug greatly reduces estrogen levels, it does cause hot flashes and other estrogen-deprivation symptoms.

DARVON: Trade name for propoxyphene, a mild painkilling drug.

DEMEROL: Trade name for meperidine, a synthetic narcotic and strong painkiller used frequently in the first day or two after surgery.

DERMOID CYST: See OVARIAN CYST.

DES (DIETHYLSTILBESTROL): A synthetic form of estrogen commonly prescribed in the 1950s and 1960s to pregnant women at risk for miscarriage. In 1971, studies linking the drug with vaginal cancer in the daughters of DES mothers (who were pregnant with them while they were taking the drug) prompted the FDA to advise against the use of the drug during pregnancy. Subsequent studies of DES daughters found that about one in one thousand contract a rare cancer that affects the cervix or vagina; dysplasia (see below) and structural abnormalities of the reproductive organs are common among this group. In addition, DES mothers have a higher rate of breast cancer than other women, and some evidence suggests that DES sons face a higher than average risk for testicular cysts, underdeveloped testes, and low sperm counts.

DIAPHRAGM: A rubber disk that is inserted into the vagina and covers the cervical opening, thereby preventing contraception. It is used with spermicidal jelly or cream.

DNA (DEOXYRIBONUCLEIC ACID): A chemical that makes up the genes, present in all the body's cells. By dictating the structure and function of cells, genes determine our characteristics and encode information for traits passed from generation to generation. Many chemotherapy drugs work by interfering with the structure or function of DNA, thus destroying the cell.

DYSPLASIA: Abnormal development of body tissue. In cervical dysplasia, cells in the top layer of the cervix (cervical epithelium) undergo cancerlike changes that can be detected by a Pap smear. In normal epithelial tissue, new cells are produced in the bottom layer and mature as they move to the top; in dysplasia, immature cells are found throughout the tissue, including the very surface where the smear is taken. The more immature cells present, the more severe the dysplasia; when the entire epithelium consists of undifferentiated cells, the condition is called carcinoma in situ. Although dysplasia occasionally clears up on its own, treatment is usually recommended to prevent it from progressing to cancer (see CAUTERIZATION). The term dysplasia is increasingly being replaced by CIN (cervical intraepithelial neoplasia), grade 1 (mild dysplasia), grade 2 (moderate dysplasia), and grade 3 (severe dysplasia and carcinoma in situ).

D&C (DILATION AND CURETTAGE): A procedure usually performed to diagnose and treat abnormal vaginal bleeding. Women may be given general or spinal anesthesia or a paracervical block plus tranquilizers, sedatives, and the like. The cervix is gradually dilated, allowing the surgeon to insert a curette and scrape tissue from the uterus for microscopic examination.

D&E (DILATION AND EVACUATION): An abortion method most often used if the fetus is more than twelve weeks old. The procedure is similar to a D&C: the difference is that a flexible suction hose is used, perhaps in conjunction with the curette and/or forceps.

ECTOPIC PREGNANCY: This occurs when a fertilized ovum becomes implanted outside the uterus, usually in a fallopian tube. If an obstetrician detects this condition early (through physical examination or by a woman's symptoms, such as pain and spotting), he or she can remove the fetus and repair any damage to the tube. However, if the fetus remains in the tube, the pressure eventually causes it to rupture, and the abdomen fills with blood. This requires emergency abdominal surgery in which the fallopian tube, and in some cases the ovary, is removed.

ELECTROCARDIOGRAM (EKG): A diagnostic test that charts any irregularities in the heart by tracing the pattern of electrical impulses that move through the heart. Electrodes are placed on the chest, ankles, and wrists. A painless procedure, the electrocardiogram is one of the standard preoperative tests.

ENCAPSULATED: Enclosed in a capsule or sheath. The term is used to refer to those malignant ovarian tumors that have not ruptured, thus have a better prognosis; however, certain ovarian tumors with an intact capsule may shed cells, which can spread cancer to other areas, according to Hugh Barber, M.D., director of the Department of Obstetrics and Gynecology at Lenox Hill Hospital.

ENDOCRINOLOGY: The branch of medicine focusing on hormones, metabolic disorders, and certain disturbances of body chemistry.

ENDOMETRIAL BIOPSY: A procedure in which a curette is used to scrape off a sample of the uterine lining, usually for evaluation of abnormal bleeding or fertility problems.

ENDOMETRIOSIS: A condition in which the type of tissue that lines the uterus (endometrium) grows in other parts of the body, usually the ovaries, uterine surface, fallopian tubes, and bowel. The implants bleed during menstruation, which can trigger an inflammatory reaction and, later, scarring. As a result, patients may have severe menstrual cramps, pain during intercourse, and decreased fertility. The cause of endometriosis is unknown, but the mechanism is thought to be a kind of reverse menstruation, in which the endometrial lining backs up in the uterus and passes through the fallopian tubes rather than through the vagina.

ENDORPHINS: Chemicals considered to be the body's natural opiates because they inhibit the conduction of pain messages between nerves in the brain and spinal cord. Researchers who are exploring ways to use this response to provide natural pain relief have found that endorphins are stimulated by states of relaxation and inhibited by fear and tension.

ENEMA: A procedure in which fluid is injected into the colon through a tube inserted into the rectum. Enemas may be used to stimulate a bowel movement in order to empty the colon for a diagnostic test (see BARIUM ENEMA). Patients also are given enemas before gynecological and other surgeries in the bowel area because the resulting trauma reduces bowel functioning for several days following surgery.

EPIDURAL: Anesthesia in which the drug continuously drips through a small tube placed in the epidural space, which is outside the dura, the protective membrane of the spinal canal. The drug produces numbness by bathing nerve endings leading to a large area of the body, such as the area from the knees to the abdomen. Epidural anesthesia may be chosen as an alternative to spinal anesthesia (see below) because it numbs a smaller area, doesn't cause a headache, and has less effect on circulation. (Both types reduce blood pressure.) However, epidural anesthesia involves a greater risk for toxicity because larger doses of anesthetic are necessary.

EPISIOTOMY: A procedure in which an incision is made in the perineum (the area between the vagina and anus) during labor to enlarge the vaginal opening. Considered routine for women in their first childbirth.

ESTROGEN: A hormone produced primarily by ovarian follicle cells; the adrenal glands and body fat also manufacture estrogens, even after menopause. In addition to prompting monthly thickening of the uterine lining and increases in cervical mucus (see FOLLICLE STIMULATING HORMONE for description of cycle), estrogen causes the development of female characteristics at puberty.

ESTROGEN REPLACEMENT THERAPY: A hormonal treatment program for women who experience symptoms due to decreased estrogen levels after natural menopause or removal of the ovaries. It is used as a short-term therapy to reduce hot flashes and other disruptive symptoms and as a long-term therapy for women at high risk for osteoporosis (see below) and those who experience sexual dysfunction due to vaginal dryness. To minimize the risk of endometrial cancer associated with estrogen use, the drug is given in cycles with monthly breaks, and progesterone is added to the treatment regimen. However, estrogen's detractors point out the risks associated with ERT won't be fully understood for years.

FALLOPIAN TUBES: Four- to five-inch tubes extending from each side of the uterus. The ends of the tubes, which lie near the ovaries, have fingerlike projections that pull in the egg after its release from the ovary. Fertilization usually occurs in the tube as the egg is traveling to the uterus.

FENTANYL: Generic name of a narcotic pain reliever considered to be a morphine substitute. It is often given during surgery to enhance the effect of anesthetic gases.

FIBEROPTICS: A system in which light is transmitted along hairthin fibers of glass or other transparent material by thousands of successive internal reflections. This technology is used in endoscopes (arthroscopes, hysteroscopes, laparoscopes, and so forth), which allow physicians to directly view and correct internal defects due to injury and disease. These instruments are inserted into the body through a natural opening or small incision.

FIBROID TUMOR: Benign tumor of the uterus. It is the most common type of pelvic tumor, occurring in one out of every four or five women over the age of thirty-five. A fibroid is usually embedded in the uterine wall (intramural) or may grow from the uterine lining into the uterus (submucous). Tumors may also project from the outer surface of the uterus (subserous) and grow into the ligaments that support the uterus (intraligamentous). In some cases, fibroids are attached to the uterus by a stem (see PEDUNCULATED FIBROIDS). They can be pea size or larger than grapefruits and most often occur in groups of varying sizes. Although most fibroids produce no symptoms, large growths may press on other organs, causing pain and pressure in the abdomen or lower back and frequent urination; fibroids growing into the uterus often bleed. If symptoms are present, or if the tumor is so large it distorts the abdomen, a myomectomy (removal of tumors only) may be performed. However, if a woman doesn't want children, a hysterectomy is often recommended because fibroids frequently recur: in a study of 2,554 patients who underwent myomectomy, 15 percent had recurrence of tumors, according to *Current Therapy in Surgical Gynecology* (B. C. Decker Inc., 1987). Also, when several fibroids are removed, there's a high risk of postoperative adhesions and bowel obstructions. Fibroids shrink on their own after menopause.

FOLLICLE STIMULATING HORMONE (FSH): A hormone produced by the pituitary gland. FSH begins the monthly menstrual cycle by stimulating the egg-forming cells in the ovaries (follicles) to mature. The cycle is controlled through an elaborate feedback system in which several hormones turn each other off and on: FSH, LH, and estrogen peak during the first half; progesterone peaks during the second half. If fertilization does not occur, progesterone and estrogen drop off, inducing menstruation.

GAS PAINS: Discomfort caused by a buildup of gas in the abdominal cavity. They can occur during surgery if the intestines are shocked into paralysis or inhibited by painkillers; pain persists until the intestines start moving. Remedies recommended by the women interviewed include milk of magnesia, Maalox, and rolling on the back from side to side. Louis Lapid, M.D., suspects that the gentler the surgeon, the milder the shock to the intestines. He suggests that patients limit foods to clear soups, liquids, gelatin, and the like for a few days following surgery.

GASTROENTEROLOGIST: A physician who treats diseases of the stomach, esophagus, small and large intestines, liver, and pancreas. This specialist may be called in to help find the cause of abdominal pain.

GASTROINTESTINAL (G.I.) SERIES: An examination of the entire digestive tract, consisting of a barium enema and upper G.I. X-rays. In the latter, patients drink a chalky-tasting barium milkshake, which coats the lining of the esophagus, stomach, duodenum, and small intestines. The patient leans against an X-ray table, which is tilted in several directions so the barium will flow into different organs.

GURNEY: Roll-away stretcher used in hospitals to transport patients.

HEMATOCRIT: A test done as part of a complete blood count that measures the relative volumes of red blood cells to total blood. A reading of 38 to 47 percent is normal for women; a lower hematocrit signals anemia.

HERNIA: Protrusion of an organ or tissue through the surrounding structures, due to weakness or rupture in the structure. Commonly refers to a rupture in the muscular wall surrounding the abdominal cavity, allowing the intestine or other abdominal organs to protrude. Hernias can occur after surgery at the site of incision.

HERPES: a contagious viral infection that causes fever blisters or cold sores around the mouth or painful blisters in the genital area. Genital herpes, usually caused by herpes simplex type 2, is spread by sexual contact, but oral herpes virus (type 1) can also affect the genital area. Herpes outbreaks may occur periodically and are sometimes accompanied by a flulike illness. Although there is no cure for herpes, a relatively new drug called acyclovir can relieve symptoms and decrease outbreaks.

HORMONE: A chemical substance produced by the body that can turn organs on and off, thus regulating many body functions, such as digestion, growth, and sexual functioning. Synthetic forms of many hormones are used to treat hormone deficiencies caused by illness or, in the case of menopause, aging.

HOT FLASHES: A feeling of warmth that begins on the face and radiates to the chest, accompanied by flushing and sweating. According to *Obstetrics and Gynecology* (J. B. Lippincott, 1986),

75 to 85 percent of women experience this symptom following menopause. Many women have only occasional episodes; a minority experience attacks that are frequent and intense enough to interfere with normal functioning. Although the cause of hot flashes is not certain, many believe they are due to a misfiring of glands involved in temperature regulation in an attempt to reactivate the ovaries.

HYPERPLASIA: An increase in the number of cells in any tissue of the body. Although this condition is not malignant, in certain areas of the body, including the uterus (endometrial hyperplasia), it occasionally progresses to cancer. Endometrial hyperplasia is due to an increased level of estrogen and often causes abnormal bleeding.

HYSTERECTOMY: Surgical removal of the uterus and adjacent structures. Total or complete hysterectomy, in which the entire uterus is removed, may be performed to remove symptomatic fibroids or a sagging uterus or to correct severe bleeding. A complete hysterectomy (known technically as a "hysterectomy with bilateral salpingo-oophorectomy") involves removal of the uterus, fallopian tubes, and ovaries. When the uterus only is removed, a woman still produces estrogen and ovulates, but the ova are absorbed by the body. When the ovaries are removed, "surgical" menopause occurs.

HYSTEROGRAM: A procedure in which X-rays are taken of the uterus after it has been filled with a dye. This is essentially the same procedure as the hysterosalpingogram (see below) because the dye automatically flows into the fallopian tubes.

HYSTEROSALPINGOGRAM: Usually done to investigate the cause of infertility, the test can detect fibroids, structural defects, and obstructions of the uterus and fallopian tubes. With a speculum in place as in a pelvic exam, the physician injects dye through a small tube placed in the cervix. X-rays follow the path of the liquid through the uterus and out the fallopian tubes.

HYSTEROSCOPE: A slender fiberoptic instrument with magnifying lenses used to visualize the cervical canal and uterus in order to evaluate or treat infertility or abnormal bleeding. After the vaginal walls are separated with a speculum, the hysteroscope is inserted through the cervix into the uterus. The physician may also have to dilate the cervix and inflate the uterine cavity with gas or a glucose solution to perform treatments. An experimental treatment, first described by Robert S. Neuwirth, M.D., head of obstetrics and gynecology at St. Luke's Hospital in New York City, involves removing submucous fibroids during hysteroscopy rather than abdominal surgery. (See FIBROID TUMOR.)

INTUBATION: Placement of a tube in the windpipe (trachea) before surgery to create an airtight pathway to the lungs for oxygen and anesthetic gases and to prevent patients from aspirating gastric juices. This is more likely to be done for major surgeries, such as hysterectomies, which require a deep state of anesthesia over a long period.

IUD (INTRAUTERINE DEVICE): A small loop or coil that fits into the uterus to prevent pregnancy. Although no one is certain how it works, the most popular theory is that it causes a chronic inflammation because the body recognizes it as a foreign body. The white blood cells involved in the reaction may interfere with uterine lining buildup necessary for fertilization, destroy sperm, and/or destroy the fertilized egg.

IV (INTRAVENOUS): A needle inserted into a vein to administer blood products, nutrients, and medications directly into the blood. The IV is usually placed in the crook of the elbow or the top of the hand.

IVP (INTRAVENOUS PYELOGRAM): A test that reveals the structure and function of the kidneys, ureters, and bladder; in gynecology an IVP may be performed to detect distortion or obstruction of the ureters by pelvic masses and damage due to complications of a hysterectomy. A dye is injected through a vein in the arm, and X-rays are taken as it travels through the urinary system.

KELOID: An overgrowth of scar tissue, appearing as thick, raised, and red, which can occur during healing of wounds or surgical incisions. Injections of cortisone may reduce tissue buildup and flatten existing keloids.

KIDNEYS: Two lima bean–shaped organs about four inches long and three inches wide located on either side of the spine, just above the waistline. By forming and excreting urine, the kidneys maintain the proper fluid and electrolyte levels and rid the body of metabolic wastes.

LAMAZE: A method of preparing a pregnant woman to deliver her baby without anesthesia (natural childbirth). Beginning in about the seventh month, the woman attends classes with a partner and learns how to breathe, push, and relax during labor.

LAPAROSCOPY: A procedure in which a hollow fiberoptic instrument with magnifying lenses is used to visualize the outer surface of the uterus, fallopian tubes, and ovaries. The test may be performed to evaluate pelvic pain or infertility or when the physician suspects endometriosis, ectopic pregnancy, or adhesions. Also, certain treatments can be performed during laparoscopy, including tubal ligation, lysis of pelvic adhesions, biopsy of the ovaries or other tissues, aspiration of benign ovarian cysts, or retrieval of a lost IUD. To move the intestines and abdominal wall away from the pelvic organs, the body is tilted so that hips are raised, and gas is infused through a needle in the abdomen. The surgeon makes a tiny incision below the navel to insert the laparoscope; if other instruments are used, they may be inserted through the laparoscope or through another incision near the pubic hair. Laparoscopy may be performed with a general or local anesthetic.

LASER (LIGHT AMPLIFICATION BY STIMULATED EMISSION OF RADIATION): A concentrated light beam that is used to vaporize tissues. This technology is used for vaginal and cervical abnormalities (see CAUTERIZATION for treatment method) as well as gynecological surgeries, such as myomectomy, cone biopsy, and as an alternative to hysterectomy to stop uterine bleeding. Laser's advantages over traditional surgery include greater precision and less bleeding and infection risk.

LEIOMYOMA: Fibroid tumor.

LEIOMYOSARCOMA: A rare type of uterine cancer, originating from leiomyomas or uterine muscle, most frequently found in postmenopausal women.

LUTEINIZING HORMONE (LH): A hormone produced by the pituitary gland that peaks in the middle of the menstrual cycle, prompting the follicle to release a mature egg (see FOLLICLE STIMULATING HORMONE for description of cycle). LH also causes luteinization, the process in which the empty follicle becomes the corpus luteum, which produces progesterone, causing the uterine lining to mature. If pregnancy does not occur, the corpus luteum shrinks in about fourteen days.

MACROBIOTICS: A severe vegetarian diet that claims to have powers to prevent as well as cure illness. The regimen emphasizes brown rice and other grains, cooked vegetables, beans (including soybeans), and seaweed; it restricts raw fruits and vegetables and suggests avoiding citrus fruit in any form and the "nightshade" vegetables (tomatoes, potatoes, zucchini, and eggplant).

MAMMOGRAM: A breast X-ray that can detect tumors that are too small or too deep in breast tissue to be felt. With the patient sitting or standing in front of the X-ray machine, each breast is flattened against an X-ray plate. Because they detect breast cancer at such an early stage, regular mammograms can significantly reduce a woman's risk of dying from breast cancer, according to the American College of Obstetricians and Gynecologists. X-ray exposure is minimal as long as the test is done with modern equipment designed specifically for mammography.

MAO INHIBITOR: A group of antidepressant drugs that inhibit the action of monoamine oxidase, an enzyme that breaks down norepinephrine, which helps transmit nerve impulses. The result is an increase in norepinephrine at nerve junctions, which is believed to help relieve depression. Because of their side effects, MAO inhibitors are only given to people who can't take or don't benefit from other antidepressants.

MENOPAUSE: The end of a woman's reproductive capabilities, in which the elaborate interactions between glands that produced fertility change dramatically, producing a period of readjustment during which the body establishes a new hormonal balance. During the transition period, women may experience hot flashes, night sweats, or other symptoms. According to the American Medical Association, menopause usually occurs between ages forty-five and fifty-five and lasts two to three years; however, it can last from ten to fifteen years. During the postmenopausal period, many women experience symptoms due to decreased estrogen production, including osteoporosis (see below) and thinning and drying of the vagina.

MICROSURGERY: Technique in which tiny structures, such as blood vessels and nerves, can be surgically manipulated using an operating microscope, ultrathin fibers for suturing, specialized microinstruments and, in recent years, lasers. Light from the microscope's lenses is projected into the surgical area, which the surgeon views through an eyepiece. Microsurgical techniques to open fallopian tubes have been a boon to infertility treatment. (See TUBOPLASTY.)

MORPHINE: A narcotic pain reliever derived from opium. It is sometimes given before surgery to sedate patients and reduce the amount of anesthesia required.

MOTRIN: Prescription brand of the drug ibuprofen, also sold in lower, over-the-counter doses as Advil, Nuprin, and others. This medication is especially effective against menstrual cramps because it inhibits prostaglandins, substances present in many body tissues that play a role in inflammatory reactions. High levels of prostaglandins, which are released as the endometrium is sloughed off in menstruation, can cause uterine spasms.

MYOMECTOMY: Removal of fibroid tumors from the uterus. The procedure usually involves an abdominal incision and postoperative recovery similar to that for abdominal hysterectomy. (See FIBROID TUMOR.)

NECROSIS: Tissue death.

NEOPLASM: A growth or tumor that serves no useful function; it may be malignant or benign (polyps, uterine fibroids). Both types of growths use nutrients meant for normal tissues and can press on other organs, but small benign neoplasms usually don't pose a serious health hazard. Malignant neoplasms, however, invade other tissues and have a grave effect on body functioning.

NOVOCAIN: Brand name of procaine, which blocks nerve impulses to a specific area of the body. It may be used as a local anesthetic at the site of incision during a surgical procedure or for regional anesthesia, in which it is injected near a major nerve to numb a large area of the body.

ONCOLOGY: The medical specialty dealing with cancer.

OOPHORECTOMY: Surgical removal of the ovaries.

OPHTHALMOLOGY: The medical specialty dealing with the eye.

OSTEOPOROSIS: The gradual loss of bone mass in women as they age, which can result in fractures and/or curvature of the spine. Osteoporosis is most common in slender white women; other risk factors include a family history of the disease, undergoing early menopause, smoking, and lack of exercise. The disease is partially preventable by a calcium-rich diet, weight-bearing exercise, and, after menopause, taking estrogen replacement therapy.

OVARIAN CYST: A cyst is a sac filled with fluid, and there are more than two hundred kinds that appear on or near the ovaries. Most common are functional cysts, which are formed during ovulation from a follicle that fails to dissolve. These usually cause no symptoms and shrink on their own after one to three months. Dermoid cysts, or teratomas, which comprise about one-fifth of ovarian cysts, are believed to originate from embryonic cells meant to become various body structures, such as skin, nerve tissue, salivary and sweat glands. As a result, tumors may contain teeth, tangled masses of hair, and other body structures. These cysts frequently are on a stalk (pedunculated) and can twist, causing pain, but they usually don't cause menstrual irregularities. Almost all ovarian cysts are benign, according to the American College of Obstetricians and Gynecologists.

OVARIES: Oval-shaped organs about one inch by one and one-half inches that lie adjacent to each side of the uterus below the fallopian tube (see above). The ovaries release eggs, estrogen, and progesterone.

PAP TEST: A screening test that can detect vaginal and cervical infections as well as cervical cancer and precancer at an early stage when cure is almost certain. The test is done during a pelvic exam after the physician has inserted a speculum to spread the vaginal walls apart. He or she then uses a plastic or wooden stick to take a sample of cervical secretions, which is smeared on a slide and sent to a lab for analysis. George Papanicolaou, M.D., who developed the test in 1928, devised a system in which smears were categorized from Class I to V:

I: no atypical or abnormal cells;
II: atypical cells but no evidence of malignancy;
III: suggestive but not conclusive of malignancy;

IV: strongly suggestive of malignancy;

V: conclusive of malignancy.

Many labs now report findings in diagnostic terms, such as "consistent with infection," "dysplasia," and so on, which are more descriptive and of greater use to physicians.

PEDUNCULATED FIBROID: A fibroid tumor growing on a mushroomlike stem. The tumor may twist on its stem, cutting off its own circulation and causing severe pain, nausea, fever, and vaginal bleeding. When these project into the uterine cavity (submucous), they can be removed vaginally. (See HYSTEROSCOPE.)

PERCODAN: Trade name for drug that contains oxycodone (a narcotic for the relief of moderate pain) and aspirin.

PERCOCET: Trade name for a drug that contains oxycodone and an aspirinlike drug called acetaminophen.

PERITONEUM: The membrane lining the abdominal cavity and covering its organs.

PESSARY: In uterine prolapse, the ligaments holding the uterus and vagina in position are so stretched out from repeated childbirth, aging, innate weakness or overweight that the uterus descends into the vaginal canal. Removal of the uterus is one solution. Another is the use of the pessary, a ring used to catch the uterus at the top of the vagina, preventing it from dropping into the canal. Pessaries used to be made of rubber; the new ones are of plastic and may be left in place for as long as a year.

PHLEBITIS: An inflammation of the veins, usually in the leg, involving small blood clots. Because estrogen can exacerbate clotting problems, women with this condition should not take birth control pills or estrogen replacement therapy.

PID (PELVIC INFLAMMATORY DISEASE): A general term for infections of the reproductive organs. The disease is usually rooted in a sexually transmitted infection, but the microorganisms causing it can enter the body during any gynecological procedure. The condition is treated with antibiotics, and many women require intravenous administration to deliver sufficient concentrations of medication. Scar tissue formation and other pelvic damage from

PID can result in infertility, increased risk of tubal pregnancy, and lingering pelvic pain; the condition can be life-threatening if infection spreads to the abdominal cavity.

PILL: Colloquially, the Pill refers to birth control pills, the most common reversible method of contraception. Two kinds of pills are available today: those that contain estrogen and progesterone prevent the monthly growth and release of eggs from the ovaries; progesterone-only pills (mini-Pill) interfere with buildup of uterine lining and changes in cervical mucus that permit sperm penetration. After one year of use, women taking the mini-Pill have about a 3 percent chance of becoming pregnant, compared with a 2 percent pregnancy risk among women taking the combination pill.

PITOCIN: Trade name for the synthetic form of oxytocin, a hormone that stimulates the uterus to contract. The drug is used to accelerate labor.

PLATELETS: Blood cells that play a major role in blood clotting. A count of 150,000 to 350,000 is considered normal for adults; platelet levels may be reduced (thrombocytopenia) due to anemia or certain cancers or increased (thrombocytosis) following surgery or injuries.

POLYP: Common growth, usually on a stem (pedunculated), protruding from the cervix, cervical canal, uterine lining, or other mucous membranes. These are almost always benign but may cause bleeding. Cervical polyps may be twisted off during an office procedure; uterine polyps are often diagnosed and removed during a D&C or hysterectomy. Uterine polyps frequently occur with fibroid tumors and, in about 10 percent of cases occurring in postmenopausal women, with endometrial cancer, according to *Obstetrics and Gynecology* (J. B. Lippincott, 1986).

PREMARIN: Trade name for the most commonly prescribed form of synthetic estrogen.

PRITIKIN: A program designed by Nathan Pritikin aimed at improving health through regular aerobic exercise and abstention from alcohol, tobacco, and caffeine and following a carbohydrate-based diet that allows only small amounts of fat (10 percent of total daily calories) and protein (13 percent of daily calories). Studies have shown that the diet can reduce cholesterol, blood pressure, and arteriosclerosis, and control glucose in people with adult-onset diabetes. An inventor who developed patents for several corporations, Nathan Pritikin had no formal training in medicine. His diet, which he developed when he was diagnosed with heart disease at age forty, was based on the theories he formulated through extensive nutrition and health reading. Before his death in 1985, Pritikin founded several centers where people follow his diet and exercise program under medical supervision. Some physicians criticize his diet as being too restricted to provide a balance of nutrients.

PROGESTERONE: A hormone produced mainly after ovulation by the corpus luteum and in lesser amounts by the adrenal glands (see FOLLICLE STIMULATING HORMONE for description of cycle). It prepares the uterus to nourish a fertilized egg by causing the lining to thicken and develop new glands and blood vessels.

PROPHYLACTIC: A preventive measure, as in prophylactic antibiotics administered before any sign of infection.

PROVERA: Trade name for the most commonly used form of synthetic progesterone.

RHYTHM METHOD: A birth control method based on avoiding intercourse during the woman's fertile period. Failure rate is high because most women can't accurately determine the parameters of that period.

SEROTONIN: A substance found in the intestines, platelets, brain, and certain cancers. Although its basic purpose is not understood, serotonin is known to constrict the blood vessels and is involved in such diverse functions as digestion, transmission of messages in the brain, and inflammation of tissues following injuries.

SIMONTON: Carl Simonton, M.D., is a Texas oncologist who, with his social worker wife, Stephanie Matthews, developed a highly controversial approach to cancer treatment, which they use in conjunction with conventional methods. Their work is based on theories that cancer is the result of great stress and enormous life changes. The Simontons theorize that people with a "cancer personality" (emotionally inexpressive and given to helplessness and hopelessness) are particularly prone to the disease. The Simontons train cancer patients to visualize themselves as powerful fighters. They will ask them, for instance, to imagine their cancer cells as weak and disorganized and their chemotherapy as a white knight riding in to destroy the enemy. The Simontons have not been able to persuade the medical establishment that their work is effective. They are also criticized for seeming to hold the cancer patients responsible for their illness.

SODIUM PENTOTHAL: A barbiturate given intravenously, usually to put patients to sleep before anesthetic gases are given.

SONOGRAM: A test in which sound waves are used to create an image of a fetus or view internal organs. It may be used to determine the size, age, growth rate, and position of the fetus or to detect an ectopic pregnancy, fibroids, or ovarian masses. About an hour before the test, the patient drinks 8 eight-ounce glasses of liquid in order to fill the bladder, which pushes the bowel away from the pelvic organs, helps transmit sound, and provides a point of reference with which to compare the density of any cysts found. High-frequency sound waves are emitted and received by a device resembling a microphone called a transducer, which is moved along the abdomen.

SPINAL: A procedure that numbs and temporarily paralyzes the lower half of the body. A local anesthetic solution is injected into the subarachnoid space, a fluid-filled envelope outside the spinal cord. A spinal is commonly given for procedures involving the lower abdomen, pelvis, and lower extremities and for vaginal deliveries.

STAPLES: Metal staplelike clips sometimes used instead of sutures to close skin and internal tissues following surgery. These are inserted with a type of staple gun that can place up to one hundred at a time. Proponents of staples claim that they are less likely to cause infection, less painful to remove, and produce a smaller scar than sutures, but, according to Dr. Norbert Gleischer, chairman of the Department of Obstetrics and Gynecology at Mount Sinai Hospital in Chicago, their only real advantage over sutures is speed.

TERATOMA: See OVARIAN CYST.

THC (TETRAHYDROCANNABINOL): The active ingredient in cannabis, or marijuana. A synthetic form (brand name: Marinol) is sometimes given to patients undergoing chemotherapy to reduce nausea and vomiting. According to Lester Grinspoon, associate professor of psychiatry at Harvard Medical School and author of *Marijuana Reconsidered* (Harvard University Press, 1977), smoking cannabis is considerably more effective.

THRUSH: A painful infection of the mouth and gums with the fungus *Candida albicans,* which can cause redness and swelling, blisters, and patchy white areas. *Candida* normally lives in the mouth and other mucous membranes without causing illness, but it can become infectious when the natural balance of the body's organisms is upset by taking antibiotics, which kill off certain species that normally "compete" with *Candida* or when the immune system is depressed, as during chemotherapy.

TRANSDERMAL PATCH: A new method of taking estrogen replacement therapy that delivers the drug through the skin instead of orally. It looks like a Band-Aid, is worn on the abdomen, and requires less estrogen. This system has the advantage of allowing the estrogen to bypass the liver, which minimizes the risk of many Pill complications, including hypertension and gallstones, and side effects, including bloating, nausea, and headaches.

TUBAL LIGATION: Surgery to prevent pregnancy by blocking or closing the fallopian tubes so sperm cannot reach the egg. The tubes can be cauterized (see above), cut or pinched shut with a clip or band. According to *The New Our Bodies, Ourselves,* (Simon & Schuster, 1984), the most common surgical approach is through laparoscopy (see above); the surgical instruments are inserted either into the laparoscope or through a second incision. The procedure can also be performed through an incision in the vagina or abdomen (minilaparotomy). The patient is usually given general anesthesia for a tubal ligation.

TUBOPLASTY: Delicate surgery performed using a microscope or magnifying glasses worn by the surgeon to repair fallopian tubes damaged by infection, abortion, or ectopic pregnancy or to reverse a tubal ligation (see above). Depending on their location, adhesions or blockages can be vaporized with a laser, cut out, or, in an experimental procedure, blown out using a catheter with a balloon on the end. Tuboplasty to reverse sterilization is only recommended when the original surgery didn't involve removal of a significant portion of the fallopian tube and the tissue at the severed ends is normal. In most cases, tuboplasty is a tedious procedure that can take up to seven hours.

TYLENOL: Brand name of acetaminophen, a mild, aspirinlike drug.

URETHRA: A small tube that carries urine from the bladder out of the body. In women the urethra measures about one to one and one-half inches and lies in front of the vagina.

URETERS: Ten- to twelve-inch tubes that carry urine from each kidney to the bladder.

UTERUS: The hollow organ where the fetus develops. Commonly called the womb, the uterus is pear-shaped, measuring about three inches across (at its widest) and three inches in length. Powerful uterine contractions expel the fetus at birth.

VAGINAL WARTS: Small growths in or on the vagina or other genital areas caused by human papilloma virus (HPV), which is transmitted during sexual activity. Warts may itch, sting, or bleed or may cause no symptoms; frequently they are too small to be visible and are detected by a Pap smear. According to the American College of Obstetricians and Gynecologists, office visits for genital warts have increased by 400 percent in the past fifteen years, and studies have linked the presence of warts to cervical cancer. They may be removed by cryotherapy, cauterization, laser treatments, or application of caustic chemicals; however, treatment can't eliminate the virus, so warts may recur.

VALIUM: Trade name for diazepam, a common sedative tranquilizer. It is preferred by many anesthesiologists as a preoperative medication because of its specific antianxiety effect.

VASECTOMY: Male sterilization. One or two incisions are made in the scrotum to allow access to the vas deferens, the tube that carries sperm from the testes to the penis. The tube is cut, and the ends are tied off or cauterized. Vasectomy does not interfere with sexual functioning.

VISTARIL: Trade name for hydroxyzine pamoate, a drug used to relieve anxiety and itching. The drug may be given as a preoperative sedative.

VULVAR WARTS: See VAGINAL WARTS.

YOGA: A Hindu system of breathing and stretching exercises combined with meditation to develop spirituality as well as health. According to *The New Our Bodies, Ourselves* (Simon & Schuster, 1984), yoga has been shown to reduce blood pressure, lower pulse rates, diminish stress, increase joint movement, and improve hormonal functioning. Yoga advocates have suggested that it can strengthen the immune system and improve general health and may be used as an alternative or adjunct to traditional medical treatments to relieve feelings of pressure in the abdomen caused by fibroids.

BIBLIOGRAPHY

American Cancer Society Cancer Book, The. Doubleday, Garden City, NY, 1986.

Choices: Realistic Alternatives in Cancer Treatments, by Marion Morra and Eve Potts, Avon, New York, 1987 (rev. ed.).

Columbia University College of Physicians and Surgeons Complete Home Medical Guide, The. Crown Publishers, New York, 1985.

Complete Book of Medical Tests, The, by Michael E. Osband, M.D. W. W. Norton & Company, NY, 1984.

Complete Guide to Women's Health, The, by Bruce D. Shephard, M.D., F.A.C.O.G., Carroll A. Shephard, R.N., Ph.D. Plume Books, published in the United States by New American Library, New York, in arrangement with Mariner Publishing Co., Inc., 1985.

Coping with a Hysterectomy, by Susanne Morgan, Ph.D. New American Library, New York, rev. ed., 1985.

"Current Concepts in Endometriosis," by Craig A. Molgaard, Ph.D., MPH, Amanda L. Golbeck, Ph.D., and Louise Gresham, MPH. *Western Journal of Medicine,* 1985, July 143: 42–46.

Current Therapy in Surgical Gynecology, by Celso-Ramon Garcia, M.D., John J. Mikuta, M.D., and Norman G. Rosenblum, Ph.D., M.D. B. C. Decker Inc., Philadelphia, 1987.

Every Woman's Health: The Complete Guide to Body and Mind by 18 Women Doctors, by D. S. Thompson, M.D., consulting editor. Doubleday & Company, Inc., Garden City, NY, 1985 (3rd ed.).

"Hysterectomy as a Social Process," *Women & Health,* volume 10 (1) Spring, 198: pages 109–127. The Haworth Press, Inc.

Medical Access, by Richard Saul Wurman, ACCESSPRESS Ltd., 1985.

Memory Bank for Chemotherapy, by Fredrica A. Preston, Cecilia

Wilfinger, Williams & Wilkins, 428 East Preston Street, Baltimore, MD 21202; 1988.

New Our Bodies, Ourselves, The, by the Boston Women's Health Book Collective, Simon & Schuster, New York, 1984.

Obstetrics and Gynecology, by David Danforth, M.D., and James Scott, M.D., J. B. Lippincott Co., Philadelphia, 1986.

Ovarian Carcinoma: Etiology, Diagnosis, and Treatment, by Hugh R. K. Barber, M.D. Masson Publishing USA, Inc., New York, 1982.

Oxford Companion to Medicine, The, Volume II. Oxford University Press, Oxford/New York, 1986.

"Perioperative Antibiotics for Hysterectomy," by David L. Hemsell, in *Antibiotic Chemotherapy,* volume 33: 73–89. Karger, Basel, 1985.

Taber's Cyclopedic Medical Dictionary, Davis, Philadelphia, 1985 (5th edition).

"Tubal Pregnancy Treated by Laparoscope," by Charles A. Tietz, M.D., F.A.C.O.G. in *Minnesota Medicine,* volume 69, February 1986: 75–76.

Understanding Your Body: Every Woman's Guide to Gynecology and Health, by Felicia Stewart, M.D., Felicia Guest, Gary Stewart, M.D., and Robert Hathcer, M.D. Bantam, New York, 1987.

Webster's Medical Desk Dictionary. Merriam Webster, Springfield, MA, 1986.

INDEX